what
the thunder
really
said

A Retrospective Essay on the Making of
The Waste Land

ANNE C. BOLGAN

what
the thunder
really
said

McGill—Queen's University Press

Montreal and London 1973

© McGill—Queen's University Press 1973
ISBN 0-7735-0165-7
Library of Congress Catalog Card Number 73-79500
Legal Deposit 4th quarter 1973

This book has been published with the help of
a grant from the Humanities Research Council
of Canada, using funds provided by the
Canada Council.

Designed by Susan Mcphee

Printed in the U. S. A. by R. R. Donnelley and Sons Company

Grateful acknowledgement is made to the following for kind permission to reprint excerpts from publications in copyright:

Faber and Faber Ltd. for excerpts from the works of T. S. Eliot.

Harcourt Brace Jovanovich, Inc., for excerpts from the poetry and essays of T. S. Eliot and from *The Waste Land: A Facsimile and Transcript of the Original Drafts Including the Annotations by Ezra Pound;* copyright, 1932, 1936, 1950, by Harcourt Brace Jovanovich, Inc.; copyright © 1960, 1963, 1964, by T. S. Eliot; copyright © 1971 by Valerie Eliot.

Farrar, Straus & Giroux, Inc., for excerpts from the following titles by T. S. Eliot: *Knowledge and Experience in the Philosophy of F. H. Bradley,* copyright © 1964 by T. S. Eliot; *To Criticize the Critic,* copyright © 1965 by Valerie Eliot; *On Poetry and Poets,* copyright © 1943, 1945, 1951, 1954, 1956, 1957 by T. S. Eliot.

Mr. M. B. Yeats, the Macmillan Co. of London & Basingstoke, the Macmillan Co. of Canada Ltd., and the Macmillan Publishing Co., Inc., for excerpts from "The Statues" and from "Lapis Lazuli" from *The Collected Poems of W. B. Yeats;* copyright 1940 by Georgie Yeats, renewed 1968 by Bertha Georgie Yeats, Michael Butler Yeats and Anne Yeats.

Faber and Faber Ltd. and New Directions Publishing Corporation, New York, for excerpts from *The Selected Letters of Ezra Pound: 1907-1941,* edited by D. D. Paige, copyright 1950 by Ezra Pound.

George Allen and Unwin Ltd. and Atlantic-Little, Brown for an excerpt from *The Autobiography of Bertrand Russell,* vol. II.

In Memoriam Matris Amabilis

. . . in my turning world
the still point which is now forever still

contents

"The Three Voices of Poetry" ∾ *The Waste Land*—"an artistic failure" ∾ genetic and biographical criticism as aids to understanding how and why the poem failed ∾ Eliot's own critical theory ∾ explanation *vs* understanding ∾ the entelechy concept ∾ *The Waste Land* as it is, measured against the criterion of what it was "aiming to be"—that is, a neo-epic of the interior life ∾ the character, theme, and form generic to such a neo-epic ∾ the three major unresolved conflicts underlying the poem's genesis ∾ some critical issues revolving around the use of biographical material ∾ Pound's annotations to the original drafts of the poem

∾ "the voice of the poet talking to himself—or to nobody" ∾ the "voice of the poet addressing an audience" ∾ the mythical scaffolding ∾ the "rude unknown *psychic material*" ∾ failures in adjustment between the two ∾ significant alterations to the myth ∾ the poem's protagonist—who? ∾ not Tiresias ∾ the crossing of diffuse impulses—surface and submerged ∾ the first unresolved conflict underlying the poem's genesis—a conflict between two voices, one public, the other private ∾ new directions

dialectical hero ∾ Tiresias, the symbol of the Transcendent Self ∾ the Quester Hero, the symbol of the empirical self ∾ the "two souls" in Eliot's poem disjoined ∾ thus, a third unresolved conflict underlying the poem's genesis revealed ∾ the conflict not one between time-logic and space-logic, as Frank suggests ∾ the conflict one between the "two souls" and the two kinds of time and vision proper to them ∾ the resolution Eliot arrived at in his philosophical writings ∾ minimal changes required for an equally viable poetic resolution of the problem

∾ A. The Historical Background to Bradley's Formulation ∾ B. The Principle of Trichotomy ∾ C. The Concrete Universal and its "Two Souls" ∾ D. The Process of Empirical Self-Development or of Soul-Making ∾ 1. The Doctrine of Immediate Experience ∾ 2. The Phenomenal Realm of Subject-Object Correlation ∾ 3. "Degrees of Truth and Reality and the Internality of Relations" ∾ Bradley's philosophy diagrammed ∾ E. The Dialectical *vs* the Byronic Hero, or Bradley *vs* Hegel ∾ implications of for *The Modern Tradition* ∾ implications of for *The Waste Land* ∾ the third unresolved conflict underlying the poem's genesis—a conflict between romantic and modern philosophical postulates

∾ philosophical beginnings and poetic ends ∾ the paradoxical relation between the "two souls" once again ∾ diagram of Bradley's philosophy elaborated ∾ temporal appearances of the Absolute ∾ minimal changes required in poetic treatment of Tiresias figure ∾ the point of intersection between the "two souls" ∾ service of Bradley's philosophy to Eliot's poetry as a whole ∾ Eliot's major poems—four quadrants in search of Bradley's circle of the Absolute ∾ "The Love Song of J. Alfred Prufrock ∾ *The Waste Land* ∾ *Ash Wednesday* ∾ *Four Quartets* ∾ Eliot's artistic failure in *The Waste Land,* a failure only within the context of the Absolute

prefatory note

The world of literary esoterica has long had *The Waste Land* as one of its central exhibits. It is time we had another look. What is offered here is a retrospective view of *The Waste Land* and one which, according to Flint's own prescript, is determined if possible to see the object as it really is" (*TSW* 15)—to see it, that is, in a way that will relate it not only to its maker and his material, but to its reader, to its time and place in literary history, and to its own informing spirit as well.

acknowledgements

The publication of even a small book provides various kinds of relief not the least of which is the opportunity to acknowledge one's primary debts. It was in the remarkable seminar on The Origins and Development of Romanticism which was given by Professor A. S. P. Woodhouse at the University of Toronto during 1950-51—one which was further enhanced by the lively intellectual presence of F. E. L. Priestley—that I was first introduced to the full liberating force of the history of ideas. Because it is that seminar which has provided both model and inspiration for the present volume, I can only offer it to Professor Woodhouse in grateful memory of a man whose extraordinary impact still remains vivid, even after nearly a quarter of a century.

To Professor Northrop Frye I owe so many kindnesses that were I simply to list them they might "exhaust time and encroach upon eternity" somewhat in the manner of The Faerie Queene to which he introduced me in those same exciting days at the University of Toronto. Not the least of my debts to Professor Frye, however, is that he managed to suppress his natural antipathy to T. S. Eliot sufficiently to guide me with expert control through the doctoral dissertation on Bradley and Eliot from which the present study has developed.

Even gratitude must become mute in the face of what I owe to two others of the province's great teachers—Professor David Savan of the Department of Philosophy in the University of Toronto and Professor Norman MacKenzie of the Department of English at Queen's University. The former was willing to devote four hours every Saturday morning for almost a year to a student of English with no prior training in philosophy and just for the unpaid pleasure and profit—assuredly dubious on his side—of reading and discussing Bradley's philosophy together. Professor MacKenzie, on the other hand, has not only been willing to read my manuscript repeatedly, and then painstakingly to guide me through its revision for publication, but he has also devoted himself to the unlikely process of recreating my soul sufficiently to make it presentable in print. In return for these manifold and generous efforts, I can only wish that I had a better book to offer and one more worthy of the humanistic spirit so admirably expressed by these, the veritable princes of academe.

I must proffer my thanks as well to Miss Carolyn E. Jakeman who, for more years than I care to remember, has been unfailingly kind in answering to my endless requests for material from the Eliot collection of the Houghton Library of Harvard University; to Jan Harding and Margaret Moses for typing and retyping the manuscript repeatedly, and without demur; and to Robin Strachan and his colleagues at McGill-Queen's University Press for their expert care and assistance in seeing the manuscript through its various stages to publication.

In addition to these who have sustained the spirit in various ways, I acknowledge no less gratefully the extensive financial assistance which I have received from several sources and which has helped to sustain the even more demanding flesh. I am grateful to the American Association of University Women which awarded me the Charlotte Dickson Fisher Fellowship for 1963-64 and to the Canada Council for a Leave Fellowship awarded for 1968-69. These fellowships made possible two uninterrupted years of post-doctoral study and research, the first at the University of Toronto and the second in England and Italy. I am grateful as well to the Humanities Research Council of Canada for providing funds to assist in the publication of this book and, finally, I must extend my thanks to the University of Western Ontario for the consistently generous support it has given to my project through the supplementary research grants it has awarded me yearly since 1966.

abbreviations

The abbreviations below, followed immediately by the appropriate page or section number, serve to identify those works of T. S. Eliot cited within the body of the accompanying text:

Cor	"Coronation"
HM	The Hollow Men
TWL	The Waste Land
AW	Ash Wednesday
BN	Burnt Norton
EC	East Coker
DS	Dry Salvages
LG	Little Gidding
TSW	The Sacred Wood [1920] (New York: Barnes and Noble University Paperbacks, 1964).
SE	Selected Essays [1932] (New York: Harcourt, Brace and Company, 1950).
OPP	On Poetry and Poets (London: Faber and Faber, 1957).
TCTC	To Criticize the Critic (London: Faber and Faber, 1965).
Use of	The Use of Poetry and the Use of Criticism (London: Faber and Faber, 1933).
KE	Knowledge and Experience in the Philosophy of F. H. Bradley (London: Faber and Faber, 1964).

Other books frequently referred to and cited in the same way are the following:

AR F. H. Bradley, *Appearance and Reality,* 2nd. ed., Ninth impression Authorized and Corrected (Oxford: Clarendon Press, 1955).

ETR ————, *Essays on Truth and Reality* (Oxford: Clarendon Press, 1914).

PIV Bernard Bosanquet, *The Principle of Individuality and Value* (London: Macmillan, 1912).

FF Sergei Eisenstein, *Film Form* [*1949*], edited and translated by Jay Leyda (New York: Meridian Books, 1957).

FS ————, *The Film Sense* [*1942*], edited and translated by Jay Leyda (New York: Meridian Books, 1957).

In all other cases, a conventional footnote has been used.

. . . bodiless childful of life in the gloom
Crying with frog voice, 'what shall I be?'

T. L. Beddoes, *Death's Jest-Book*

introduction

In his essay, "The Three Voices of Poetry," Eliot has discussed the number of voices which a sensitive ear can normally distinguish in the reading of poetry:

The first voice is the voice of the poet talking to himself—or to nobody. The second is the voice of the poet addressing an audience, whether large or small. The third is the voice of the poet when he attempts to create a dramatic character speaking in verse; when he is saying, not what he would say in his own person, but only what he can say within the limits of one imaginary character addressing another imaginary character. (*OPP* 89)

This last is, of course, the most easily discernible involving, as it does, the direct speech of characters in a play or poem, but Eliot goes on to complicate the discussion of the dramatic voices of the poet by asking further whether we are not able in poetic drama to distinguish, not only "the voice of each character—an individual voice different from that of any other character" but also "from time to time . . . the voices of the author and the character in unison, saying something appropriate to the character, but something which the author could say for himself also" (*OPP* 100). Eliot quotes the famous "To-morrow and to-morrow and to-morrow" as an example of the kind of line in which he hears "Shakespeare and Macbeth . . . uttering the words in unison, though perhaps with somewhat different meaning" (*OPP* 100). Finally, Eliot completes the catalogue of voices to which his ear has become attuned by

1

taking note of a third variant of the dramatic voice—thus bringing the total number of distinguishable voices to five: "And finally there are the lines, in plays by one of the supreme poetic dramatists, in which we hear a more impersonal voice still than that of either the character or the author" (*OPP* 100). Having introduced this impersonal voice, and the god-like presence behind it, Eliot says nothing more about it. I suggest that we label it "the voice of the prophet," thus adding to it that fine air of remoteness which is no doubt proper to its speaking.

Having taken considerable pains to distinguish the many voices of poetry it is possible to discriminate, Eliot then concludes with the admission that these five voices are not to be thought of as mutually exclusive and "that in every poem, from the private meditation to the epic or the drama, there is more than one voice to be heard" (*OPP* 100). It would seem that what Eliot has really been concerned to discriminate in this essay is not so much "the three voices of poetry" as it is the varying tonalities of *one* voice—the voice of the poet orienting itself to the differing formal requirements of the poem he is seeking to write. His concern is with the three (or more accurately the five) voices of the *poet* which he has come gradually to hear in the course of his poetic development. Surely the poet he is speaking of is himself and moreover, I would suggest, himself after a rereading of *The Waste Land* for in the concluding paragraph of his essay he says somewhat defensively: "If you complain that a poet is obscure, and apparently ignoring you, the reader, or that he is speaking only to a limited circle of initiates from which you are excluded—remember that what he may have been trying to do, was to put something into words which could not be said in any other way, and therefore in a language which may be worth the trouble of learning" (*OPP* 101-2). I believe that Eliot's language is worth the considerable trouble it takes to learn it, and I submit that the most fruitful exercise yet to be performed upon *The Waste Land* is to apply to it the aural discriminations he has put forward in this essay.

If we proceed in this aurally alert manner two things will be evident immediately. One is that, formally speaking, *The Waste Land* reveals itself to be a collage of voices—the many voices of one poet looking for a new brand of structural glue. The second is that he never quite found it. That a dazzling and abundant poetic power lies behind these fragments is, I think, unquestionable. What those fragments went in search of, and at least to some extent found, was a "better craftsman." If Eliot, in dedicating the poem to Ezra Pound, gave to him that enviable accolade, it is only now that we have Valerie Eliot's handsome edition of *The Waste Land: A Facsimile and Transcript*[1] that we can judge for ourselves the nature and full extent of Pound's contributions to the poem, and thus perceive how justly deserved the tribute really was.

Pound himself, of course, always maintained a modest reserve as regards his skilful rescue of the poem from Eliot's hands. He characterized his own efforts on its behalf, perhaps somewhat quaintly, as involving a kind of surgical midwifery. He it was, he tells us, who delivered "the printed infancies" to an unbelieving world, and the difficult labour had finally to be eased by Caesarean section. The unfortunate suggestion in such cases (and one which, in this instance, is amply supported by the transcript of the text now before us) is of a forced and somewhat premature birth. Indeed, so acute do one's aural sensibilities become under Eliot's own tutelage that at times one can almost hear this particular poem of his cry out in irritation against its maker, feeling itself perhaps, like the bastard Richard,

> Deform'd, unfinish'd, sent before my time
> Into this breathing world scarce half made up,
> And that so lamely and unfashionable
> That dogs do bark at me as I halt by them.
> (*Richard III*, I.1.20-3)[2]

1. Valerie Eliot, ed., *The Waste Land: A Facsimile and Transcript of the Original Drafts Including the Annotations of Ezra Pound* (London: Faber and Faber, 1971).
2. The correspondence between Eliot and Pound on the subject of *The Waste Land* may be found in D. D. Paige, ed., *The Letters of Ezra Pound: 1907-1941* (London: Faber and Faber, 1941), pp. 233-37. At the conclusion of one of his letters to Eliot, Pound included the following:

SAGE HOMME

These are the poems of Eliot
By the Uranian Muse begot;
A Man their Mother was,
A Muse their Sire.

How did the printed infancies result
From Nuptials thus doubly difficult?

If you must needs enquire
Know diligent Reader
That on each Occasion
Ezra performed the caesarean Operation.

A fuller understanding of Pound's efforts, however, is now readily available to those willing to apply themselves diligently to a study of his annotations as these appear

In his essay on "The Frontiers of Criticism," Eliot has told us that to "understand a poem," it is necessary not only to see it as it is but also to see what it was "aiming to be" (OPP 110), and I would venture to suggest that in the disfigured lineaments of "the printed infancies" now before us it is possible to see, not only the poem which with poetic grace it might well have become, but also the various kinds of creative distemper which make it most certainly, far from being Eliot's masterpiece, his most significant "artistic failure," to use the phrase Eliot himself applied to Hamlet (SE 123). If the failure consists in Eliot's inability to fuse the materials of The Waste Land into one harmonious and self-sustaining whole, the critical task, on the other hand, is one of determining just how and why the failure occurred. This task is one which has been immensely forwarded by the appearance of that genetic and biographical material which has recently been put before us, both in the Facsimile Edition of The Waste Land and in Robert Sencourt's T. S. Eliot: A Memoir.[3] The latter book, if it is embarrassingly flossy in treatment and banal in judgment, yet is the first to provide us with a great many of those useful (and generally reliable) factual details of the poet's life without which the scholarly enterprise can very often not go forward. It is worth noting that it was Eliot himself who, in so many of his critical essays, emphasized the fallacy inherent in just that kind of genetic approach to literary works of art as will undoubtedly be given further inpetus by these recent publications. The approach of which Eliot disapproved was one of attempting to understand a poem "by explaining its origins" (OPP 110), or by examining "its sources" (OPP 112), or by directing attention to "the feeling or emotion or vision in the mind of the poet" instead of to "the feeling, or emotion, or vision resulting from the poem" (TSW x).

Commenting on one such endeavour involving Wordsworth, Eliot began by referring to "such information or conjecture" (OPP 112) as had then recently been provided by Sir Herbert Read and by Mr. F. W. Bateson. The former had "explained the rise and fall of Wordsworth's genius by the effects upon him of his affair with Annette Vallon" (OPP 111), whereas the latter had maintained that

---

in the Facsimile Edition. The reader may also consult Hugh Kenner, *The Invisible Poet: T. S. Eliot* (London: Methuen, 1965), pp. 125-31, for a secondary account of the matter.

3. Donald Adamson, ed., *T. S. Eliot: A Memoir, by Robert Sencourt* (New York: Dodd, Mead and Company, 1971).

"the real secret" (*OPP* 112) behind that rise and fall lay, not in the Vallon affair, but in Wordsworth's incestuous love for his sister Dorothy instead. At this point, Eliot was led to remark a little sadly that "a knowledge of the springs which released a poem is not necessarily a help towards understanding the poem" (*OPP* 112) and then to conclude with the following remarkable paragraph— one whose central idea was in large part responsible, not only for establishing the formalist platform of the New Criticism in 1920, but for launching thereby the new and counter-romantic literary theory that would later develop out of it:

I am not maintaining that there is *no* context in which such information or conjecture as that of Sir Herbert Read and Mr. Bateson may be relevant. It is relevant if we want to understand Wordsworth; but it is not directly relevant to our understanding of his poetry. Or rather, it is not relevant to our understanding of *the poetry as poetry*. I am even prepared to suggest that there is, in all great poetry, something which must remain unaccountable however complete might be our knowledge of the poet, and that that is what matters most. When the poem has been made, something new has happened, something that cannot be wholly explained by *anything that went before*. That, I believe, is what we mean by 'creation'. (*OPP* 112)

In this paragraph, Eliot is merely re-echoing the stand he had elaborated much earlier when he said, in his preface to the 1928 edition of *The Sacred Wood*, that "the problem appearing in those essays, which gives them what coherence they have, is the problem of the integrity of poetry, with the repeated assertion that when we are considering poetry we must consider it primarily as poetry and not another thing" (*TSW* viii). It was for this reason that it seemed "a laudable aim" to Eliot in 1919 to "divert interest from the poet to the poetry" (*SE* 11) and to redirect the critical practice of his day by insisting upon a new point of departure for literary criticism, and one that would be genuinely literary rather than biographical or psychological instead. The shift of alignment he effected was so forceful that *The Sacred Wood*, in which he first signalized it, sometimes takes on the air and tonality of a great critical manifesto: "The best that we can hope to do is to agree upon a point from which to start, and that is, in part, the subject of this book" (*TSW* x). Eliot is completely unambiguous as to that starting point. It resides in the poem itself. The aspiration of "The Perfect Critic" (*TSW* 1-16), as opposed to the "Imperfect Critics" (*TSW* 17-46) Eliot scores so vividly in *The Sacred Wood,* must be to look "solely and steadfastly at the object" (*TSW* 11) and, by using the invariable "tools of the critic: comparison and analysis" (*TSW* 37), simply to "elucidate" (*TSW* 11) and thus assist the reader "to see the object as it really is" (*TSW* 15). Thus, literary criticism that is properly *literary* will restrict itself to the poem which "in some sense, has its own life" (*TSW* x) and "its own existence, apart from us" (*Use of* 34).

Eliot's appeal for a new focus or orientation in critical practice was, as I have also suggested above, invariably accompanied by the negative counterpart of it which, in his eyes, had equal importance. If the function of literary criticism *per se* is always "the elucidation of works of art" (*SE* 24), what that function is *not* must be given equal attention, and this aspect of his argument Eliot also puts forward most vigorously. The permanent wedge which Eliot sought to drive between the poet and the poem has perhaps nowhere been made more explicit than it is in the following statement:

But if, either on the basis of what poets try to tell you, or by biographical research, with or without the tools of the psychologist, you attempt to explain a poem, you will probably be getting further and further away from the poem without arriving at any other destination. The attempt to explain the poem by tracing it back to its origins will distract attention from the poem, to direct it on to something else which, in the form in which it can be apprehended by the critic and his readers, has no relation to the poem and throws no light upon it. (*OPP* 99)

It was basically for this reason that Eliot believed that "Honest criticism and sensitive appreciation is directed not upon the poet but upon the poetry" (*TSW* 53).

It is precisely because the poem cannot, *as a poem,* be "explained by anything that went before" (*OPP* 112) that the attention of "The Perfect Critic" must be focused upon it, rather than upon the poet who served as the vehicle of its "creation." Thus the fresh bias of what John Crowe Ransom would later designate as the New Criticism, in his book of that title,[4] would seem to be unmistakably clear. It was, as I have already said, a bias which sought to redirect attention from "the feeling or emotion or vision in the mind of the poet" to "the feeling, or emotion, or vision resulting from the poem" (*TSW* x) and one which insisted that, not only are the two radically different in kind, but that it is only the latter which can be of real concern to the literary critic and provide him with the proper ground for aesthetic valuation.

When Eliot, in his Preface to the 1928 edition of *The Sacred Wood,* emphasized the importance of "considering poetry . . .

4. J. C. Ransom, *The New Criticism* (Norfolk: New Directions, 1941).

primarily as poetry and not another thing" (*TSW* viii), he was concerned that the uses of poetry, whatever they may be, be sought wholly from within the poetic object. The primary assertion was that the poem "has its own life" (*TSW* x), and "its own existence, apart from us" (*Use of* 34), and is ultimately to be evaluated, therefore, in terms of what it is in itself rather than in any referential terms which would focus upon its serviceability to morals, politics, religion, psychology, or history (*TSW* ix). What poetry can do, Eliot everywhere insists, it can do only by being what it is "and not another thing" (*TSW* viii). The ground of its real value is to be sought in the kind of thing it is and, when we know this, we will know as well why it can also do some of the other things it does. Thus, what we may call the formalist bias of the New Criticism, together with its rigorously textual approach, was launched and it was this, I believe, which led the New Criticism generally to "restrict the scope of criticism" and to confine its strategy, as Stallman for example has told us it does, "to the literary work itself."[5] If there was any one course upon which the New Criticism was originally set, and upon which there was a large area of agreement in critical purpose, it was one of restoring emphasis to the work of art as an autotelic whole independent of its maker and in no sense to be conceived as a mere extension or reflection of him or of his personal life. The New Criticism, in short, became a criticism largely preoccupied with the means and ends of poetry rather than with its sources.

In becoming so, it may have seemed admirably obedient to Eliot's expressed preferences in *The Sacred Wood* but, in fact, this restriction of critical interest (in which Eliot himself, in virtue of his accounts of the creative process, has never shared) represented only a partial realization of his dictum that it is the poem itself which must provide the literary critic with the material of his analysis and evaluation. In the second edition of *The Sacred Wood,* Eliot indicated that the formalist bias of that book merely represented for him "logically and chronologically the beginning" of critical inquiry, not its end and certainly not its totality (*TSW* viii). He indicated further that he had himself already moved on "to another problem not touched upon in this book: that of the relation of poetry to the spiritual and social life of its time and of other times" (*TSW* viii). Thus, on the very same page, we find Eliot asserting the

5. R. W. Stallman, *Critiques and Essays in Criticism: 1920-1948* (New York: Ronald Press Company, 1949), p. 9.

autotelic nature of the poem on the one hand and its referential thrust on the other. He has given witness both to the centripetal nature of poetry and to its centrifugal force as well and if, at the level of statement, a contradiction seems to appear, yet I would suggest that the contradiction is more apparent than real and is nothing to boggle over at the more imperious level of the realities involved.

In order that this may be shown, let us first consider *all* of the possibilities which may be thought to exist for the literary critic simply in virtue of the four central and coordinate terms which mark the limits of literary criticism as a humanistic discipline—that is, the work of art itself, *the poem;* its maker, *the poet;* the audience to which it is in some sense addressed, *its reader;* and the all-embracing *whole of reality* within which, first, it is made and, second, it continues to exist. I can perhaps recapitulate the entire scope of critical interrelationships by which the limits as well as the major preoccupations of various literary critics and their schools may be defined in a mnemonically helpful Reality-Poet-Poem-Reader-Reality trope which, if schematically diagrammed, would look like this:

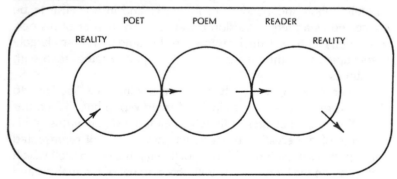

It was in 1956, in his essay on "The Frontiers of Criticism," that Eliot addressed himself to the question: "when is criticism not literary criticism but something else?" (*OPP* 106), and the answer he arrived at was that "The critic accordingly is a *literary* critic if his primary interest, in writing criticism, is to help his readers to *understand and enjoy*" (*OPP* 116). The remainder of Eliot's essay makes it abundantly clear that what they are "to understand and enjoy" is the work of literature itself—that signified by the third term in our suggested trope and by the central circle in our diagram.

8

The attack Eliot launches against those "Imperfect Critics" pilloried in *The Sacred Wood*, on the other hand, rests on the fact that they "are often interested—but not quite in the nominal subject, often in something a little beside the point" (*TSW* 24). Eliot does not condemn their variant interest and he indicates that such critical activity may still be "legitimate and useful" (*OPP* 116) but, in this case, the result "is to be judged as a contribution to psychology, or sociology, or logic, or pedagogy, or some other pursuit—and is to be judged by specialists, not by men of letters" (*OPP* 116-17). There is not for Eliot, as he says himself, any such thing as "forbidden ground" (*OPP* 114)—just ground that is sometimes literary, sometimes not. When it is not, the critic using it—whatever else he may be—is not primarily a *literary* critic. Eliot's final stand in the matter was formulated in 1955 and he put it this way: "Literary criticism is an activity which must constantly define its own boundaries; also, it must constantly be going beyond them: the one invariable rule is, that when the literary critic exceeds his frontiers, he should do so in full consciousness of what he is doing" (*OPP* 215). Eliot's own practice as a critic was always consonant with the implications of this statement and, as a consequence, his criticism exhibits a catholicity of interest which the work of many other New Critics has hardly managed to suggest. It is a catholicity which led him in the course of his literary life to range freely that entire spectrum of interrelationships involved in the perceptive practice of literary criticism which I have attempted to schematize in the diagram provided above.

It has been necessary to mention this apparent inconsistency in Eliot's critical theory not only because it has plagued so many of the earlier commentators on his criticism but because the particular kind of critical enterprise attempted here derives its impetus, as well as its principle of organization, from the triadic relationships everywhere underlying Eliot's literary theory and implicit in the diagram schematized above. In short, what the present study will attempt to do is to emulate Eliot's own critical practice by seeking a thoroughly comprehensive version of *The Waste Land*. It will try to gather together in a single picture the various results that can be derived from an exploration of the complex interrelationships in which the poem is involved and which are delineated by our four terms of critical inquiry. Given such aspirations, then, how must one proceed?

9

Clearly one must begin and end, as the New Critics tend to do, with "the literary work itself" and, therefore, with its already structured and formed matter. In the case of *The Waste Land*, this can only mean the poem itself just as the poet finally left it to us. Just as clearly, however, it is important to notice with what inevitability one's critical energy begins to run backwards and forwards into a consideration first of the matter so formed and then of the kind of activity required of the poet to effect the transformation from one to the other. At such a juncture, the centre of interest may be seen to shift from "the literary work itself" to the poet conceived in some sense as its source. In short, it is the psychology of poetic creativity rather than the poem itself which then compels critical interest. It does so, of course, because that psychology includes within itself and relies so extensively upon the Janus-faced distinction between what is "given" to the poet and what is "made" from it. Thus the critic's interest may be either with the poet as maker of the poem, or it may be with his material—the material given to him by his "nature," his personal life, his total universe of "experience," the material upon which he works and to which he is somehow related. It follows too that the possibility of extending critical interest from poem to poet, on the one hand, immediately opens up the possibility of a similar extension in the direction of the reader on the other. In this case, the critical enterprise shifts to a concern with the poem as the vehicle of certain effects, as the purveyor of an aesthetic experience, or of that "art emotion" (*SE* 10) in which the poem's primary value for the reader interested "in poetry and not another thing" resides. What the relation of that "art emotion" as finally objectified and arrested in the poem is to the "personality and emotions" (*SE* 11) of "the man who suffers" (*SE* 8) or to "the mind which creates" (*SE* 8) is a further possible consideration and it is one by which the circle arbitrarily drawn by the strictly practical critic around "the literary work itself" may be brought to a full close.

Eliot has told us many times that "the essential function of literary criticism" is to "promote the understanding and enjoyment of literature" (*OPP* 115). He has also frequently warned us against "mistaking explanation for understanding" (*OPP* 109), a distinction which alerts us to the fact that Eliot is using the word "understanding" in its classical sense and with a meaning, therefore, which to many modern readers will appear highly restricted and special—if, indeed, not wholly occult. If Eliot is hardly expansive or even clear concerning this special meaning, he is nonetheless certainly explicit enough: "By *understanding* I do not mean *explanation* though explanation of what can be explained may often be a necessary preliminary to understanding" (*OPP* 115). Eliot's fullest statement on the matter, however, is perhaps the following: "One can explain a poem by investigating what it is made of and the causes that brought it about; and explanation may be a necessary preparation for understanding. But to understand a poem it is also necessary, and I should say in most instances still more necessary, that we should endeavour to grasp what the poetry is aiming to be; one might say—though it is long since I have employed such terms with any assurance—endeavouring to grasp its entelechy" (*OPP* 110).

The essential distinction to which Eliot is pointing here is the distinction between "explanation" of a work of art and an "understanding" of it vis-à-vis its own "entelechy." But what, we may well ask, is a poem's "entelechy" and how is one in fact "to grasp" it? At this point, Eliot's philosophical writings can be of assistance to us inasmuch as the concept of the "entelechy" is clarified for us there by Eliot's contrast of Aristotle's original use of that word with Leibniz's later obscuration of it. Eliot says: "In the *De Anima* the soul is called the first entelechy of body. . . It is difficult, it is true, not to think of the soul as something added to the body (as to Galatea) or else to identify soul with the (living) body. Soul is to body as cutting is to the axe: realizing itself in its actions, and not completely real when abstracted from what it does" (*KE* 195).

It would seem, then, that the "entelechy" of a poem is that which turns the wheel of its own becoming and Eliot would add that such an entelechy is "only actual when it energizes" (*KE* 195). Just as the axe is really an axe only when it is cutting and thereby "realizing itself" (or making itself really what it is) "in its actions," so the entelechy of a poem is that which inspirits the process whereby it becomes what it is itself "aiming to be"—that is, a poem "and not another thing." The entelechy of a poem is not to be identified with the realized poem—"the (living) soul." It is not, in short, the Word made Flesh, but rather the spirit impelling the Word to *become* Flesh—to become actualized or materialized in time and thus to fulfil the potency it has for temporal and verbal incarnation. It is the entelechy of the poem which vitalizes its parts, informs the composition of the whole, and guides the creative process to its consummation. Both poet and poem, though in different senses, are but vehicles in service to that entelechy, and once the creative process is completed and the poem finally achieved, it is certainly not the

11

poet who stands revealed or objectified within it. It is instead that entelechy or informing and vitalizing spirit of which the poem is a revelation and to which it points. Commenting on one occasion on some stimulating letters of D. H. Lawrence, Eliot expressed this semi-mystical view of poetry as follows:

This speaks to me of that at which I have long aimed, in writing poetry; to write poetry which should be essentially poetry, with nothing poetic about it, poetry standing naked in its bare bones, or poetry so transparent that we should not see the poetry, but that which we are meant to see through the poetry, poetry so transparent that in reading it we are intent on what the poem *points at*, and not on the poetry, this seems to me the thing to try for. To get *beyond poetry*, as Beethoven, in his later works, strove to get *beyond music*. We never succeed, perhaps, but Lawrence's words mean this to me, that they express to me what I think that the forty or fifty original lines that I have written strive towards.[6]

What the present study seeks to do is to "understand" *The Waste Land* in that particular sense which Eliot has applied to the word "understanding." It will, in short, measure and evaluate the poem *as it is* against the criterion provided by what it was "aiming to be." It will "endeavour to grasp"—and to say—just what it was that the poem was "aiming to be," and to do so by addressing itself not only to the poem's centripetal core but by exploring the universe of its centrifugal relations as well. What it hopes finally to delineate thereby are not Eliot's intentions but those of his poem—the poem that "has its own life" (*TSW* x), and "its own existence, apart from us" (*Use of* 34). We shall see later that within Eliot's philosophical world there is no other way than that—the way of relations—for exploring or understanding anything, but for now it may be well to resume briefly what the reader will find developed hereafter in much greater detail.

The conclusion at which the present study arrives is that *The Waste Land* was "aiming to be" an extended interior monologue but not quite in the sense that such other Eliot monologues as "The Love Song of J. Alfred Prufrock," "Portrait of A Lady," and "Geron-tion" are. Unlike those earlier poems, *The Waste Land* aspired to epic status but it was inevitable—given such an aspiration—that Eliot would eschew those classical or Miltonic precedents for the epic which, if they might provide him with earlier paradigms for the concept of the epic hero, yet could no longer serve the ideological

6. These remarks of Eliot's are taken from an unpublished lecture which he delivered in New Haven, Connecticut. They are quoted by F. O. Matthiessen in his *The Achievement of T. S. Eliot* (London: Oxford University Press, 1947), p. 90.

and imaginative requirements of a genuine modernity in defining later ones. What Eliot would seek instead was to create for his time a neo-epic of the interior life—an epic, that is, mounted upon *le paysage intérieur*. In his attempt to do so, Eliot was in fact joining issue with some of his earlier romantic predecessors as well as with some later modern contemporaries such as Ezra Pound, Hart Crane, William Carlos Williams, and Wallace Stevens.

The landscapes of the mind, however, together with the drama implicit within them, could attain such epic proportions only if the mind being dramatized was of far greater significance than is that of the merely empirical self or phenomenal ego conventionally found at the base of the poetic monologue—whether in its nineteenth-century dramatic, or in its twentieth-century interior, form —and this is the peculiar dilemma residing at the ideological core both of the romantic epic and of its "hero" as well. It was a dilemma that defeated Eliot's romantic predecessors, and must inevitably have done so, because of the fatal disjunction between the two selves and their respective worlds—phenomenal and noumenal—which they inherited from Kant and which, as a consequence, made it impossible for them ever after to create a viable methodology of transcendence from the phenomenal world of one to the noumenal world of the other. It was, in short, the metaphysical dualism underlying romantic thought which enervated the aspirations of the romantic hero and at the same time obviated the possibility of structuring an epic of the interior life around him, or around what Keats designated as "the wordsworthian or egotistical sublime."[7] Those merely phenomenal heroes of the post-Cartesian world could never satisfy that "spirit unappeased and peregrine / *Between* two worlds" (*LG* II italics mine) in whom Eliot would seek, and eventually find, his own generic literary persona—the persona, that is, of the dialectical hero central to post-Hegelian English and American philosophy and central as well to the formation of all Eliot's major poems from *The Waste Land* on.

It is one of the major achievements of *The Waste Land* that Eliot found for himself and his time the dialectical hero wanted by his poem. If in that poem Eliot's epic aspirations remained—like those of the romantics before him—similarly unfulfilled, yet the fault was not finally (as it was with them) to be found in his philosophy. It was to be found instead in an unfortunate, and indeed fatal, coincidence

7. Hyder E. Rollins, ed., *The Letters of John Keats: 1814-1821* (Cambridge: Harvard University Press, 1958), 1, 387.

13

between the poet as maker of his poem and the poet as persona within it—a coincidence similarly known to many of Eliot's romantic predecessors and similarly debilitating to their creativity. It was that coincidence which was largely responsible for Eliot's inability to internalize within *The Waste Land* in a formally successful way the philosophical resolution of the romantic dilemma which, under Bradley's tutelage, he had already worked out for himself in his early philosophical writings. It is in those writings that we may see provided the ideological base for the correlative literary creation of "the generic Eliot character"[8] or persona, the generic Eliot theme, and the generic Eliot form whose embodiment would become the informing spirit (or entelechy) behind everything Eliot wrote, once he had completed his doctoral dissertation on *Knowledge and Experience in The Philosophy of F. H. Bradley* in 1916.[9] It was, however, the successful integration of those three constituent aspects of his poem—hero, theme, and form—that eluded Eliot in 1921 and 1922, and kept *The Waste Land* from becoming the neo-epic of modernity I think it was "aiming to be."

I can only suggest here, and in brief, the view I shall defend more fully later on—the view, that is, that at the core of such a modern epic poem must be a persona consonant with the lineaments of post-Hegelian dialectical thought. Such a persona cannot be conceived in terms of that "metaphysical theory of the substantial unity of the soul" which Eliot must inevitably have found himself "struggling to attack" (*SE* 9) in 1918, for that earlier Aristotelian theory could not accommodate the more dynamic features of the post-Hegelian dialectical hero. Instead, that hero must reveal an essentially transcendental (rather than transcendent or already fully existent) nature and, further, his transcendentalism must involve him to some extent at least in that paradox of the "two natures" —both man and god, human and divine, "Torn and most whole" (*AW* 11)—which would seem to make him a prime candidate for Christianization. What Eliot in fact did by telescoping in the persona of his poem the formerly disjoined mythical existents of Fisher King and Quester Hero was to Christianize that myth which provided him with the scaffolding of his poem in precisely the way that,

8. The phrase is Hugh Kenner's but I would disagree with his identification of that character with Prufrock. See Kenner, *The Invisible Poet: T. S. Eliot*, p. 35.

9. See T. S. Eliot, *Knowledge and Experience in the Philosophy of F. H. Bradley* (London: Faber and Faber, 1964). See Appendix II for an account of some of the problems involved in using Eliot's philosophy as a critical vehicle for enlarging our understanding of his poetry and criticism.

under the tutelage of Josiah Royce, he had earlier Christianized "the philosophy of F. H. Bradley." In this venture, the transmutation of Bradley's philosophy is so nearly complete as almost to transform it into something other than itself and, accordingly, there will be those who believe that in this regard Eliot (and Royce before him) have arrived equally at a point of irremediable inconsistency in their philosophical positions. I cannot entirely concur in such a view, but I can well understand the considerations which might prompt someone to formulate it.[10]

If "the generic Eliot character" is to be identified as the dialectical hero of Hegel and Bradley, the generic theme proper to the modern long poem at the centre of which he might comfortably reside can only be identified with that dialectical and transubstantiatory process whereby the new and more heroic substance is achieved. Hero and theme, in short, are yoked together by virtue of that process they equally express, albeit in slightly different ways. What that process yields to the poem's persona is the new substance of the Pauline "new man," whereas what it gives to the poem itself is its theme—that theme which, when fulfilled, yields to its reader that equally new and never before existent "substance of the poem" to which Eliot misleadingly refers in one of his notes to it.

If, so far as *The Waste Land* goes, hero and theme are both seriously obscured, the cause in some measure is to be found in the enormous difficulties Eliot faced in creating a wholly new methodology of literary form that would be consonant with the structure of the philosophy he had come to espouse. In short, the literary form generic to post-Hegelian dialectical philosophy is a form whose lineaments will retrace with precision the triadic nature of the experiential process involved in creative becoming. It is one of Eliot's major achievements in *The Waste Land* that he did in fact create such a form and did to some extent use it in his poem. One of Eliot's major failures, on the other hand, derives from his inability to sustain that achievement throughout the poem as a whole.

If for the moment, then, one can accept the working hypothesis that *The Waste Land* was "aiming to be" a neo-epic of modernity, the next task becomes one of determining precisely how and why the poem foundered. In my first chapter I have addressed directly the first of those three major unresolved conflicts which, lying at the core of the poem's genesis, are in my view responsible for the

10. See my account of Bradley's own position in chap. VII, and also p. 153, n. 1.

15

poem's failure to fulfill its own aims more completely. What I attempt to show there is the nature of the artistic problem which was created for Eliot by that crippling coincidence which seems to me to exist between the poet-maker of his poem and the poet-protagonist of it. Because of it, the poem divides rather than unifies itself between the two distinct "voices" which Eliot developed as a way of expressing the variant impulses by which the poem was being energized—one public, and the other private to Eliot himself.

The second major unresolved conflict which the poem's formation reveals has to do with the formal incongruity existing between Parts I, III, and V of *The Waste Land* on the one hand, and Parts II and IV on the other. I have outlined the nature of that conflict in my second chapter and have done so by way of the distinction Eliot has himself drawn between the second and third of "The Three Voices of Poetry" he has described in that essay. Whereas one can see quite clearly in Parts I, III, and V of the poem the emergent form of an extended interior monologue, its second and fourth parts (and even some of the individual frames within Part I) stand in its midst like fully formed globules of independent matter, but matter formed to other and more dramatic ends than those which can be served by *le paysage intérieur* and by a narrative monologue expressive of them.

My third chapter is more generalized in treatment and historical in design. It provides an account of the common effort made by many modern artists at the turn of the century to create a new post-Hegelian, and consequently postexpressionistic, aesthetic theory which would be consonant with the ideological requirements of their own time and significantly different, therefore, from that of the romantics before them. It is the work primarily of Eisenstein, Joyce, and Eliot which, in that chapter, provides some of the more instructive examples we have of the difficulties involved, first, in delineating the concept of dialectical form and, then, in applying it to the making of genuinely modern works of art.

If my earlier chapters make use of the perspectives provided to the literary critic by the first three of our critical terms—that is, Reality, Poet, and Poem—my fourth goes on to concern itself with the relational perspective created by that of the Reader. It deals, in short, with some of the practical implications which the concept of dialectical form has for the post-Hegelian reader of modern poetry and it attempts to provide an example of the actual difference made to the reading of such a poem as *The Waste Land* by applying to it the import of those dialectical principles which are seen as informing its composition. Then, leaving behind them the problem of the poem's dialectical form, my fifth and sixth chapters return to a further consideration of the artistic problems surrounding both the formation and the presentation of its dialectical hero. That consideration is set against the historical background of those ideological developments in philosophy which separate the romantic and the modern irrevocably from one another as regards their divergent conceptions of the nature of heroism. It is the Keatsian concept of "Soul-making" which in those chapters provides me not with the chronological but with the ideological point of transition from one to the other, for almost a hundred years had to pass before the importance of Keats' intuitive insights were to be fully recognized and then taken up by The New Idealism of Bradley and Bosanquet as the core concepts around which they would systematize their philosophy. If my fifth chapter is concerned specifically with the historical emergence of the concept of dialectical becoming or of "Soul-making," the sixth has to do with Bradley's historic formulations of the logical and metaphysical base necessary to support that concept successfully.

Finally, having derived from Eliot's own philosophy the material necessary to a fuller understanding of the nature and extent of his creative enterprise, my study concludes with an application of that understanding to the last of those three unresolved conflicts which served to bereave *The Waste Land* of the complete success it might otherwise have achieved. If one would perceive the nature of that third unresolved conflict clearly, however, it is imperative to understand that within post-Hegelian philosophy god is dead—at least, in the traditional Christian and transcendent form delineated by an earlier philosophy. What exists instead at the centre of a dialectical universe is a perpetually dying and reviving god and one who ceaselessly turns the wheel of its becoming as he continually passes out of and regains himself at a higher level. It is that spiralling process which drives him to his own ever-expanding integrity or wholeness and which confers on the dialectical hero the only principle of divinity which can possibly exist in a post-Hegelian world. In specific terms, my seventh and final chapter is concerned, then, with those minimal changes which were still required even after "the better craftsman" had completed his work, if the earlier romantic disjunction of the "two souls" (*KE* 206)—phenomenal and noumenal—was to be resolved in the spiralling continuities of the dying and reviving god Eliot tried, but with only partial success, to put at the centre of his poem.

It is perhaps unfortunate that the spiral of the dialectical hero begins within the "the man who suffers" rather than within "the mind which creates" (*SE* 8), for it is that circumstance that necessitates at least some mention in the present study of that highly restricted biographical material which has recently been the cause of so much furor in the world of Eliot scholarship. A word must be said now concerning some of the critical issues surrounding the use of that material.

Eliot's reservations concerning biographical criticism are, as I have tried to point out earlier, grounded finally in literary principle, but they are also—and I think undoubtedly—the result of his well-known personal reticence as well. One need only recall Eliot's comments on John Middleton Murry's account (in his *Son of Woman: The Story of D. H. Lawrence*) of "the emotional dislocation" Lawrence underwent as the result of his "mother-complex" to perceive the lineaments of Eliot's own fear. Eliot says: "Mr. Murry has written a brilliant book . . . . It is a definitive work of critical biography, or biographical criticism. It is so well done that it gives me the creeps: probably these matters matter no longer to Lawrence himself; but any author still living might shudder to think of the possibility of such a book of destructive criticism being written about him after he is dead."[11] It is this compound of literary principle and personal reticence which must have led Eliot to restrict as emphatically as he did in his will the use of all genetic material by students of his work. The following letter, written by his publisher and making Eliot's position unequivocally clear, was printed in *The Daily Telegraph* on 23 July 1970:

SIR—We have been interested to read the letter from Mr. T. S. Matthews (July 7) concerning his proposed biography of T. S. Eliot.

In a memorandum dated Sept. 30, 1963, attached to his will, Eliot wrote: "I do not wish my Executors to facilitate or countenance the writing of any biography of me": and we as his publishers are honouring his request. On the other hand he authorised us to publish his letters, and this we are planning to do at the earliest possible moment.

P. F. DU SAUTOY
Vice-Chairman. Faber & Faber Ltd.

11. T. S. Eliot, [A review of] *Son of Woman: The Story of D. H. Lawrence*, by John Middleton Murry, *Criterion* X, 41 (July 1931), 768-69.

That Eliot's restrictions are not limited solely to the biographical form of genetic criticism is clear from the letter he wrote to John Quinn on 22 September [1922] concerning the manuscript and typescript material he presented to Quinn at that time—material which included the various drafts of *The Waste Land* now put before us by Mrs. Eliot in her Facsimile Edition. In a part of that letter which Mrs. Eliot does not quote for us in her introduction, Eliot says: "You will find a great many sets of verse which have never been printed and which I am sure you will agree never ought to be printed, and, in putting them in your hands, I beg you fervently to keep them to yourself and see that they never are printed."[12]

If, in publishing the Facsimile and Transcript of *The Waste Land,* Mrs. Eliot would seem to have abrogated her late husband's wish that his manuscript and typescript material should never be printed, it can only be because of a second wish, not altogether consonant with the first, which Eliot expressed in another part of this same letter to Quinn which Mrs. Eliot *does* quote and which reads as follows:

> I am quite overwhelmed by your letter, by all that you have done for me, by the results that you have effected, and by your endless kindness. In fact, the greatest pleasure of all that it has given me is the thought that there should be anybody in the world who would take such an immense amount of pains on my behalf. The thought of this will be a permanent satisfaction to me.
>
> My only regret (which may seem in the circumstances either ungracious or hypocritical) is that this award [The annual Dial award of $2000 for service to letters in America] should come to me before it has been given to Pound. I feel that he deserves the recognition much more than I do, certainly 'for his services to Letters', and I feel that I ought to have been made to wait until after he had received this public testimony. In the manuscript of *The Waste Land* which I am sending you, you will see the evidences of his work, and I think that this manuscript is worth preserving in its present form solely for the reason that it is the only evidence of the difference which his criticism has made to this poem. . . .[13]

If one requires a further example of this same ambivalence in Eliot's desires as regards Pound's annotations, one has only to recall the statement he made in 1946 while discussing those same annotations in *Poetry.* On that occasion, he put it this way: "I should like to think that the manuscript, with the suppressed passages, had disappeared irrecoverably: yet on the other hand, I should wish the

12. B. L. Reid, *The Man from New York: John Quinn and His Friends* (New York: Oxford University Press, 1968), p. 540.
13. Valerie Eliot, ed., *The Waste Land: A Facsimile and Transcript,* xxiv.

blue penciling on it to be preserved as irrefutable evidence of Pound's critical genius."[14]

What we are given in these two instances are not uncharacteristic examples of that yeastiness which enables anyone and everyone to quote Eliot with ease ever after and to derive from him whatever leaven is required for his own particular loaf. If, in short, "the difference which . . . [Pound's] criticism has made to this poem" is a significant difference—and Eliot has repeatedly assured us that it is—and if the evidence for that difference is "worth preserving," then it can only be for the purpose of *demonstrating* "the difference . . . made to this poem" by it. It must be this latter motive which has prevailed most strongly upon Mrs. Eliot and which has prompted her wise decision to publish Eliot's manuscript material despite Eliot's own earlier caveats about the wisdom of doing so. It is a decision for which all students of Eliot's work can only be enormously grateful.

A word must be said finally concerning the original drafts of *The Waste Land* and Pound's memorable annotations of them. In my view, the contributions Pound made to the poem's unity and integral wholeness—two of the more central concerns of the present study—derive from, and are limited to, two specifics:

1. his excisions of all material extraneous to that unity—excisions amounting to almost three hundred lines of verse, and

2. his insistence that the Phlebas passage constituting Part IV of the poem be retained in its present form when Eliot, depressed by his ruthless excision of the eighty-three lines precedent to that passage, wanted to excise it as well. Pound's comment on this point is worth repeating both for its inimitable style and for its importance to the argument which will eventually follow: "I DO advise keeping Phlebas. In fact I more'n advise. Phlebas is an integral part of the poem; the card pack introduces him, the drowned phoen. sailor. And he is needed ABSOLOOTLY where he is. Must stay in."[15] In short, the effect of the excisions was, in Eliot's own words, to reduce "a sprawling, chaotic poem called *The Waste Land* . . . to about half its size"[16] and thus to rid it not only of all verse that was merely derivative or of secondary intensity but to rid it as well of such material as could only obscure further the lineaments of the poem's own informing vision and integrity.

14. T. S. Eliot, "Ezra Pound," *Poetry* LXVIII, 6 (September 1946), 330.
15. Paige, ed., *Letters of Ezra Pound: 1907-1941*, p. 237.
16. Eliot, "Ezra Pound," 330.

It is noteworthy that Pound, in describing *The Waste Land* to some of Eliot's friends, spoke of it as: *"a series of poems* [italics mine] possibly the finest that the modern movement in English has produced, at any rate as good as anything that has been done since 1900, and which certainly loses nothing by comparison with the best work of Keats, Browning, or Shelley."[17] The concern of "the better craftsman" was directed primarily to *"the poetry as poetry"* (*OPP* 112)—"poetry," that is, "as excellent words in excellent arrangement and excellent metre" (*TSW* ix)—and does not, therefore, deal significantly with the problems of structure and form more central to the designs and purposes of the present study. What Pound's marginalia—now so decisively preserved—really bear witness to is not only what Eliot has described as Pound's "critical genius" but also to just how unbelievably banal some of Eliot's verse could be. With a little help, however, Eliot managed to get rid of such detritus, for example, as "When Lil's husband was coming back out of the Transport Corps"[18] in favor of Pound's "When Lil's husband got demobbed." It is great fun to go through the Facsimile Edition and watch Pound's critical pencil at work, guided as it always and unerringly was by his impeccable sense of rhythm, and by his unrelenting demand both for the visually specific and for the maximum concentration derivable from the use of the exact, rather than the nearly exact, word. Henceforward, that edition can only be regarded in the way that Eliot himself used to look upon Pound's *Cantos*—that is, as "indeed a mine for juvenile poets to quarry."[19] Frequently the changes seem so slight, and yet how beautifully advantaged the various passages emerge. Sometimes the change or suppression of merely one word is enough to release a line from bondage and to transmute the banal into the poetic as, for example, in the designation of Mr. Eugenides' French as "demotic" instead of as "abominable," and also as did the suppression of "black" from the line "Only a [black] cock stood on the rooftree."[20] One needs, however, in conclusion, to remark on Eliot's occasional—and, in this reader's view, justified—resistances to some of Pound's suggestions as well. When Pound would have deleted the Shakespearean "Those are pearls that were his eyes," Eliot left the line in, and the typist scene continues to be played out

17. Paige, ed., *Letters of Ezra Pound: 1907-1941*, p. 241.

18. Valerie Eliot, ed., *The Waste Land: A Facsimile and Transcript*, p. 13.

19. T. S. Eliot, "Introduction," *Ezra Pound: Selected Poems* (London: Faber and Faber, 1928), p. 19.

20. Valerie Eliot, ed., *The Waste Land: A Facsimile and Transcript*, p. 87.

during the "violet hour" despite Pound's objection to the visual imprecision of the phrase.[21]

When the most important poem of the century has been designated "an artistic failure," it is necessary, if not to be guarded, at least to be clear—in any event, clearer than Eliot was before me in designating Shakespeare's *Hamlet* in that way (*SE* 123). The judgment of failure is, as I have tried to show earlier, one derived from and shored against the poem's own aspirations. What that poem is, is not quite what it was "aiming to be" and, as a consequence, if it is a poem that has attained a large measure of notoriety in the half-century of life it has already had, and has also been much enjoyed, yet it is a poem that has all too frequently been enjoyed for the wrong reasons. This returns us at last to the point from which we began, and to Graham Hough who can be of service here because he has put the matter of the poem's failure, together with some of the reasons for it, most simply and directly. He begins with the straightforward and emphatic assertion: "I cannot think that the problems raised by the structure of *The Waste Land* have been faced"[22] and he ends by committing himself to the view "that for a poem to exist as a unity . . . , we need the sense of one voice speaking, as in lyric or elegiac verse; or of several voices intelligibly related to each other, as in narrative with dialogue, or drama."[23]

Basically I feel committed to the same view and well understand the extent and depth of the frustrations that curl the edges of Hough's book. The "sense of one voice speaking" throughout, or of "several voices intelligibly related to each other," *is* indispensable to the integrity of this poem and this is not what we are in fact given in *The Waste Land.* I would suggest, however, that if we were to apply to the poem the aural discriminations Eliot put forward in his essay on "The Three Voices of Poetry," it is possible to gain not only "the sense of one voice speaking" but the sense as well of how other voices in the poem might be "intelligibly related" to it. Such a procedure cannot make the poem any more organically successful than it now is but it can serve to illumine both what the poem was "aiming to be" and some of the difficulties on which it foundered.

21. Ibid., pp. 7 and 43 respectively.
22. Graham Hough, *Reflections on A Literary Revolution* (Washington, D.C.: The Catholic University of America Press, 1960), p: 28.
23. Ibid., p. 34.

1

"what shall I be?"

It will be remembered that the major distinction Eliot makes between poetry of the first voice and poetry of the second is the
distinction between poetry addressed to oneself "or to nobody,"
and poetry addressed "to other people." That lyric poetry can be
defined in other ways, Eliot is aware but his concern here is to
identify it with the voice that is properly the poet's own. He pref-
aces this section of his essay therefore with the following statement:
"It is obviously the lyric in the sense of a poem 'directly expressing
the poet's own thoughts and sentiments' . . . that is relevant to my
first voice—the voice of the poet talking to himself—or to nobody.
It is in this sense that the German poet Gottfried Benn, in a very
interesting lecture entitled *Probleme der Lyrik,* thinks of lyric as the
poetry of the first voice" (*OPP* 97). Eliot goes on then to discuss
Herr Benn's lecture and to give an account, which for convenience
I shall abbreviate, of the particular kind of human situation which,
if it involves a poet, is likely to result in the writing of lyric poetry:

What, asks Herr Benn in this lecture, does the writer of such a poem,
'addressed to no one,' start with? There is first, he says, an inert embryo
or 'creative germ' . . . and, on the other hand, the Language, the resources
of the words at the poet's command. He has something germinating in him
for which he must find words; but he cannot know what words he wants
until he has found the words; he cannot identify this embryo until it has
been transformed into an arrangement of the right words in the right order.
When you have the words for it, the 'thing' for which the words had to

23

be found has disappeared, replaced by a poem. What you start from is nothing so definite as an emotion, in any ordinary sense; it is still more certainly not an idea; it is—to adapt two lines of Beddoes to a different meaning—a

> bodiless childful of life in the gloom
> Crying with frog voice, 'what shall I be?'

I agree with Gottfried Benn, and I would go a little further. In a poem which is neither didactic nor narrative, and not animated by any other social purpose, the poet may be concerned solely with expressing in verse—using all his resources of words [sic], with their history, their connotations, their music—this obscure impulse. He does not know what he has to say until he has said it; and in the effort to say it he is not concerned with making other people understand anything. He is not concerned, at this stage, with other people at all: only with finding the right words or, anyhow, the least wrong words. He is not concerned whether anybody else will ever understand them if he does. He is oppressed by a burden which he must bring to birth in order to obtain relief. Or, to change the figure of speech, he is haunted by a demon, a demon against which he feels powerless, because in its first manifestation it has no face, no name, nothing; and the words, the poem he makes, are a kind of form of exorcism of this demon. In other words again, he is going to all that trouble, not in order to communicate with anyone, but to gain relief from acute discomfort; and when the words are finally arranged in the right way—or in what he comes to accept as the best arrangement he can find—he may experience a moment of exhaustion, of appeasement, of absolution, and of something very near annihilation, which is in itself indescribable. And then he can say to the poem: 'Go away! Find a place for yourself in a book—and don't expect *me* to take any further interest in you.' (*OPP* 97-8)

It is noteworthy in this context that the point of Eliot's remarks on *Hamlet* is to suggest that that is at least one play which finds its origins in the particular kind of experience he and Herr Benn are describing here: "*Hamlet,* like the sonnets, is full of some stuff that the writer could not drag to light, contemplate, or manipulate into art" (*SE* 124). Alternatively, I believe that whether or not this is true of *Hamlet,* it is certainly true of *The Waste Land.* As with the earlier work, I think that "we must simply admit that here . . . [Eliot] tackled a problem which proved too much for him" (*SE* 126). The remainder of this chapter will be concerned with some of the internal evidence by which these assertions may be gounded but we may as well add here Eliot's own admission of the point in a brief commencement address he delivered at Concord Academy in 1947. On that occasion, he said that he had written *The Waste Land* primarily "to relieve my emotions" and as "a purely personal act."[1] To this we may now add the further evidence provided by Mrs. Eliot's epigraph to the Facsimile Edition of the poem. That epigraph consists of the following statement made by Eliot during a lecture at Harvard University and recorded by his brother: "Various critics have done me the honour to interpret the poem in terms of criticism of the contemporary world, have considered it, indeed, as an important bit of social criticism. To me it was only the relief of a personal and wholly insignificant grouse against life; it is just a piece of rhythmical grumbling. T. S. E."

It would seem quite clear that what Eliot was mainly intent on doing when he wrote *The Waste Land* was to exorcise his own private demons and that, I would suggest, is assuredly one of the reasons why this poem had bedevilled his critics ever since. It would not, however, have done so if its lyricism were pure, and if Eliot had really been "talking to himself—or to nobody" but a writer who is "going to all that trouble, not in order to communicate with anyone, but to gain relief from acute discomfort" does not then go on to lay his oppressive burden before the public, supplemented with notes. In other words, if it is clear that the "obscure impulse" is there, it is equally clear that this is a poem animated—at least in part—by other, and more social, purposes as well. As a consequence, what we hear when we listen to *The Waste Land* are two voices which Eliot at the time was not able to fuse successfully—that is, "The voice of the poet talking to himself—or to nobody," and also "the voice of the poet addressing an audience, whether large or small." If *The Waste Land* remains flawed as a work of art, at least part of the problem resides in the implications of that "also," for what finally results from the crossing of these diffuse impulses is a poem that, while it hopes to communicate, is determined not to communicate too much. In order that this may be seen more clearly, we must concern ourselves next with the mythical scaffolding upon which the poem is said to be constructed and all commentary on that aspect of the poem must, of course, begin with Eliot's own headnote to *The Waste Land:*

Not only the title, but the plan and a good deal of the incidental symbolism of the poem were suggested by Miss Jessie L. Weston's book on the Grail Legend: *From Ritual to Romance* (Cambridge). Indeed, so deeply am I indebted, Miss Weston's book will elucidate the difficulties of the poem much better than my notes can do; and I recommend it (apart from the great interest of the book itself) to any who think such elucidation of the poem worth the trouble. To another work of anthropology I am indebted in general, one which has influenced our generation profoundly; I mean

1. Recorded by Richard Chase in "T. S. Eliot in Concord," *American Scholar* XVI (Autumn 1947), 441.

The Golden Bough; I have used especially the two volumes *Adonis, Attis, Osiris.* Anyone who is acquainted with these works will immediately recognize in the poem certain references to vegetation ceremonies.

Anyone who consults Jessie Weston's *From Ritual to Romance* and Frazer's *The Golden Bough* as Eliot suggests here may indeed "recognize in the poem certain references to vegetation ceremonies," but it is hardly likely that they "will elucidate the difficulties of the poem" to any great extent inasmuch as anyone familiar with the works Eliot cites will also be aware that "The Grail Legend" *as such* does not exist. It is a construct made up of what Miss Weston herself calls "a congeries of widely differing elements"[2] which poets and scholars tend to assemble in markedly differing ways. It is in these novelties of composition and treatment rather than in the "elements" themselves that one is likely to find the more trustworthy indices of what the poem was "aiming to be" as well as "the plan" which Eliot tells us it has. Nonetheless, and despite the enormous number and variety of extant versions, it is true that certain features of the Grail story do appear often enough and with such salience as to distinguish themselves from peripheral and inconstant accretions. When these are taken together, the skeleton of a "story" does begin to emerge—a story that goes back to time immemorial and one which has appeared in countless diverse times and places.

The first of these more or less constant features of the legend concerns the land. It is, we are told, languishing under a prolonged drought which has destroyed all life and all vegetation. In some versions of the legend, the land is called the Waste Land and its ruler, the Fisher King, is also wounded, and wounded in the sexual organs. In most versions, the plight of the land is closely linked with that of its ruler whose infirmity is a cause or an extension or a sign of the sickness of the land. As Miss Weston herself puts it, "for some mysterious and unexplained reason [the king's infirmity] reacts disastrously upon his kingdom, either depriving it of vegetation, or exposing it to the ravages of war."[3] In short the Fisher King's sexual impotence is correlative to the dryness of the land and it is in the inability of either to produce that the vegetative and fertility elements of the myth come together. Not only, however, is the Fisher King sexually impotent but he is also impotent to do

2. Jessie Weston, *From Ritual to Romance* [1920] (Garden City: Doubleday, 1957), p. 2.
3. Ibid., p. 20.

26

anything either for the land or for himself directly and it is because of this that the Grail Hero, rather than the Fisher King, dominates the action which the legend encompasses. The Quester, a knight of surpassing purity, must undergo a ritual quest which always involves a series of temptations and terrifying trials culminating in a nightmarish ordeal at the Perilous Chapel to which he must finally repair in order to ask certain specific questions. If he asks these properly, the healing waters flow and both the King and the Waste Land are restored.

These four features of the legend then—the land that is waste, the impotent Fisher King, the Quester Hero and, finally, his ritual quest culminating in the ordeal at the Perilous Chapel—remain surprisingly constant and define the mythical pattern which Eliot doubtless saw as providing the linear or narrative "plan" of the poem he was writing. At least, these are the features which he does in fact take over from the books he cites. Other features, equally central to the legend, such as "The Hidden Castle with its solemn Feast, and mysterious Feeding Vessel, the Bleeding Lance and Cup,"[4] he disregards, but the existence in the poem even of the four constants is not to be taken for granted. The Fisher King, for example, is nowhere mentioned in the poem itself but only in Eliot's supplementary notes. It is noteworthy too that the only observable relation between the Perilous Chapel which Miss Weston describes and "the empty chapel" which appears in line 388 of the poem is that both serve as the place wherein the Quester asks his questions. I am suggesting, in short, that the relations which exist between "The Grail Legend" and Eliot's poem, if they are suggestive, are also quite tenuous and that critically speaking it is perhaps more important to concern ourselves with the remarkable changes Eliot forced upon the myth so that it might serve his own special, and indeed very private, needs rather than with those elements which he merely took over from it. It is in these alterations that we shall find the surest evidence we have for the intrusion of that "obscure impulse" which "the writer could not drag to light, contemplate, or manipulate into art" as successfully as he might otherwise have done.

Before bringing his essay on "The Three Voices of Poetry" to a close, Eliot makes a very interesting comment on the relationship that exists between the experiential material within him which the poet is seeking to transform into art and the "set of objects . . . [the] situation . . . [the] chain of events" (SE 124-5) which he seeks as

4. Ibid., p. 3.

a mode of effecting that transformation. He says: "It is likely, of course, that it is in the beginning the pressure of some rude unknown *psychic material* that directs the poet to tell that particular story, to develop that particular situation (*OPP* 101)." A full account of the "rude unknown *psychic material*" which impelled Eliot to seek out and use the myth of the impotent Fisher King must await the publication of the poet's biography but a brief mention of that long–drawn–out private tragedy which darkened the middle years of Eliot's life so unmercifully and left such a deep impression on his poetry will perhaps be allowed here.

Most of the *The Waste Land* was written during the autumn of 1921 when Eliot, on the verge of a breakdown and now under the care of a specialist in Lausanne, was taking a rest cure there: "By the waters of Leman I sat down and wept." Six years earlier, he had entered into a disastrous marriage with Vivienne Haigh-Wood, a pretty ballet dancer who, from the very early days of their marriage, began to exhibit the emotionally and sexually disordered behaviour which led ultimately to her confinement in a private institution. It was these early years of their marriage, apparently the most difficult, which gave to Eliot the searing blueprint for the unforgettable and seemingly relentless portraits of the death-in-life of sexual sterility which we find in the poetry he wrote between 1915 and 1930. It was in that year, 1930, when the last of a series of temporary separations from his wife was about to become permanent that Eliot, in a state of bewildered misery, could say in *Ash Wednesday* with full knowledge and resignation as to what lay ahead:

> Because I know I shall not know
> The one veritable transitory power
> Because I cannot drink
> There, where trees flower, and springs flow, for there is nothing
> again.
>
> (*AW* 1)

His wife's illness was a costly one both in terms of money and in terms of the sexual and emotional bankruptcy into which he was driven by it during the years of "this our exile,"

> . . . the years that walk between, bearing
> Away the fiddles and the flutes.
>
> (*AW* IV)[5]

5. D. D. See Paige, ed., *The Letters of Ezra Pound: 1907-1941* (London: Faber and Faber, 1941), pp. 238-41, for evidence of the efforts Pound made to relieve at least the financial side of Eliot's distress by pleading, badgering, and bullying thirty

It is clearly in his own "inveterate scars" (*BN* 11) that the very moving source and more than adequate cause may be found for the rawness, the shuddering distaste, which characterize both Eliot's 1920 volume and *The Waste Land* as well and which generate that sense of futility and dry despair the reader responds to in the inner voice of the poet-protagonist who speaks the entire interior monologue which *The Waste Land* was "aiming to be." His "story," if it is not quite that of the Fisher King, is yet close enough but the difficulty Eliot encountered with it is one which he encountered again later when he wrote *The Family Reunion,* a play elaborative of similar themes, although the difficulty expresses itself somewhat differently in each case. He has himself analysed the failure in craft which prevented that play from becoming what it was "aiming to be" and the same failure applies to *The Waste Land:* "But the deepest flaw of all, was in a failure of adjustment between the Greek story and the modern situation. I should either have stuck closer to Aeschylus or else taken a great deal more liberty with his myth" (*OPP* 84).

It was this same inability to make a firm choice between viable alternatives which deflected *The Waste Land* from becoming as much of a success as it might otherwise have been. And again, as Eliot said earlier of *Hamlet,* "It must be noticed that the very nature of the *données* of the problem" (*SE* 125) precluded his resolution of it. Had Eliot "stuck closer" to the myth of the Fisher King, he might well have produced a more public and social poem but he could not then have gratified so well the needs of his private voice. Alternatively, had he "taken a great deal more liberty with his myth," he could have gratified little else. But what changes did Eliot in fact make in the Grail Legend and what, if anything, do those changes reveal of that "rude unknown *psychic material*" which at least in part was directing his creative energies?

The first notable alteration in the myth concerns that vegetation aspect of it which all but disappears in Eliot's treatment in favour of the theme of sexual sterility. Thus the theme of the *waste land* itself and of its Fisher King is subordinated not so much to that of the heroic quest (as in the Grail Legend itself) but rather to the barrenness, animality, and sexual perversion of its inhabitants. The few allusions Eliot does make to the *waste land* itself in such

---

of his friends to put up £ 10 each yearly for the remainder of Eliot's life so that Eliot might leave the employ of Lloyd's Bank. Also see Appendix I with regard to the present situation concerning an Eliot biography.

images, for example, as those of "the dead land" (line 2), the "stony rubbish" (20), "the cracked earth (369), and "the arid plain" (424) all undergo a significant sea-change by being introjected finally within the personalized metonymy of the line: "Shall I at least set my lands in order?" (425). This highly selective emphasis, innovative in itself, is all the more remarkable when it is seen in conjunction with the second, and perhaps even more important, alteration which supports it and which concerns the two wholly distinct figures central to the Grail Legend and its mythical action—that is, the Fisher King whose lands it is that are waste, and the Quester Hero through whom they are finally to be restored. What Eliot does in the poem itself (as apart from the Notes to the poem) is to telescope these two mythical figures into one—a union for which there is (as also with Eliot's other change) no precedent whatever in any of the several hundred versions of the Grail Legend collated by Frazer and Weston.

It was this yoking together in one identity of both agent and patient, healer and healed, Quester Hero and Fisher King—a yoking which gives to the mythical archetype of the dying and reviving god the all-inclusive redemptive pattern essential to its later Christian variants—which gave to Eliot the persona required by "the bodiless childful of life" germinating within him and wanted by his poem. Through that persona—so manifestly and intuitively right for his purposes—"the voice of the poet talking to himself—or to nobody" and "the voice of the poet addressing an audience" could come together in a poetically viable way. If successfully fused with one another, what the reader would then hear is something like what Eliot said he sometimes hears in the plays of Shakespeare—that is, "the voices of the author and the character [speaking] in unison, saying something appropriate to the character, but something which the author could say for himself also" (OPP 100).

It would seem that if the myth of the Fisher King was not, as it stood, quite able to furnish Eliot with an adequate vehicle for the successful fusion of his private and public voices, yet that myth in its adjusted form certainly was. Technically speaking, all that was required of Eliot further was the consistent diminution of the Fisher King aspect of the Grail Legend in favor of that of the Quester Hero —a diminution already prepared for in the original by the inherent passivity of the sexually maimed Fisher King's role within it. In the ways of mythology, it is only a short step from being diminished to

30

being subsumed and that is the step Eliot takes in "The Fire Sermon." The Fisher King is presented there as the "I"–protagonist of the poem but only by way of the lines: "While I was fishing in the dull canal / On a winter evening round behind the gashouse" (189-90) and again, later in the poem, by way of the lines: "I sat upon the shore / Fishing, with the arid plain behind me" (423-4). Neither the obvious parody implicit in the first reference (a further Eliot innovation and perhaps the most important innovation of all) nor the climactic seriousness of the second is intended to establish, or is capable of establishing, with any finality, the character of the Fisher King as a separate entity within the poem. What interests Eliot is not the character of the Fisher King but his disease, together with the fact that that disease has reacted so disastrously upon his "lands" both public and private.

I have been suggesting that Eliot's alterations in the myth were not only innovative and purposive but significant and promising as well. By means of them, Eliot created the persona he needed in order to fuse his material—again both public and private—into a unified whole. Moreover, that persona could, in addition to its other assets, provide for the reader "the sense of the one voice speaking" required by Hough and required as well by the form of the extended interior monologue Eliot had already used with such success in earlier poems and which one can see emerging here once again—at least, in some parts of the poem if not always, or quite so clearly, in others.

If one agrees that the indispensable formal requirement of an extended interior monologue such as *The Waste Land* was "aiming to be" is, in this case, a persona undergoing the redemptive mythical action of heroic transformation on the pattern of death and rebirth, and if one agrees further that Eliot, by way of his adjustments to the myths he was using, had in fact found the persona proper to such a poem, where then does the artistic problem which it posed for Eliot lie? To begin with, the problem lies in the fact that, having found the persona wanted by his poem, Eliot was unwilling to accept him as such and that he has—because of that unwillingness—disabled many of his readers from finding him at all. And in this matter too Eliot has achieved an unwarranted success for even such sensitive and astute critics of his poetry as Leavis and Kenner have allowed themselves to be sufficiently misled by one of Eliot's controversial notes to *The Waste Land* as to accept Tiresias, rather than the poet-protagonist of the poem, as providing "the poem with a nameable point of view"[6] and therefore, by extension, as its central personage. Here is Eliot's note: "Tiresias, although a mere spectator and not indeed a 'character', is yet the most important personage in the poem, uniting all the rest. Just as the one-eyed merchant, seller of currants, melts into the Phoenician Sailor, and the latter is not wholly distinct from Ferdinand Prince of Naples, so all the women are one woman, and the two sexes meet in Tiresias. What Tiresias *sees,* in fact, is the substance of the poem."[7] This could not be more misleading if it were intended by its author as a deliberate piece of obfuscation and that, I would suggest, is precisely what it is.

In another place, Eliot has given an account of how these notes to *The Waste Land* came to be written. Because I cannot make sense of the poem except by disregarding them completely in this instance, I must first at least quote the passage in its entirety:

> Here I must admit that I am, on one conspicuous occasion, not guiltless of having led critics into temptation. The notes to *The Waste Land!* I had at first intended only to put down all the references for my quotations, with a view to spiking the guns of critics of my earlier poems who had accused me of plagiarism. Then, when it came to print *The Waste Land* as a little book—for the poem on its first appearance in *The Dial* and in *The Criterion* had no notes whatever—it was discovered that the poem was inconveniently short, so I set to work to expand the notes, in order to provide a few more pages of printed matter, with the result that they became the remarkable exposition of bogus scholarship that is still on view to-day. I have sometimes thought of getting rid of these notes; but now they can never be unstuck. They have had almost greater popularity than the poem itself —anyone who bought my book of poems, and found that the notes to *The Waste Land* were not in it, would demand his money back. (*OPP* 109-10)

However this may be, it must be unequivocally asserted here that it is not what Tiresias sees but what the poet-protagonist of the poem sees that is "the substance of the poem" and that Tiresias is not, and could not possibly be, that protagonist. Tiresias, being a seer and prophet—a "mere spectator"—and therefore external to the mythical action of death and rebirth enjoined upon the protagonist, cannot be "the most important personage in the poem" and the one "uniting all the rest." Eliot's confusion of the two is, in my

6. H. Kenner. *The Invisible Poet: T. S. Eliot* (London: Methuen, 1965), p. 129. See as well, F. R. Leavis' attempt to read the poem as "an effort to focus an inclusive human consciousness" in his *New Bearings in English Poetry,* 2nd ed. (London: Chatto and Windus, 1961), p. 95.
7. See Eliot's note to line 218 of the poem.

view, not only—and perhaps even deliberately—misleading, but also an admission of artistic failure as well. It is little more than an attempt, after the fact, to superimpose on the poem from without —and merely by means of an appended authorial fiat—a unifying force that is felt to be lacking within, and to find that force, further-more, in a figure who can serve as a convenient shield for the poet hiding behind him. The nub of one of Eliot's major problems as craftsman is here but it was clearly "the man who suffers" rather than "the mind which creates" (*SE* 8) which led him to attempt such a desperate remedy.

The problem, in short, resides in the reader's difficulty in locating the poem's central persona and thus in identifying himself with the point of view through which his experience of the poem will first be generated and then progressively expanded. The problem of point of view is, of course, one of the central problems any writer faces for it is ultimately the problem of determining what eye or mind it is that is capable of ordering the material of the poem— "these fragments"—into a unified whole, thus endowing it with its integrity "as poetry and not another thing" (*TSW* viii). The attempts made by critics to read the poem in terms of its thematic unity, or the unity of its emotional effect, or that provided by its images, or by its mythical scaffolding, have all been generous in the extreme but they leave me, as they do Graham Hough and others, with the conviction that the solution to the poem's structural problem can only really be found by way of the one single personage who from beginning to end moves through the poem and finally emerges in sight of, if not yet perfectly endowed with, "The Peace which passeth understanding." I would locate that personage in the com-posite and thereby Christianized mythical figure of the poet-protagonist—a personage who, at the poem's beginning and while looking back upon Marie's arid monologue, can ask of the prophet the question: "What are the roots that clutch, what branches grow / Out of this stony rubbish?" (19-20) and then, having undergone the *askesis* of a journey through his own interior *waste land,* can answer it for himself in the dazzling if somewhat bizarre tour de force with which the poem ends:

I sat upon the shore
Fishing, with the arid plain behind me
Shall I at least set my lands in order?
London Bridge is falling down falling down falling down
Poi s'ascose nel foco che gli affina

Quando fiam uti chelidon—O swallow swallow
Le Prince d'Aquitaine à la tour abolie
These fragments I have shored against my ruins
Why then Ile fit you. Hieronymo's mad againe.
Datta. Dayadhvam. Damyata.
                    Shantih   shantih   shantih
                              (423-33)

Lines like these have satisfied the sleuthing instincts of at least two generations of readers and tend to make of this poem a piece which passeth understanding indeed, but the difficulty they pose is really of another kind, not so easily soluble as are the problems of language and source.

The gratuitous difficulty created by Eliot's note as regards the protagonist of *The Waste Land,* if it is disruptive and mischievous at the same time, is not finally as damaging to the potential unity of the poem's structure, however, as is the internal failure to fuse completely the needs and purposes of his private with his more public voice. It is because of this that the poem is allowed to provide us with two quite distinctive protagonists—the one called for by the mythical scaffolding and the other required "to relieve my emotions"—rather than with the single unifying persona suggested by its incipient form. If the two may be said to coexist with one another, yet they are not as wholly annealed as they would be in a more organically unified poem. Instead, the twin personae and their respective plots tend either to stand side by side, as Eliot's early poems today stand incongruously by the side of the later ones, or sometimes even to pull apart from one another. When, on the other hand, the two personae do converge, they do not so much fuse as blur into one another. Thus the difficulty I have been elaborating faces the reader in the form of just such a blurred focus together with the sense of obscurity and further sense of a dislocation in perspective which is usually consequent upon it. Alternatively, if one's knowledge of the poet's material—both mythical and biographical—is more nearly complete, the fusion of the two which the poem's integrity requires and towards which Eliot was obviously moving is also more nearly achieved.

The crossing of the first two of "The Three Voices of Poetry" Eliot identified in that essay—the voice of the poet, that is, which is wedded to the "rude unknown *psychic material*" and the voice of the poet which is wedded to his more social and satiric purposes—becomes evident to the reader in those lines of the poem in which what its protagonist says is not really appropriate to his

34

character and conventional role as mythic persona at all but is more nearly expressive of what "the author could say for himself." As such, what he says is not really available to the reader or at least not as fully as would otherwise be the case. When, as with the romantics, the coincidence between the poet and his persona is virtually complete and when, as a consequence, it is no longer possible to distinguish "the man who suffers" from "the mind which creates" (*SE* 8), the meanings wanted by the words are no longer suitably generalized and applicable to all. Because they are being energized from a biographical rather than from a mythical core, their meaning is extraneous to the poetry "as poetry and not another thing" (*TSW* viii). The effect, consequently, is one of shrinkage rather than of symbolic expansion—a kind of unweighting as regards the suggestiveness and universality of the mythic dimension. It is as if one were seeing in reverse a video replay of a stone being thrown into a pool of water. The direction of flow, instead of being outward from centre to circumference, is reversed and we see the ever-widening circles disappear into the whirlpool of its own dark centre.

This is what happens, for example, in the conclusion of the poem which as a consequence is as cryptic as it could possibly be. What we find there is one of several examples of the disruptive change in point of view which is forced upon the reader as a result of the crossing of the diffuse impulses underlying the poem and of the two quite different voices and stories giving expression to them. We also find there an example of the frequent dependence of the poem for its meaning on material that is not fairly within it, or in it only in a submerged form. What one would normally expect at this juncture in the poem, if it were really being developed according to the mythical "plan" that Eliot says it has, would be to have the mythic persona arrive at the contemporary equivalent of the Perilous Chapel, ask of its god in a generalized form the ritualistic questions whose answers would lead us all to salvation, and then to have the regenerative rains come.

What we find instead is that the second and submerged poet-protagonist of Eliot's poem, unlike the legendary hero of Frazer and Weston, arrives at the "empty chapel" laden with a deep and personal guilt—a guilt wholly unknown to his mythical counterpart. Unlike him too, he does not question the god of Thunder but instead internalizes by way of reminiscence the three injunctions— Give, Sympathize, Control—which he recalls from a Hindu fable.

35

With regard to his own marital situation, he goes on then to excoriate himself in an act of self-searching which makes him question—not of the god, but of himself: "What have we given?" What he had given was obviously not enough, for what he had given was not really himself but only

> . . . blood shaking my heart
> The awful daring of a moment's surrender
> Which an age of prudence can never retract.
>   (402-4)[8]

His death-in-life "existence" he owed to that one moment, a moment which would never be revealed, as indeed it was not, either

> in our obituaries
> Or in memories draped by the beneficent spider
> Or under seals broken by the lean solicitor
> In our empty rooms
>   (406-9)

When, secondly, sympathy and compassion had been asked of him —a movement out of himself and into another's room—it was the pride of a Coriolanus which had restrained and locked him forever in his own:

> I have heard the key
> Turn in the door once and turn once only
> We think of the key, each in his prison
> Thinking of the key, each confirms a prison
>   (411-14)[9]

And when, finally, he sees that his boat responds "Gaily to the hand expert with sail and oar," (419) he realizes that her heart too

8. Eliot has revealed this sense of guilt concerning his first wife and also his feeling of personal responsibility for the failure of their marriage in numerous letters to Bertrand Russell and to others as well. One of the more revealing of these is perhaps the one he wrote to Russell on 7 May [1925]—a letter which Russell published in *The Autobiography of Bertrand Russell: 1914-1944*, (London: George Allen & Unwin Ltd., 1968), II, 174, but which cannot be quoted here because of copyright restrictions. We may add to the view Eliot has there expressed Sencourt's perhaps less reliable impression concerning the first Mrs. Eliot that "Tom's decision to go to America without her [to deliver the Charles Eliot Norton lectures at Harvard] certainly pushed her further over the confines of sanity." Donald Adamson, ed., *T. S. Eliot: A Memoir*, by Robert Sencourt (New York: Dodd, Mead and Company, 1971), p. 150.

9. Eliot's note to these lines refers the reader first to the forty-sixth line of the thirty-third canto of the *Inferno* and then to a passage from F. H. Bradley's *Appearance and Reality*. See Appendix II for an account of the philosophical implications which Eliot's reference to Bradley has for a more accurate reading of *The Waste Land*.

"would have responded / Gaily, when invited" (421). It too would have been "obedient / To controlling hands" (421-2) had she been "invited" and had there been "controlling hands," but there were none. The "arid plain" (424) of his past, however, is now all behind him and he has felt on the pulse the agonizing sterility which follows upon the failure of romantic love to live up to the idyllic expectations of "the hyacinth garden" (37). The sea is "waste and empty" (42) and everywhere about him the temptations which attend the man necessarily committed to celibacy: the fornication of the "nymphs" "And their friends, the loitering heirs of city directors" (179-80); the "jug jug jug jug jug jug" (204) of rape; the homosexual weekends "at the Metropole" (214) with "Mr. Eugenides, the Smyrna merchant" (209); the inclination to "The sound of horns and motors, which shall bring / Sweeney to Mrs. Porter in the spring" (197-8) and, finally, even the pederastic inclination to *"those children's voices singing in the dome!"* (202). It was not to Carthage Eliot came, but to Leman,

Burning burning burning burning
(308)

and it was in Leman that Augustine's words became applicable to his own situation:

O Lord Thou pluckest me out
O Lord Thou pluckest

burning
(309-11)

That *The Waste Land* represents the turning point of Eliot's life is evident in the new directions the poem announces both for Eliot the man and for Eliot the poet as well. If he would in fact put his "lands in order," he must needs accept for himself the wisdom retained in those "fragments" which he has now, as the fruit of his journey through *The Waste Land,* "shored against . . . [his] ruins." Those fragments enjoin two things upon him: one, the acceptance of and a Christian resignation to the purgatorial fires of Arnaut through which the all-consuming fires of his own lust will be transformed and, two, a return by way of identification with *"Le Prince D'Acquitaine à la tour abolie"* (429) to the tradition of the troubadours, the lyric poet-musicians of Provence who were the predecessors of Dante and the formulators of a lyric tradition very different from that of such contemporary romantics as Gottfried Benn. De Nerval, in his sonnet *El Desdichado* (*The Disinherited*

37

One), represents himself as the neglected and outcast heir of that earlier tradition.

Thus, in the hope that he too might once again "be as the swallow" and attain "The peace which passeth understanding," Eliot determined to move forward by moving back—back to the orthodoxy of a Christian faith which earlier he had scorned and back to a lyric tradition of poetry which was precedent to that of the romantics and whose tower was now in ruins. If it was so, it was because lyricism "In the sense of a poem 'directly expressing the poet's own thoughts and sentiments'" reveals an almost irresistible tendency to become merely a monologue of the personal ego and to invite that coincidence of poet and persona that Eliot found so dangerous to "the mind which creates," whereas that earlier lyricism which Eliot was to find again and admire so profoundly in the later poetry of Yeats would enable him, not to *express* "his personal and private agonies," but to serve as the vehicle within which they might be transmuted "into something rich and strange, something universal and impersonal" (*SE* 117).

"There are two forms of impersonality" (*OPP* 255), Eliot tells us in his essay on Yeats. One is mounted upon the rejection of or the escape from the personal; the other on a progressive transubstantiation of it. What Eliot would continue to seek after *The Waste Land,* as he had done before it, was a poetic formula for the second— one consonant with the innovative "programme for the *métier* of poetry" (*SE* 6) he had announced in "Tradition and the Individual Talent" but had not yet fulfilled in practice and one which would enable him to achieve the impersonality "of the poet who, out of intense and personal experience, is able to express a general truth; retaining all the particularity of his experience, to make of it a general symbol" (*OPP* 255). Such a formula would enable him to present his material as Yeats did—"not . . . for its own sake, but as a vehicle for a situation of universal meaning" (*OPP* 260). In order to find that formula, however, Eliot would have to cut behind that lyricism of the romantics which, according to one of its finest critics, "tends to move inside and downward instead of outside and upward"[10] in seeking for the source of its own creativity.

It is instead the counter-romantic movement which Eliot would continue to explore, together with the dynamics of expansion central to a post-Kantian Anglo-American Idealism—an idealism which

10. N. Frye, "The Drunken Boat," *Romanticism Reconsidered* (New York: Columbia University Press, 1963), p. 16.

not only reverses the romantic direction of flow but mounts it on the action, both mythical and dialectical, of death and rebirth at a higher plane. All of Eliot's fragments directed him backwards to a pre-Cartesian and preromantic past in search of redemption rather than extinction: "There is only the fight to recover what has been lost" (*EC* V). Eliot's later poetry presents us with the record of that recovery but, for him, it was necessary first to feel on the pulse the full force of personal and poetic failure. Eliot would live to rise from that failure like the phoenix reborn of its own ashes or like a modern Fisher King redeemed but it must have been "the voice of the prophet" in his poem—that "more impersonal voice still than that of either the character or the author"—which spoke to him at that time and from whom he learned the way. That, in fact, may well be what the thunder really said to T. S. Eliot in 1922.

2

the
sense of
one voice
speaking

In the previous chapter, we have heard Eliot refer to the likelihood that it is "some rude unknown *psychic material*" that, in the beginning, directs the poet to tell some "particular story" or to develop some "particular situation." At another time and in another place, Eliot has re-enforced this view by telling us as well that "What every poet starts from is his own emotions" (*SE* 117). If, within his own account of the creative process, Eliot has insisted that this is true, yet he has also indicated within that same account that neither the poet nor his poem ends with those emotions. What happens in between, on the other hand, Eliot has described in terms of a "struggle": "the struggle—which alone constitutes life for a poet— to transmute his personal and private agonies into something rich and strange, something universal and impersonal" (*SE* 117). Given this view, it might well be that the most rewarding ground for further exploration into the making of *The Waste Land* lies neither in its beginnings nor even in its end but somewhere in that vivid in-between.

If our account of the poem in the preceding chapter has had to begin where the poem itself began—that is, in the "personal and private agonies" of "the man who suffers" (*SE* 8), our concern now must be instead with "the mind which creates"—the mind involved in the struggle to transmute those agonies "into something rich and strange, something universal and impersonal." Before proceeding further, however, it might be well to recapitulate briefly the conclusions at which our previous chapter arrived.

Our primary concern there was not only to locate the first of those three unresolved conflicts which underlie the poem's genesis and contribute to its partial failure but also to identify the poet-maker's major achievements as well. With regard to the former, we may say that the particular "voice" which Eliot was seeking to create and to utilize in *The Waste Land* was that Shakespearean voice he had himself first isolated, and then described, as one in which "the author and the character [are speaking] in unison, saying something appropriate to the character, but something which the author could say for himself also, though the words may not have quite the same meaning for both" (*OPP* 100). I tried to suggest that Eliot's motive in seeking to develop such a voice was that it would enable him to adjust to one another, in a poetically viable way, the needs of two other of those three "voices" he tells us he had come to discern in his reading—that is, his own personal and private voice ("the voice of the poet talking to himself—or to nobody") and his more public voice ("the voice of the poet addressing an audience, whether large or small") (*OPP* 89). I also suggested that, whereas Shakespeare may in fact have been able to create such a voice and to make skilful use of it, Eliot at this stage was not, and that those lines in which he attempts to do so (particularly those near the poem's close) become merely cryptic instead. If this was one of the poet-maker's failures, what then were his successes?

Eliot's major success was in telescoping the persona of the maimed Fisher King with that of the redemptive Quester Hero, thus creating the persona wanted by his poem and wanted for the resolution of his own private situation as well. Not only could that persona simultaneously gratify the poet's public and private needs; it could also serve to unify his poem by generating in the reader "the sense of one voice speaking" which its integrity as a poem requires and which is required as well by the form of the extended interior monologue which three-fifths of the poem, at least, reveals as its own. Because of the coincidence, however, between the poet-maker of the poem and the poet-protagonist of it, what was required further if the poem was to unify itself successfully was that the poet-protagonist of the poem and his private "story" should be totally subsumed within that of the mythical and more public hero provided to Eliot by Frazer and Weston. Eliot was partially successful in achieving the transmutation necessary to his material, and would perhaps have been more so had he not obscured the emerging identity of the poem's real protagonist by elevating Tiresias to that central role instead, thus serving further the forces of disruption and disunity rather than those of progressive unification.

Before returning to an even more detailed analysis of the poem's central persona and of the form through which he is presented to the reader, we must dispose first of the troublesome structural problem created for that reader by the presence in *The Waste Land* of a host of "imaginary characters" whose relation to the poet-protagonist of the poem is perhaps not as immediately clear as it should be. Having dealt already with the first two of Eliot's "Three Voices of Poetry," we may turn now, in the second phase of our inquiry into the making of *The Waste Land,* to an account of his third—that is, the voice the poet uses "when he attempts to create a dramatic character speaking in verse; when he is saying, not what he would say in his own person, but only what he can say within the limits of one imaginary character addressing another imaginary character" (*OPP* 89).

It is possible, I think, to distinguish several "imaginary characters" in *The Waste Land* of the kind Eliot has described here—each with a distinct and easily discriminable voice of his own but with varying and decidedly uneven degrees of substantiality. Some of the more memorable voices we hear in the poem are perhaps those of: Marie (1-18) and of the Lithuanian whose voice she hears in the Hofgarten (12); those of the girl and boy recalling their return from the hyacinth garden (35-41); the voice of Madame Sosostris (46-59); those of the wife and husband in "A Game of Chess' (111-38) —her lines (as earlier with the girl and boy) distinguished from his by being enclosed in quotation marks; the voice of Lil's friend (139-67)—her lines interrupted and then completed by those of the bartender (141, 152, 165, 168-71); the voice of the typist muttering her one unforgettable line (252); and finally the voices of the three Thames daughters speaking in turn (292-95, 296-99, 300-5 respectively). These are some of the people who live in Eliot's poem and several of his most memorable characters are among them— particularly the neurasthenic wife, her lifeless husband, Lil's unnamed friend, the synthetic typist, and even her "young man carbuncular." The voice they share in common is assuredly Eliot's "third" voice—that is, the voice a poet uses "when he attempts to create a dramatic character." A further word might well be said here, however, concerning Eliot's technique of characterization. The creation of fully rounded viable characters is an art which Eliot never mastered in his poetic drama but it must be noted that it is an art to which he never aspired and had no need to aspire before he started to write plays. Indeed, it is an art which is not at all congenial to the satiric and meditative purposes his poetry is primarily made to serve. One has only to think of the characters of Chaucer and Shakespeare to perceive what is missing, and yet the particular kind of actuality which Eliot's army of characters has is equally memorable and represents an equally impressive achievement, although of a very different kind. If, as George Wright suggests, and I think quite correctly, Eliot's personae are "of an importance subordinate to that of their gestures and to that of the color, the tone, the 'idea' of their action,"[1] that is not to say, as he also does, that they are "type" characters or that "what . . . [Eliot] cares about is their relationship to certain enduring archetypal roles."[2] No one who has ever experienced the surprised delight or the shock of recognition which comes when Eliot nails a character to the wall *in saecula saeculorum* could possibly feel that.

The dexterity of Eliot's characterization is remarkable and, when it is coupled with the remorseless accuracy of his vision, the result is a highly unusual but completely achieved art—and an art so rare in English literature that some of the characters of Ben Jonson provide almost the only analogues for comparison. From the very early verse, one need not think only of Prufrock. There is the lady in "Portrait of a Lady", "(slowly twisting the lilac stalks)," and her young man whose "smile falls heavily among the bric-à-brac"; there is Bleistein whose "lustreless protrusive eye / Stares from the protozoic slime / At a perspective of Canaletto" and his friend, the Princess Volupine, who "extends a meagre, blue-nailed, phthisic hand / To climb the waterstair"; there are the incomparable Grishkin and Sweeney, the delightful Doris who "towelled from the bath, / Enters padding on broad feet" and, in *The Waste Land* as we have just seen, there is the unforgettable typist who "turns and looks a moment in the glass, / Hardly aware of her departed lover," then "smoothes her hair with automatic hand, / And puts a record on the gramophone." And there are others as well.

1. George Wright, *The Poet in the Poem* (Berkeley: University of California Press, 1960), p. vii.
2. Ibid., p. 63.

These characters, if of simpler mould than Shakespeare's, are no less vivid and that surely is the significant point to be made. Eliot always relies on the single observed impression, the characteristic detail or gesture which sets one man or woman apart from every other of his kind—a far cry from "type" characterization indeed. J. Alfred Prufrock is not a "type"; nor is the typist, though both are representative of something permanent in human nature. As is not unusual, Eliot himself indirectly provides the most reliable commentary on the particular techniques of characterization involved. In his essay on Ben Jonson, Eliot says of him that

His characters are and remain . . . simplified characters, but the simplification does not consist in the dominance of a particular humour or monomania. That is a very superficial account of it. The simplification consists largely in reduction of detail, in the seizing of aspects relevant to the relief of an emotional impulse which remains the same for that character, in making the character conform to a particular setting. This stripping is essential to the art, to which is also essential a flat distortion in the drawing; it is an art of caricature. (SE i38)

Jonson was able to utilize this art in the making of great plays; Eliot was not. To use a phrase of his own which he applied to Browning, Eliot remains a dramatic poet "whose dramatic gifts are best exercised outside the theatre" (OPP 94). Basically, the reason for this is that Eliot's control of descriptive elements is sure and unwavering whereas his control of dialogue is not.[3] When it comes to things seen and heard—that is, to the characteristic detail or gesture by which a character reveals himself—Eliot's instinct is unerring. So also is the gift for arresting that detail with such concentration in a precise visual image that the contained intensity explodes into generality as soon as the reader confronts it. The typist herself says almost nothing but everything around her speaks with eloquence and finality of what she is. She stands wholly and completely revealed and one is all but impaled by the vision. If one examines this scene carefully, one will see that the "flat distortion in the drawing," the simplification and the "stripping," is essential to the particular art which the poet is seeking to realize, but our more immediate concern here is not so much with Eliot's technique of characterization as it is with the place such "imaginary charac-

3. To my mind, the most memorable bit of dialogue Eliot ever wrote is that found in the pub scene in "A Game of Chess." In her Editorial Notes to the Facsimile Edition (p. 127, 5), Mrs. Eliot has indicated, however, that the passage was transcribed from a story actually recounted to the Eliots by their maid, Ellen Kellond.

ters" and "scenes" as those cited are intended to have in the total structure of *The Waste Land*.

If these dramatic characters together with the "scenes" in which they appear are not intended to be elements in a verse play of the traditional kind, and clearly they are not, then what kind of existence is the reader supposed to attribute to them in the poem in which they appear? The problem presents itself in its clearest form as soon as we become aware that the dramatic voices of these imaginary characters are enclosed in a larger nondramatic and narrative frame that requires from the reader a shift in point of view. Such shifts in point of view, when they occur *within* any given scene, present no problem. For example, we move from the voice of Lil's friend to that of the bartender and back again with no difficulty but who is it, we are required to ask, at the conclusion of her monologue who speaks the poignant and memorably ironic line "Good night, ladies, good night, sweet ladies, good night, good night," and what are we to make of it? And is the speaker of that line to be identified with the speaker of the brilliantly sardonic preface to the "nerves" passage (77-110) and with the equally sardonic narrator who tells us that "Madame Sosostris, famous clairvoyante, / Had a bad cold"?

Let us assume, at least for the moment and as if it were self-evident, that all those lines in the poem (such as the one just quoted) which are not spoken by "one imaginary character addressing another" are to be attributed instead to one voice—the voice of the poet-protagonist of the poem. This leaves us still with the central problem of determining the exact principle of relation which polarizes the dramatic voices of the imaginary characters from the voice of the protagonist and which sets and maintains the distance between them. That principle, a principle of objective-subjective correlation, will be familiar to students of Eliot's early poems. It will also be known to those familiar with the theories of perception which were current at the time Eliot was writing them—the theories that lie behind the dynamic art "of transforming an observation into a state of mind" (*SE* 249) or an "objective correlative" (*SE* 124) into its own subjective correlate. It was this particular art which guided Eliot in the formation of his first volume of poetry (entitled significantly enough *Prufrock and Other Observations*) and, clearly, was guiding Ezra Pound as well when he said the following for example: "In a poem of this sort one is trying to record the precise instant when a thing outward and objective transforms itself, or darts into

45

a thing inward and subjective."[4] It was that moment or "precise instant" which poets like Pound and Eliot sought to arrest, particularly in their early verse, together with the geometry of "exact equivalence" (SE 125) which they internalized in their poems as a way of evoking and sustaining such moments. The equational aspect of the literary theories involved is the aspect to which Eliot gave particular emphasis in his now famous and, indeed, notorious rubric that: "The only way of expressing emotion in the form of art is by finding an 'objective correlative'; in other words, a set of objects, a situation, a chain of events which shall be the formula of that particular emotion; such that when the external facts, which must terminate in sensory experience, are given, the emotion is immediately evoked. If you examine any of Shakespeare's more successful tragedies, you will find this exact equivalence" (SE 124-5). I would suggest, therefore, that the dramatic voices we hear in The Waste Land must be seen as the formulaic correlates of the "particular emotion" they serve to generate in the poem's poet-protagonist. To this matter we shall return in considerable detail later but, for now, we must leave our account of the poem's dramatic voices and attend once again to its poet-protagonist for it is only from that persona that we can hope to derive the "sense of one voice speaking" which we continue to seek.

Thus far we have been concerned with the third of Eliot's "Three Voices of Poetry" and I have indicated that, if these voices are "dramatic" in the sense that their words are not to be taken as those of the poet-protagonist himself, that is not to say that they have a locus independent of his. In short, I am suggesting that so far as the poem itself goes they must be seen as constituting the residual data of his consciousness, and this despite the fully developed and seemingly independent scenic form in which they are presented to us. They are voices heard by the protagonist with his inner ear or recalled in his memory and, as such, they must be carefully distinguished from his own. Thus, the juxtaposition in The Waste Land of the individual frames which make up the first two sections of the poem, and which account for somewhat less than half of the total 433 lines of the poem, constitute a series of particulars which cannot exist in a vacuum; nor can they "be accorded independent status," to use a phrase of Hugh Kenner's.[5] They can be justified

4. Ezra Pound, Gaudier-Brzeska: A Memoir [1916] (Hessle: The Marvell Press, 1960), p. 89.
5. H. Kenner, The Invisible Poet: T. S. Eliot (London: Methuen, 165), p. 128.

46

psychologically only as the data of consciousness, as something once actually perceived or felt or acted upon, for the indispensable formal requirement of the poem as a whole is, as was indicated earlier, a consciousness which either presides over it or else moves progressively through it—a consciousness in which these fragments of psychic experience inhere or can come together. That consciousness we have attributed to the persona of the poem's poet-protagonist.

Although the poet-protagonist's voice appears several times in the first two sections of the poem (five to be exact), it nowhere appears with sufficient salience to make it stand out among the poem's dramatic voices, and this is a notable defect. It is in the opening passage of "The Fire Sermon," the climactic centre of the poem, that we really meet the poet-protagonist of the poem in his own unique and discriminable character for the first time, and it is here that we enter directly into the stream of his rich and allusive consciousness. Having met him in line 173, with the first two sections of the poem already completed, we never depart from his consciousness again until we lay the poem aside and return to ourselves. Because this frame of the poem is central to it in every way and because it is here, if anywhere, that we gain "the sense of one voice speaking," we must quote the passage entire:

The river's tent is broken: the last fingers of leaf
Clutch and sink into the wet bank. The wind
Crosses the brown land, unheard. The nymphs are departed.
Sweet Thames, run softly, till I end my song.
The river bears no empty bottles, sandwich papers,
Silk handkerchiefs, cardboard boxes, cigarette ends
Or other testimony of summer nights. The nymphs are departed.
And their friends, the loitering heirs of city directors;
Departed, have left no addresses.
By the waters of Leman I sat down and wept . . .
Sweet Thames, run softly till I end my song.
Sweet Thames, run softly, for I speak not loud or long.
But at my back in a cold blast I hear
The rattle of the bones, and chuckle spread from ear to ear.

A rat crept softly through the vegetation
Dragging its slimy belly on the bank
While I was fishing in the dull canal
On a winter evening round behind the gashouse
Musing upon the king my brother's wreck
And on the king my father's death before him.
White bodies naked on the low damp ground

47

And bones cast in a little low dry garret,
Rattled by the rat's foot only, year to year.
But at my back from time to time I hear
The sound of horns and motors, which shall bring
Sweeney to Mrs. Porter in the spring.
O the moon shone bright on Mrs. Porter
And on her daughter
They wash their feet in soda water
Et O ces voix d'enfants, chantant dans la coupole!

(173-202)

Within this brilliant cross-montage of voices, the flat—somewhat sardonic—first voice we hear is easily distinguishable from the muted *cri du coeur* which begins by counterpointing it and then goes on to modulate sensitively into the restlessly urgent rhythms of a man with a mission. The use of the term "voices" may be confusing here, however, if it suggests the separate and distinct voices of separate and distinct dramatis personae. What we are in fact concerned with now is the variant tonalities of "one voice"— the voice of the poet-protagonist of the poem which is signalized for the reader hereafter by his deliberate, if not quite consistent, use of the first person pronoun. The movement arrested for us by the collision of one particular tonality of that voice with another is a movement from one level of sensibility to another within the same persona, and what the poem in fact does is to define its own progress and enact its own meaning by way of these astonishingly subtle aural gradations.

This returns me to the assumption with which I began—the assumption that, in *The Waste Land,* tone is a primary determinant of meaning and that the poem relies to an unprecedented degree on aural discriminations which are at once indispensable and yet highly elusive. An adequate sensitivity to them is the indispensable requirement for perceiving that this poem does in fact have the makings of a beginning, a middle, and an end. If we add a small measure of divination, it may even be possible to trace a consistent linear progress from one to the other which leaves its protagonist a very different man at the end of the poem than he was at its beginning. The turning point in that developing drama of consciousness which the poet-protagonist is enacting and which the reader simultaneously enacts with him will be found at the conclusion of "The Fire Sermon" in the words:

To Carthage then I came

Burning burning burning burning
O Lord Thou pluckest me out
O Lord Thou pluckest

burning

(307-11)

Let us return therefore to the earlier passage cited from "The Fire Sermon" and analyse it carefully for, if we cannot discriminate the variant tonalities of the poet-protagonist's voice in isolation from one another, we shall not be able to relate each of them in turn to what we shall find in our sixth chapter is the dialectical process of "soul-making" that Eliot derived from the philosophy of F. H. Bradley and which, I shall eventually attempt to show, he is dramatizing in this poem by way of their interaction.

The first of these three variant tonalities can best be distinguished from its accompanying tonalities by likening it to that flat, somewhat tired, voice used by a mere observer figure or by a cinematic narrator as he unrolls a series of shots in a documentary film. Its pitch is established in such lines as:

The river's tent is broken: the last fingers of leaf
Clutch and sink into the wet bank. The wind
Crosses the brown land, unheard. The nymphs are departed.

(173-75)

For greater clarity, I shall henceforth refer to this variant of the poet-protagonist's voice simply as the voice of the observer. His is primarily a descriptive voice whose dual function it is, on the one hand, to describe the tableaux of aimlessness and dry despair which in memory unroll themselves before the eyes of the poet-protagonist and, on the other, to do whatever link work it is necessary to do as well. It is an anonymous voice which never makes use of any personal pronouns and its limits or borders in any given passage are often set by the introduction of a personal pronoun signalling the entry into the poem, either of one of the dramatic voices, or of one of the two other variants of the protagonist's voice. If anonymous, however, the voice of the observer figure is hardly atonal. It is characterized by a sardonic quality which, if it does not make a point of calling attention to itself, yet is highly coloured and unmistakably ironic in its rhetorical shading:

The nymphs are departed.
And their friends, the loitering heirs of city directors;
Departed, have left no addresses.

In the poem, the voice of the observer *in isolation from the two other variants of the protagonist's voice* is heard only three times. It is heard first in the flatly dissonant description of Madame Sosostris (43-46) and then it shades quietly into the background as she enters with her own voice, precious with the illusion of hidden meanings. The longest descriptive passage given to the observer is that which introduces the wife in "A Game of Chess" (77-110). We hear the isolated tonality of the observer for the last time in "Death by Water" which is also spoken by him.

If the dry, seemingly disinterested, voice of the observer figure represents the poet-protagonist in all the essential passivity of a computer merely perceiving or recording data, the plaintive lyric voice he uses represents and defines his passional response to that data. This variant of the poet-protagonist's voice, once heard, is unmistakable. Its pitch is established for us in such affective lines as:

By the waters of Leman I sat down and wept . . .
Sweet Thames, run softly till I end my song,
Sweet Thames, run softly, for I speak not loud or long . . .
(182-84)

and in the hauntingly beautiful line cited earlier, "Good night, ladies, good night, sweet ladies, good night, good night." Mainly, however, it is as a refrain on the City that we hear the moving reverberations of the lyric voice (60, 207, 259-65, and 376), and it is possible, by way of that refrain, to trace the growing tension which insinuates itself progressively into the action of the poem and helps to define thereby the rhythm of linearity referred to earlier. It is a tension which reaches its highest pitch of intensity in the lines yoking the poet-protagonist with St. Augustine (307-11) and consequently announcing the turning point in the drama of his transformation—lines in which what we are hearing is the fusion of the lyric voice with the third and final variant of the poet-protagonist's voice, the voice of *the significant self-in-becoming* or Quester Hero.

This variant of the poet-protagonist's voice is the one which makes use of the first person pronoun and which is further characterized by a mounting sense of urgency related to and developed from the anterior instruments of perception and response:

> But at my back in a cold blast I hear
> The rattle of the bones, and chuckle spread
>   from ear to ear.
>
>   (185-86)

It is this urgency which will finally impel the poet-protagonist to undertake the quest delineated in the poem's concluding section and to endure in the course of it "the agony in stony places" through which the fires of his own consuming lust will be transformed *"nel foco che gli affina"*—in the purgatorial "fire which refines them." The voice of the Quester Hero which dominates the entire fifth section of the poem shades tonally now and then, either into the voice of the observer ("A woman drew her long black hair out tight") or into the lyric voice ("Shall I at least set my lands in order?"), but never for more than a moment and never in such a way as to relax the compelling linear thrust demanded by the action of the quest.

An anticipation of the voice of the Quester Hero is heard in the badly misplaced last frame of "The Burial of the Dead" (60-76)—that first in a series of hallucinatory passages which belongs properly with the others of its kind in the concluding section of the poem. Eliot, however, no doubt sensed the need and the propriety of introducing his protagonist's voice to the reader in its own distinguishable character somewhere in the first section of the poem but, because that voice has not been differentiated from the many voices around it in any notable way, the device fails. Although the reader senses the intended yoking of his point of view with that of the speaker when, in the last line, he is shatteringly addressed by him as " 'hypocrite lecteur!—mon semblable,—mon frère!' " he has some difficulty in accepting the allegations and in understanding just what he has done to deserve them because the yoking has not been adequately prepared for.

It has been necessary to examine these three variant tonalities of the poet-protagonist's voice in isolation from one another primarily because they often appear in the poem in isolation from one another, and it is this parcelling out—this deliberate fragmentation of the "one voice speaking"—which makes it so difficult to determine in any given instance whether it is in fact the voice of the poet-protagonist we are hearing or one of those dramatic voices which are impinging on and affecting his consciousness instead. Before proceeding further, therefore, we may conclude this section of our argument by identifying specifically those lines spoken by the

51

poet-protagonist of *The Waste Land* and by isolating thus the "one voice speaking" through which alone the poem can unify itself and become what it is "aiming to be." That protagonist is the Quester Hero whose voice, in all its various gradations, the reader hears uninterruptedly from line 173 to the end of the poem. He hears it as well, in one or other of its triadic range of tonalities, six times during the first two sections of the poem where it is found interspersed with the poem's "dramatic voices": lines 1-7, 19-20, 43-46, 60-76, 77-110 and, finally, in line 172. The reader able to maintain this point of view as he reads will find little that is structurally unsound within it for he will have perceived that what Eliot set out to write, and what *The Waste Land* was generically "aiming to be," was an extended interior monologue, and he will have little difficulty in perceiving the stages in its dramatization. By way of summary, then, let us be clear as to just what it is that Eliot has done in this important passage from "The Fire Sermon."

Interested as he is primarily in what we have referred to as the process of "soul-making" and in what Eliot has elsewhere described as the "unification of sensibility" (*SE* 248) which plays such a substantive part in its progressive achievement, Eliot has sought to delineate that process by arresting it in *the very mode of its operation.* To each of the variously distinguishable, but hardly distinct, aspects of that sensibility, he has accorded, therefore, if not a separate voice, then at least the distinctive and readily identifiable tonality proper to it. These three tonalities we have designated as those of the protagonist as observer, as lyrist, and as Quester Hero and we may relate them now to the dialectical movement from sensuous perception through passional response to final act. Because the total drama which the poem enacts is the self-generative drama of the "development of sensibility" (*SE* 245), the interweaving of these tonalities as they modulate sensitively into one another parallels the disposition of the interior "action" of the poem and represents the various stages in the enactment of that drama. The reader who, from his analysis of "The Fire Sermon," can discriminate these variant tonalities aurally from one another, and who is aware of the principle by which they are related to the poem's dramatic voices, is able at any given moment to identify his point of view as reader with that of the "one voice speaking" and to perceive the particular stage of the drama which is at that moment being unfolded.

A final point needs to be made regarding not the variant tonalities in isolation from one another but Eliot's astonishingly acute device of cross-cutting them. The rhythms of inflation and deflation which he commands by way of this expedient represent one of his most notable achievements and that he manages to create by way of them a most impressive scale of satiric effects is, I think, quite obvious. What is not so obvious is that in *The Waste Land* this cross-cutting serves as Eliot's major device for defining not only the peculiar quiddity of his protagonist but for delineating the self-generative and developmental process of its further becoming as well. It is not Everyman who, looking at a contemporary Thames with its

> empty bottles, sandwich papers,
> Silk handkerchiefs, cardboard boxes, cigarette ends
> Or other testimony of summer nights . . . ,
> (177-79)

will be impelled by indirection to recall the earlier, more graceful Thames which had served once as the harmonious and pastoral backdrop for a song in celebration of marriage, the hymeneal rights of which were then based on its life-fulfilling procreative function. The memory is a literary one but it is nonetheless vivid for that and, because it exists as a residual datum of his consciousness and has the life and force of an idyllic dream still, its *collision* in thought with the contemporary "nymphs" he observes and with "their friends, the loitering heirs of city directors," can effect for him and for us as well—and at the very moment of its happening—the response which buckles him:

> By the waters of Leman, I sat down and wept . . .

Thus far our concern has been largely with the personae inhabiting the waste land of Eliot's poem. It is, alternatively, to the principle of collision—a principle central to the post-Hegelian concept of dialectical form and to the problems Eliot had in creating such a form for his poem—that our next chapter will address itself. Before doing so we may bring the present chapter to a close by recapitulating the further stages of our argument which have been developed within it.

If, in our first chapter, we dealt primarily with the difficulties Eliot encountered in successfully integrating "the voice of the poet talking to himself—or to nobody" with "the voice of the poet addressing an audience, whether large or small" (OPP 89), our major concern in this second chapter has been to outline the problem created for Eliot's poem by his failure to relate at least some of the many voices of his "imaginary character[s]" (OPP 89) to that of the poem's poet-protagonist in a readily intelligible way. The relation is troublesome only when the voices of those imaginary characters come to us in such well-developed scenes, for example, as those given to us in both the "nerves" passage and the pub scene of "A Game of Chess," and in the Madame Sosostris passage in "The Burial of the Dead" as well—scenes so well-developed in fact that they sit in the midst of the poem like independent tableaux or set-pieces and reveal thereby a second unresolved conflict within the poet-maker as regards the poem's intention. The scenic and the psychic cannot easily accommodate to one another and these scenes—brilliant and memorable as they are—resist the psychic interiorization required by the form of an extended interior monologue which the larger portion of the poem reveals that it was "aiming to be."

If this is in fact what the poetically viable elements in the poem reveal of its own direction, we find ourselves inclined to ask why it is that a poet who had already manifested such obvious competence with the form of the interior monologue in such poems as "The Love Song of J. Alfred Prufrock," "Portrait of A Lady," and "Gerontion" failed so notably this time to model the well-wrought urn. The answer to this important question will involve us in a somewhat lengthy excursus—this time into the difficulties which must be faced by any artist working within a postromantic, and counter-romantic, philosophical tradition who would attempt to extend into the world of literary art the applied significance of the seminal insights he had derived from the dialectical philosophy of his time. It is the achievement of Sergei Eisenstein, Eliot's Russian contemporary, that he was the first to apply systematically to film theory and practice the very same dialectical principles which Eliot had absorbed from his study of the New Idealism and then tried to apply, though with uneven success, to his own poetic theory and practice as well. It is for this reason that our next chapter will begin with an account of Eisenstein's seminally important contributions to aesthetic theory rather than immediately with Eliot's own.

3

dialectical form

In his essay entitled "A Dialectic Approach to Film Form," what Eisenstein actually did was to apply the major insights of Hegel's dialectical philosophy to a consideration of the methodology of film form and then progressively construct, in a series of essays, what he rightly believed to be the new and revolutionary concept of aesthetic form implicit within it. To that concept Eisenstein gave the name of "spatial form" (*FF* 47), intending thereby to distance it, and the tridimensional space-logic on which it relies, altogether from those linear conceptions of form which had dominated earlier nineteenth century aesthetic theory and which were based on a successive time-logic instead.

It is this same concept of "spatial form" which Joseph Frank, in a serialized essay of great importance entitled "Spatial Form in Modern Literature,"[1] applied many years ago to his remarkably perceptive reading of some notable works of the period. I should at this point, however, interpolate a reservation about Frank's application to a *verbal* art of what, in Eisenstein's handling and in that of Lessing's *Laocoön* (1766) before him, is an essentially visual concept. Eisenstein derived the name "spatial form" (*FF* 47) from his observation that "the phenomenon of spatial depth" is achieved in stereoscopy from "the optical superimposition of two planes"

1. Joseph Frank, "Spatial Form in Modern Literature," *Sewanee Review* 53 (Spring 1945), 221-40; (Summer 1945), 433-56; and (Autumn 1945), 643-53.

(*FF* 49) and to my knowledge it was he, rather than Lessing as Frank erroneously suggests,[2] who coined this memorable phrase some- time in the late twenties to signalize that particular observation. From it Eisenstein then went on to derive the following conclusion: "From the superimposition of two elements of the same dimension always arises a new, higher dimension. In the case of stereoscopy the superimposition of two non-identical two-dimensionalities re- sults in stereoscopic three-dimensionality" (*FF* 49-50). Eisenstein goes on, quite properly in my view, to apply this visual conception of "spatial form" to the equally visual art of cinematography. Al- though the concept has obvious relevance to literary theory as well —a relevance Frank has exploited with great success—the use of the term "spatial form" as a way of denoting that relevance is, I think, far likelier to confuse rather than to forward its understand- ing. It is for this reason that I shall simply use instead the phrase, "dialectical form," as a way of designating that particular concept of aesthetic form which I am presently concerned to elaborate and which, in my view, underlies the literary substitution in the twen- tieth century of a post-Hegelian and dialectical theory of aesthetic form for an earlier Kantian and expressionistic theory.

However this may be, what the dialectic provided to a host of modern artists was a new, and transmutative, formula for creation. It is Eisensteins's work rather than Eliot's, however, which can lead us most clearly and directly to an understanding both of the nature of dialectical form and of the self-generative logic which supports it. We must, therefore, turn to that work directly.

The two unchanging specifics of film technique, Eisenstein tells us, are the individual shot-cipher (or frame) and montage, and if "The minimum 'distortable' fragment of nature is the shot: in- genuity in its combinations is montage" (*FF* 5). "To determine the nature of montage," Eisenstein also tells us, is therefore "to solve the specific problem of cinema" (*FF* 48) for the art of montage is none other than the art of achieving creative or self-generating combinations. Eisenstein goes on to show that there are basically only two ways to approach the theoretic as well as the practical problem of form or composition—one linear and the other spatial, and that the first of these cannot yield a genuinely *creative* aesthetic theory in the sense which both Eisenstein and Eliot insist must be given to that word.

2. Ibid., p. 225.

But let us hear Eisenstein himself on the two theories of montage which are involved—the linear (or "linkage") theory of Kuleshov and Pudovkin on the one hand, and the spatial (or particle "collision") theory which he himself evolved and which he calls "the ideographic (montage) method" (*FF* 36), on the other. Speaking specifically of Kuleshov, Eisenstein sometimes quotes his view directly and sometimes comments on it sardonically as follows:

A shot. A single piece of celluloid. A tiny rectangular frame in which there is, organized in some way, a piece of an event.
"Cemented together these shots form montage."
This, roughly, is what is taught by the old, old school of film-making, that sang:

"Screw by screw,
Brick by brick . . ."

Kuleshov, for example, even writes with a brick:
If you have an idea-phrase, a particle of the story, a link in the whole dramatic chain, then that idea is to be expressed and accumulated from shot-ciphers, just like bricks.
"The shot is an element of montage. Montage is an assembly of these elements." This is a most pernicious make-shift analysis. (*FF* 36)

A little later on, Eisenstein summarizes the earlier view once again and then uses it as a way of introducing his own alternative conception of form. He says:

The earliest conscious film-makers, and our first film theoreticians, regarded montage as a means of description by placing single shots one after the other like building blocks . . . .
A completely false concept! . . .
According to this definition, shared in even by Pudovkin as a theoretician, montage is the means of *unrolling* an idea with the help of single shots: the "epic" principle.
In my opinion, however, montage is an idea that arises from the collision of independent shots—shots even opposite to one another: the "dramatic" principle. (*FF* 48-9)

If Eisenstein believed that the linear theory of montage is an essentially noncreative and mechanical theory, that is only because it lacks the "inspired mathematics" of "the ideographic (montage) method" (*FF* 36) and substitutes for those mathematics the simple arithmetic formula of $1 + 1 = 2$. Montage, both for Kuleshov and Pudovkin, means merely "to mount," to superimpose one individual frame upon another of like kind and by this mounting gradually to unroll the thematic "idea" which, be it noted, is already implicit within it. Thus the art of composition, or fusion into a "new whole" (*OPP* 108) as Eliot describes it, is seen as an essentially accretive act and one which does not so much transmute "the particles" which are its material as collect, or group, or arrange them in such a way as to transform them and to make external and explicit what was formerly internal and implicit within them.[3] Thus the "whole" to which this additive procedure leads is one which is, and can only be, *equivalent* to "the sum of its parts" and which, therefore, is in no way either quantitatively greater than, or qualitatively distinguishable from, the content of those parts. Growth by accretion, however, is a very different thing from the creation of new substance and for this, as Pound has also told us, the progressions must be geometric rather than arithmetic and 1 + 1 must give us—not 2—but 3 instead.[4] It was Eisenstein, however, more clearly than Pound, who provided the formula for those geometric progressions when he insisted that "The basic fact was true, and remains true to this day, that the juxtaposition of two separate shots by splicing them together resembles not so much a simple sum of one shot plus another shot—as it does a *creation*. It resembles a creation—rather than a sum of its parts—from the circumstance that in every such juxtaposition *the result is qualitatively* distinguishable from each component element viewed separately" (*FS* 7-8).

Eisenstein never wearied of this important assertion nor of what was to him this "newly revealed feature of the film strips—that, no matter how unrelated they might be, and frequently despite themselves, they engendered a 'third something' and became correlated when juxtaposed according to the will of an editor" (*FS* 9).

The "third something" is quite clearly, and as Eisenstein has also indicated, the legitimate aesthetic offspring of that "third side" or "moment" in every "logical entity" which Hegel describes in his *Smaller Logic*.[5] I will attempt to show later that although F. H. Bradley (to whom Eliot is more immediately indebted for his post-

3. A pre-Hegelian and expressionistic theory of aesthetics wedded to an organic and immanental metaphysic is here clearly implied.

4. See Ezra Pound, *Gaudier-Brzeska: A Memoir [1916]* (Hessle: The Marvell Press, 1960), particularly pp. 88-94—pages which are also reprinted in R. Ellmann and C. Feidelson Jr., editors, *The Modern Tradition* (New York: Oxford University Press, 1965), pp. 145-52.

5. See especially sections 79-82 of the *Smaller Logic*, and also Eisenstein's statement that "The foundation for this philosophy is a *dynamic* concept of things: Being —as a constant evolution from the interaction of two contradictory opposites. Synthesis—arising from the opposition between thesis and anti-thesis" (*FF* 45).

Kantian philosophical insights) does not hold the formal machinery of Hegel's dialectic in any great esteem,[6] he is in principle committed nonetheless to the self-generative or triadic logic of the concrete universal which supports that dialectic. The new and characteristically different formulation which Bradley gave to that logic constitutes what will perhaps remain as his most enduring achievement and, as a consequence, renders the dialectic a much clearer and more convincing doctrine than it had been, if only by freeing it from the quasi-esoteric terminology in which Hegel had shrouded it. In any event, the question of whether the logic internal to the dialectic is ultimately of Hegelian or Bradleian derivation is of little consequence as regards the application of that logic to aesthetic theory and practice—the more so as both Eisenstein and Eliot have acknowledged that the primary influence in teaching them how to apply the dialectic *in practice* derived more from the discontinuous novelistic techniques of Flaubert than it did from the respective philosophies which underlie it.

Nor does it seem particularly worthwhile to concern ourselves with competitive priorities or with a "who was first" kind of discussion as regards the relative theoretical and practical merits of Eliot, Joyce, Pound, etc. There was clearly a great confluence of intellectual currents involved and one which just as clearly came to a head in Paris in the first two decades of the century. Dialectical modes of thought, originating in Germany, had already swept over the continent and then moved on to England and America in philosophy, but did not immediately affect the course of the English literature involved there. French literature seems to have been the first to internalize the practical effects of the dialectic and Eisenstein and Pound seem to have been the first to relate that dialectic to the sympathetic and similar logic which underlies the structural practices involved in the Chinese ideogram, the Japanese hokku, and in the Noh plays as well. Pound (himself the great vortex of those decades and living in Paris or London much of the time) was then able to influence an entire generation of writers—Eliot, Joyce, and the later Yeats preeminently among them—those, in short, who for one reason or another were susceptible to the magnetic attractions of dialectical form.

6. We may recall here without elaborating it Bradley's censure of Josiah Royce when he began moving too far towards the Hegelian left. After commenting on what he considered to be Royce's aberration, Bradley concluded as follows: "Here I join issue. I can no more accept Prof. Royce's doctrine than I can accept what is often understood as the process of Hegel's dialectic" (*ETR* 278).

Our concern for the moment, however, is in particular with Eliot and with Eisenstein—Eliot who said that "The kind of poetry that I needed, to teach me the use of my own voice, did not exist in English at all; it was only to be found in French" (*OPP* 252), and Eisenstein who said: "Strangely enough, it was Flaubert who gave us one of the finest examples of cross-montage of dialogues, used with the same intention of expressive sharpening of idea. This is the scene in *Madame Bovary* where Emma and Rodolphe grow more intimate" (*FF* 12). Eisenstein went on then to elaborate in detail the technical significance which the scene had for him. Joseph Frank's article, to which I have already referred, although it makes no reference whatever to Eisenstein's earlier endeavours, goes on independently to make a similar analysis of this very same scene and can provide us therefore with an even more convenient summary of the essential material. Frank says:

For a study of esthetic form in the modern novel, Flaubert's famous county fair scene in *Madame Bovary* is a convenient point of departure. The scene has been justly praised for its mordant caricature of bourgeois pomposity, its portrayal—unusually sympathetic for Flaubert—of the bewildered old servant, and its burlesque of the pseudo-romantic rhetoric by which Rodolphe woos the sentimental Emma. At present, it is enough to notice the method by which Flaubert handles the scene—a method we might as well call cinematographic, since this analogy comes immediately to mind. As Flaubert sets the scene, there is action going on simultaneously at three levels, and the physical position of each level is a fair index to its spiritual significance. On the lowest plane, there is the surging, jostling mob in the street, mingling with the livestock brought to the exhibition; raised slightly above the street by a platform are the speech-making officials, bombastically reeling off platitudes to the attentive multitudes; and on the highest level of all, from a window overlooking the spectacle, Rodolphe and Emma are watching the proceedings and carrying on their amorous conversation, in phrases as stilted as those regaling the crowds. Albert Thibaudet has compared this scene to the medieval mystery play, in which various related actions occur simultaneously on different stage levels; but this acute comparison refers to Flaubert's intention rather than to his method. "Everything should sound simultaneously," Flaubert later wrote, in commenting on this scene; "one should hear the bellowing of the cattle, the whisperings of the lovers and the rhetoric of the officials all at the same time." . . .

This scene illustrates, on a small scale, what we mean by the spatialization of form in a novel. For the duration of the scene, at least, the time-flow of the narrative is halted: attention is fixed on the interplay of relationships within the limited time-area. These relationships are juxtaposed independently of the progress of the narrative; and the full significance of the scene is given only by the reflexive relations among the units of meaning. In Flaubert's scene, however, the unit of meaning is not, as in modern poetry,

60

a word-group or a fragment of an anecdote, but the tonality of each level of action taken as an integer: the unit is so large that the scene can be read with an illusion of complete understanding, yet with a total unawareness of the 'dialectic of platitude' (Thibaudet) interweaving all levels, and finally linking them together with devastating irony.[7]

What Flaubert has in fact done is to manipulate a continuous parallel between the bellowings of cattle, the rhetoric of men, and the whisperings of lovers and, by so doing, he has sparked what Thibaudet has very aptly referred to as "the dialectic of platitude" interweaving all levels. What is noteworthy, however, and what Eisenstein insists upon, is that the three "particles" or "cells"[8] of the montage involved, if they may be seen as equivalent to the still-shots of cinematography—let us say, to Shots A, B, and C— do not, and cannot of themselves, unroll what he calls that sense of "monumental triviality" which constitutes the newly created aesthetic substance of the scene, and which is *qualitatively* distinguishable from the content of any one of the three "shots" taken alone or conceived of as an aggregate of the three. The whole, in this case, *is* greater than the sum of its parts and the "more" or "qualitatively different than" which that whole delivers is due to the fact, as Bradley would say,[9] that the relationship of the shots to one another is itself internal to the substance being defined or created. It is, in short, actually *constitutive* of that substance on the model provided by that concrete universal of the Idealists with which we shall be very much concerned in a later chapter.

To look, let us say, at some cinematic footage of Richard Burton and Elizabeth Taylor in a love scene is to define one kind of thematic content. To collide that footage by way of immediate juxtaposition with some additional footage of a boar nuzzling a sow is to create a satiric scale of effects (à la Flaubert or Corbière), the cause of which does not inhere in either bit of footage taken alone but in the "reflexive relations" of the two which, at the very moment of their perception, generate the wider experience one then simultaneously responds to. Separately, each unit or particle is in

7. Frank, "Spatial Form in Modern Literature," 230-32.
8. In working out for himself a literary theory and practice consonant with Bradley's theory of Internal Relations, Eliot consistently used the word "particles" (*SE* 8) for this phase of his construct, whereas Eisenstein used the word "cells" (*FF* 37).
9. This, it seems to me, is the point of the first half of Bradley's great book, *Appearance and Reality*—the half entitled "Appearance." See especially Chapters II ("Substantive and Adjective") and III ("Relation and Quality") and also Note B ("Relation and Quality") in the Appendix wherein the Bradleian theory of Internal Relations is given its best and most stunning formulation.

a sense neutral and would define a quite different thematic idea than it does in collision with the other. Such footage, within dialectical composition, will no longer be viewed as substantive or thematic in itself. Instead, it will be conceived of not as itself the thematic idea but rather as one of the stages necessary to its becoming what it is in fact "aiming to be," and thus to its apprehension as well. Artists henceforward will concern themselves not so much with the expression of a theme in the nineteenth-century manner as with the arrangement and composition of those elements which, in collision with one another, will generate it in the manner Eliot suggested by way of his chemical metaphor in "Tradition and the Individual Talent" (*SE* 7-8). It is for this reason that Eisenstein declares so emphatically that

Actually, to achieve its result, a work of art directs all the refinement of its methods to the *process.*

A work of art, understood dynamically, is just this process of arranging images in the feelings and mind of the spectator. It is this that constitutes the peculiarity of a truly vital work of art and distinguishes it from a lifeless one, in which the spectator receives the represented result of a given consummated process of creation, instead of being drawn into the process as it occurs. (*FS* 17)

One of the immediate and more important effects of this notion of the reader as one who "experiences the theme" by being drawn into the process of its creation, rather than by being told about it afterwards, is to establish the reader's status as a co-creator of the work of art. He is so simply in virtue of the fact that, each time he enters into that impersonal and relational dance of the particles, he is enabled to experience personally, without the intrusion of the artist, and at the precise moment of its happening, not only the creative and therefore self-generative collisions which the poet has arranged for him but also the moment of intense (because enlarged) awareness which results whenever they are collided into dynamic fusion with one another.

Two important innovations in aesthetic theory may be seen to follow from the observations derived from Eisenstein and detailed above—one for the artist and the way in which he composes his work, and the other for the reader or viewer and the way in which he is expected to read and, indeed, to co-create it. It is these innovations which became the twin cornerstones of modern aesthetic theory, together with the formulae, both for artistic composition and for the reader co-creation which that theory requires. Here again Eisenstein's experience can be of assistance to us inasmuch as he has described so clearly the way in which he came to discover that formula for himself.

In *The Film Sense,* Eisenstein confesses that for a time he had become so enamoured of the simple technique of juxtaposition that he neglected to turn his attention critically to the aesthetic implications of the "third something" (*FS* 9) which that device invariably generates and in which he found its real creative issue. It was not long, however, before he discovered those implications in the peculiar stance which, as film director, he had to maintain—a stance which kept him shuttling back and forth from the shot-ciphers together with their juxtapositions on the one hand, to the "third something" or "whole" which together they must serve, at the same time that they create it, on the other. For it is, Eisenstein tells us, that "third something" or what, in another context, he calls "the content of the *whole*" (*FS* 9) which must "determine both the content of the shot and that content which is revealed through a given *juxtaposition of these shots*" (*FS* 10). and which thus in fact "predetermines both the individual elements and the circum-stances of their juxtaposition" (*FS* 10).

The artist or maker, driven by what we shall hear the New Idealists describe as that "spirit of the whole" (*PIV* 267) which both underlies and informs the dialectic of becoming, keeps his eye firmly trained, now upon the "new whole" (*OPP* 108) which is coming into being (and which, be it noted, is to be the creative *result* of the compositional process he sets in motion), and alternately, upon that precise collocation of "particles" (*SE* 8) which, through experimental collision, he finds capable of eliciting the result he desires. The artist proceeds to compose his work, that is, not by expressing or externalizing anything but rather by internalizing in it the stages of its own becoming—the stages which the poet's persona and reader will then be invited to retrace. Or, as Eisenstein has put it, "*composition takes the structural elements of the portrayed phenomena* and from these composes its *canon for building the containing work*" (*FF* 151).

The modern artist, in short, will adopt the procedures of the "whodunit" which, beginning at the end ("The end is where we start from" (*LG* V)—that is, with a corpse on its hands—works its way back to those particular circumstances in which that end finds its true beginnings. Or, to put this another way, the modern artist adopts the procedures of the contemporary chemist who, when he says that he has discovered a new product or "a new compound" (*SE* 8), really means that he has discovered a particular combination of elements which he can pressure into creating that compound for him.

One of the theoretical consequences which followed from the reader's newfound status as co-creator was that the relationship of the poem to its author which had held a front and centre position on the platform of romantic literary theory was now seriously upstaged by the relationship of the poem to its reader instead, together with the concern for the differing intensities (and subsequent valuations) of poetry which that relationship engenders. The deeper and far more significant effect of this theoretical displacement, however, has been in its substitution of what is essentially a reader-oriented aesthetic of completion for the earlier romantic and poet-oriented aesthetic of expression—a displacement which manifested itself in the virtual disappearance of the author from works of modern literature, at least in his direct or omniscient form. If the theory of dialectical form were rigorously applied, even the persona or mask which almost all authors tend to use could also become expendable and disappear as completely as the poet-protagonist has done in the first two sections of *The Waste Land.*

The basic and paradoxical requirement of such a dialectical aesthetic theory as I have outlined above revolves, however, so far as the poet-maker goes, around the critical stance which he must maintain during the entire course of his creative labour—one eye, as it were, being on the poem (the "new whole" or "object") which is yet to be, and the other on those stages in its own becoming which will, if provided to the reader, enable that reader safely and inevitably to make his way towards its proper completion and enjoyment. The task of the artist, in Eliot's view, is one of insuring that "exact equivalence" (*SE* 125) between the two which is necessary to artistic success but the paradox involved in that task resides in the fact that the "new whole" on which the poet must keep his eye trained is a whole that "was not," as Eliot tells us, "in existence before the poem was completed" (*Use of* 138). It might be well here to recapitulate something of Eliot's insistence on this important point.

Throughout his literary criticism, Eliot has asserted repeatedly that genuine creative activity has not occurred unless "something comes into being which is new,"[10] something that, once it exists in time, "has its own life" (*TSW* x) and "its own existence, apart from us" (*Use of* 34). In speaking of what the poem communicates, Eliot insists that "what is there to be communicated was not in existence before the poem was completed" (*Use of* 138). When Eliot seeks to characterize the "something new" that "has happened," he invariably does so in terms of integrity or wholeness, the fusion of the many into the one, and the one he refers to always as an "object," "a thing," or a "work of art"—terms that Eliot uses interchangeably with one another. In a commentary, for example, on John Livingston Lowes' *Road to Xanadu*, Eliot tells us that we may be grateful to Lowes for showing us "once and for all that poetic originality is largely an original way of assembling the most disparate and unlikely material to make *a new whole*" (*OPP* 108. Italics mine) and, in "Tradition and the Individual Talent," he describes the poem as "a concentration and *a new thing* resulting from the concentration, of a very great number of experiences which to the practical and active person would not seem to be experiences at all" (*SE* 10. Italics mine). In the same essay, he condemns those literary productions which, in attempting to imitate, or to conform to, something which is already in existence, do "not really . . . conform at all" for such a production "would not be new, and would therefore not be a work of art" (*SE* 5). Finally, when Eliot describes the impressionistic critic as "an incomplete artist," he does so because the sensibility of such a critic "alters the object" whereas "in an artist these suggestions made by a work of art, which are purely personal, become fused with a multitude of other suggestions from multitudinous experience, and result in the production of *a new object* which is no longer purely personal, because it is a work of art itself" (*TSW* 7. Italics mine).

In summation we may say that, for Eliot, what comes into being through the instrumentality of the poet is new in the sense that it has never before had temporal existence; has integrity or wholeness in the sense that it comprises a unity; and is endowed with a mysterious and sacred viability in the sense that it has a capacity for entering into relations of its own as a consequence of having "its own life" and "its own existence, apart from us."

Interesting as these affirmations are in themselves, they hardly seem radically innovative or even particularly significant until we

10. T. S. Eliot, "Preface", *English Poetry and Its Contribution to the Knowledge of a Creative Principle* (London: Faber and Faber, [1950]), xi.

relate them to the disjunction between poet and poem which Eliot also insists upon, and to which we have already made reference in our introductory chapter. It is precisely because the "something new" that comes into being through the mediumship or instrumentality of the poet was not ever, or in any form, in existence prior to its own completion that the poem he makes cannot be conceived of or understood or evaluated in terms of its phenomenal maker or his emotions or in terms even of the process by which it was made. If, as Eliot has indicated repeatedly, "All poetry may be said to start from the emotions experienced by human beings in their relations to themselves, to each other, to divine beings, and to the world about them" (*TCTC* 38), yet that is not to say, as Eliot has also indicated repeatedly, that it is "the function of poetry . . . simply to arouse these same emotions in the audience of the poet" (*TCTC* 38). It is not such personal emotions—emotions, that is, deriving from "the history of the poet" (*SE* II)—which should be or, in fact, are of concern to the reader interested primarily in "poetry and not another thing" (*TSW* viii). What he should derive instead from his experience of reading poetry is *"significant* emotion"—emotion, that is, "which has its life in the poem" (*SE* II) and is an expression of his response to "the new (the really new)" appearance once again, and in time, of that experiential reality which poetry is and has always been.

In Eliot's view—and the matter is worth considerable emphasis —the poem does not correspond to anything that was already in existence; the poem does not imitate anything that was already in existence; the poem does not externalize or express anything that was already in existence. The impulse to create the "new (the really new) work of art" (*SE* 5), the impulse to make "a new whole" (*OPP* 108) or "a new object" (*TSW* 7), may indeed exist as one of the defining characteristics of the poet but *what* he makes is neither in him nor of him. It has no lodgement in his being whatever—neither before, nor at any point during, the creative process and that ultimately is why Eliot believes that "To divert interest from the poet to the poetry is a laudable aim" (*SE* II) and why he insists that "Honest criticism and sensitive appreciation are [and must always be] directed not upon the poet but upon the poetry" (*SE* 7).

That there is a paradox which lies at the heart of such an aesthetic theory as has been outlined here, Eliot was of course well aware. If we would probe that paradox, we need only look again at the stance of the artist in creation. Clearly "the mind of the poet"

(*SE* 7)—"the mind which creates" (*SE* 8) by fusing the many "particles" into a "new whole"—is a mind which, in order to perform its task, must somehow exist "above" both "the particles which can unite to form a new compound" (*SE* 8) and also above the "new compound" which they can in fact "unite to form." Thus the significance and creative nature of "the transforming catalyst" (*SE* 8) for Eliot is to be defined "not precisely in any valuation of 'personality' " (*Se* 7) but rather in his sensitivity to the *nisus* or "spirit of the whole" (*PIV* 267) which runs through and connects all the internally related "particles" or "elements" of his experience and which enables him *critically* to exert on "the particles," by way of their spatial adjustment and readjustment, "the pressure, so to speak, under which the fusion takes place" (*SE* 8). Thus for Eliot, as for all dialecticians, creativity is to be defined, paradoxically enough, not in terms of a *creative* process but rather in terms of that creative issue which results from what is essentially a *critical* process—that is, an intellectual process. This is surely the point of Eliot's strictures against Arnold who, it seemed to Eliot, "overlooks the capital importance of criticism in the work of creation itself" (*SE* 18) and which urged Eliot by way of contrast to say that "Probably, indeed, the larger part of the labour of an author in composing his work is critical labour; the labour of sifting, combining, constructing, expunging, correcting, testing: this frightful toil is as much critical as creative" (*SE* 18).

Within such a dialectical theory of form, what distinguishes "the mind which creates" from "the man who suffers" (*SE* 8) is clearly that vision of the whole in terms of which the creating poet is enabled to be critical during the course of his forming or composing —that whole which will serve him as the *criterion*[11] in terms of which the craftsman will make the practical judgments necessary to his craft. It is that "new whole" and its "becoming" of which the poet is the temporal agent. It is an agency he can fulfill only when he follows out the *nisus* implicit in "the particles" themselves —a *nisus* which urges them to inclusion in that larger whole within which they are not so much obliterated at they are transmuted and

11. The concept of the *criterion* is as central to the mind and art of T. S. Eliot as it is to the philosophy of F. H. Bradley from which he obviously derived it. See especially Chapter XXIV of *Appearance and Reality*, pp. 318-54, and see also a brief defence of the doctrine which Bradley makes on pp. 560-61, and which begins as follows: "The doctrine of the Criterion adopted by me has in various quarters been criticized, but, so far, I venture to think, mainly without much understanding of its nature."

made "whole" by losing their a–partness and by being made into one.

We have suggested that the paradox referred to above exists in the fact that "the whole"—the "third something" which the poet seeks to effect—is a "whole" which, if it "is not actually in existence until after the poem is completed," is yet that which must everywhere function as a guide to the agent poet in his formation of it. The resolution of that paradox is attainable only when we realize that if "the new whole" was itself "not in existence," yet its entelechy or spirit was—"the spirit of the whole" (*PIV* 267) just as Bradley and Bosanquet had delineated it for Eliot in their innovative studies, and as he himself went on to adumbrate the conception in *Four Quartets.* It is clearly that spirit which lies behind Eliot's concept of creativity for if "the end" (the "new whole") did not in some sense at least "precede the beginning" (the particles) and if "the end and the beginning were [not] always there / Before the beginning and after the end" (*BN* V), the poet could never make it as a creator and the new poetic substance would never come into being through him and his mediumship. It is only if this kind of nonlinear and timeless simultaneity or "co-existence" (*BN* V) is somehow available to man—a simultaneity within which the words "before" and "after" do not apply—that we can hope to split the mystery of creativity.

For Eliot, of course, "the mind which creates" (*SE* 8) is not—as I shall attempt to show later—the mind of man. It is a mind which is not personally the poet's own but rather "a mind which he learns in time to be much more important than his own private mind" (*SE* 6). If man does not own that mind, yet it is a mind in which he can share and in whose working he can actively participate. It is in virtue of just such participation that his life becomes progressively more and more significant because more and more god-like and creative, or co-creative. Eliot has made two statements about that mind which are apposite here inasmuch as they relate the conception to its classical source. The first is in a personal letter quoted by E. M. Stephenson[12] in which Eliot takes issue with Diels's translation of the epigraph from Heraclitus which Eliot had used as a tuning-fork for the *Four Quartets.* Diels translates the passage as follows: "Although the word is in common use for all, most men live as if they had each a private wisdom of his own." Eliot then

12. E. M. Stephenson, *T. S. Eliot and the Lay Reader,* 2nd ed. (London: Fortune Press, 1946), p. 80.

comments as follows: "I should say that Herakleitos meant a great deal more than simply 'the word is in common use.' I think that he meant rather that the reason, the Logos, or the rational understanding of the nature of things is common or available to all men." Secondly, and in a footnote in his essay "Second Thoughts About Humanism," Eliot makes the same point—this time against Norman Foerster. He says: "Mr Foerster's 'reason' seems to me to differ from any Greek equivalent (λογος) by being exclusively human; whereas to the Greek there was something inexplicable about λογος so that it was a participation of man In the divine" (*SE* 433 footnote). It is, as I have already suggested, in virtue of just that kind of participation that the artist is enabled to create—to bring into new and actual temporal being something which until then never was.

Once "the new (the really new) work of art" (*SE* 5) has been created, it becomes the responsibility of the reader/critic "to see the object as it really is" (*TSW* 15). If he would discharge that responsibility successfully, he must first co-create the poem he would respond to, or criticize, or evaluate, by retracing its relational lineaments—the relations which are internal to and actually constitutive of its own becoming. Thus meaning and theme will be sought not in the various units or particles which make up the poem's *matter* but rather, and as Joseph Frank has also pointed out, through "the reflexive relations among the units of meaning."

It is, of course, a very different, and far more dynamic, philosophy than Kant's which provides the metaphysical base for such a dialectical theory of aesthetic form as I have outlined above, and outlined in the most summary of terms, and there is also much more to be said about it than can be dealt with here. Perhaps enough has been said, however, to justify the working assumption that what Eliot may well have been about in *The Waste Land* was the creation of a poem responsive to a new and radically different concept of form than had ever been systematically utilized in English poetry before his—a concept not only consonant with the major insights of the dominant philosophy of his time but consonant as well with those conclusions he had himself arrived at—and expressed—in the philosophical writings he completed not long before he began writing *The Wast Land* in 1921. Is this, however, merely conjecture on our part, or is there some ground for assuming as we have done that Eliot was a profoundly serious artist and one very much concerned therefore with developing a new and more nearly contemporary methodology of form? I would suggest that it is in his essay, "*Ulysses,* Order and Myth" that Eliot reveals the depth and seriousness of his concern for problems of literary form, and reveals as well the method he himself developed and used in *The Waste Land* in response to that concern.

It is by emphasizing with regard to Joyce's *Ulysses* "the significance of the method employed" there—that is, "the parallel to the *Odyssey,* and the use of appropriate styles and symbols to each division"—that Eliot indirectly suggests the method he is himself using in *The Waste Land* and had used even before Joyce in his *Poems (1920).* Somewhat further on in the same paragraph, Eliot indicates that the method is one of "great importance"—so great that it seemed to him indeed to have "the importance of a scientific discovery."[13] Eliot goes on then to conclude as follows:

In using the myth, in manipulating a continuous parallel between contemporaneity and antiquity, Mr. Joyce is pursuing a method which others must pursue after him. They will not be imitators, any more than the scientist who uses the discoveries of an Einstein in pursuing his own independent, further investigations . . . . It is a method already adumbrated by Mr. Yeats, and of the need for which I believe Mr. Yeats to have been the first contemporary to be conscious. It is a method for which the horoscope is auspicious . . . Instead of narrative method, we may now use the mythical method.[14]

It is one of those extraordinary historical coincidences that "the mythical method" should have been discovered by Joyce and by Eliot at very nearly the same time and then simultaneously applied —by one to the novel, and by the other to poetry. It was during the month of October 1922 that the "existing monuments" (*SE* 5), already so comfortably established within the literary world, were unsettled—not to say, confounded—by the introduction of two really new works of art among them, for it was in that month that both *Ulysses* and *The Waste Land* were first published in London.[15]

It should be clear from what has been said above that Joyce's method in *Ulysses* and Flaubert's in *Madame Bovary* are identical

13. T. S. Eliot, "Ulysses, Order, & Myth," *Dial* LXXV, 5 (November 1923), 480.
14. Ibid., pp. 482-83.
15. One thousand copies of *Ulysses* had appeared in Paris during the preceding February but very few, if any, of these had made their way to London. Regarding the specifics of the influence of *Ulysses* on the making of *The Waste Land,* the reader should consult the excellent account provided by Robert Adams Day in his "Joyce's Waste Land and Eliot's Unknown God." See Eric Rothstein, ed., *Literary Monographs* (Madison: University of Wisconsin Press, 1971), IV, 139-226.

in principle with that formulated by Eisenstein in his book *Film Form.* Both, that is, use collision, or juxtaposition without copula, as the creative device which, of itself and progressively, generates the thematic idea or vision to which the reader is led by it. In *The Waste Land* Eliot provides us with yet another instance of that principle at work for it is his expressed intention to manipulate in his poem the same kind of "continuous parallel between contemporaneity and antiquity" that Joyce manipulated in his novel. If the two, however, everywhere run parallel to one another throughout the poem in a linear fashion, yet it must never be forgotten that it is the *collision* of the two which, in the minds of poet-protagonist and reader alike, creates that sense of shatteringly ironic dissimilarity between mythical and modern which compels us to see the latter as in fact a parody of the former. Neither the mythical dimension nor the modern, taken alone, would generate that all-pervasive sense of parody which constitutes the thematic "substance of the poem," but the dissimilarities between the two, everywhere amplified and orchestrated through the device of collision, creates the vision to which both poet-protagonist and reader alike attain—the vision of the contemporary world, its inhabitants, and their ritualistic actions as hollow at the core and reflecting an unselfconscious parody of the more meaningful ones existent within the ancient world. The vision culminates finally in an inclusive moment of shattering self-awareness by the poet-protagonist when, in full consciousness, he comes to see himself and his humiliating malaise as itself a parody of that known to his long dead exemplar.

If such deflationary self-awareness is what the Quester Hero, ironically enough, achieves at the end of his quest, yet it must also be noted that it is no Byronic kind of irony or self-mockery with which either the poem or its poet-protagonist concludes. They end instead on a note of affirmation and one which is mounted, not on that doubling and redoubling of the "static" self which grounds the fractured ironies of the Byronic hero but, instead, on the struggle towards a recreation (rather than further fragmentation) of the self. In a commentary on a book by Haakon Chevalier entitled *The Ironic Temper,* Eliot had this to say about the various uses to which irony can be put: "What we rebel against is neither the use of irony against definite men, institutions or abuses, nor is it the use (as by Jules Laforgue) to express a *dédoublement* of the personality against which the subject struggles. It is the use of irony to give the appearance of a philosophy of life, as something final and not instrumental, that leaves us now indifferent; it seems to us an evasion of the difficulty of living, where it pretends to be a solution of it."[16]

It is, then, this "instrumental" or functional irony which may be found at the core of *The Waste Land*, but it must be emphasized once again that, for Eliot, the *"dédoublement"* which effects it is neither reductionist in tendency, not to be taken "as something final." It is instead to be seen as that "against which the subject struggles" and, in short, as itself part of the generative vehicle made use of by the soul in its struggle towards its own recreation—the process we have designated as the process of "soul-making," and the process towards an understanding of which we are slowly making our way.

One cannot labour very long in the vineyards of aesthetic theory without acquiring an empathic understanding of the desire so often expressed by artists and poets alike to leave those vineyards to someone else. In a letter to me dated 18 October 1962, for example, Eliot made just such a summary dismissal of aesthetics when he said that, "In the years when I was a student of Bradley's work and was working for a doctorate in philosophy, the one branch of philosophy in which I took no interest whatever was aesthetics." In effect, this was not a little unlike the remark, attributed to Barnett Newman, that "Aesthetics is for the artist, as ornithology is for the birds."[17]

Encouraged thus by our betters, it is perhaps wise to turn now from the complexities of literary theory to those of literary practice and to attempt to apply directly to a reading of *The Waste Land* the dialectical principles we have thus far been concerned merely to elaborate. Such a dialectical reading of *The Waste Land* will perhaps illuminate more clearly than anything else can that three-sided and self-generative process of "soul-making" which is induced by the principle of particle collision and which we will seek to understand finally by relating it to the philosophy of F. H. Bradley from which Eliot, at least in part, derived it.

16. T. S. Eliot, "A Commentary," *Criterion* XII, 48 (April 1933), 469.
17. Reported by Harold Rosenberg in *The Anxious Object* (New York: Horizon Press, 1964), p. 172.

4

a
dialectical
reading of
the waste land

To read *The Waste Land* dialectically is to read it reflexively—that is, as a system of constitutive relationships both meaningful and controlled. Two major phases are involved in such a reading and derive from the particular uses to which Eliot has put "the mythical method" in *The Waste Land*—the first, linear and developing therefore along the lines provided by the successive stages in the hero's quest and progressive transformation, and the second, non-linear or dialectical and exhibiting therefore the nondiscursive form natural to psychic or interior life. If, in short, *The Waste Land* derives its linear thrust from the "continuous parallel between con-temporaneity and antiquity" of which we have already heard Eliot speak, yet it must always be remembered that the broadening perceptions generated by that running parallelism are generated dialectically and, therefore, in a nonlinear fashion.

In this respect, the form the poem would have revealed with greater sureness, had it in fact become more completely what it was "aiming to be," is not unlike that of a railroad track which moves forward assiduously but relies on the ceaseless interconnection of two rails to do so. The characteristic movement of Eliot's poet-protagonist, however, is somewhat more complex than that image will allow for, if he does indeed move forward along the linear tract provided for him by the two major planes involved in "the mythical method" and its analogues, yet he derives the impetus to do so only by moving vertically up and down across the sleepers or ties first, as it were, and by colliding those analogates with one another as he goes. The movement of the poet-protagonist, therefore, is neither wholly horizontal nor wholly vertical but one which partakes of both and, as a consequence, reveals the informing pattern of a stepladder or spiral instead. It does so when the variant movements involved—horizontal and vertical, linear and dialectical—intersect within his psyche and generate by means of that intersection those creative tensions which give continuing impetus to the progressive drama of his transformation.

What Eliot's poet-protagonist does, in short, is to retrace psychically the major moments in the process of his own becoming or "soul-making." Those moments include a record of the actual temporal and physical journey he has made through that contemporary waste land "where a cauldron of unholy loves sang all about . . . [his] ears"—a *waste land* inhabited by countless multitudes living or partly living like himself. What he comes to perceive by way of the constant collision of myth and modernity is just how great the distance really is between the world of mythical action and romance on the one hand, and the contemporary world of those ritual imitations burlesquing them on the other, and what he (rather than Tiresias) *"sees"*—and enables the reader to see through him—is, "in fact, . . . the substance of the poem." The psychic journey of Eliot's Quester Hero is not like Weston's, a journey *From Ritual to Romance* but just the reverse—a journey back from the romantic debasements of the present to the inspirited and more life-fulfilling rituals of the past.

But how, in specific terms, does the dialectic of the poet-protagonist's interior life proceed? I have already indicated that there are two aspects involved in his progressive transformation—one linear or temporal, and the other nonlinear or dialectical. I have also suggested that the first of these derives from the two planes implicit in the "continuous parallel between contemporaneity and antiquity" which it is the function of "the mythical method" first to establish and then to maintain. Eliot internalized that parallelism within his poem by way of a continuous and effective juxtaposition of mythical titles with modern texts. The mythical underpinnings of the poem, that is, are suggested to the consciousness of the poet-protagonist and to that of the reader as well by way of the poem's epigraph, and also by way of those various titles which Eliot assigned to the five sections of the poem. These can serve the reader as significant indices of that vision of the whole which generated and informed the composition of the poem, for what those titles recapitulate are the various stages implicit in the "story" of *the waste land* and implicit as well in that quest for heroic transformation through death and rebirth which is central to it.

If the mythical titles and modern texts everywhere run parallel to one another throughout the linear course of the poem, it is nonetheless the constant collision of their analogical planes which generates the poet-protagonist's ever-widening perception of the nature of the contemporary *waste land* and of its inhabitants. As indicated earlier, in our account both of Eisenstein's theoretic treatment of dialectical form and of Eliot's practical handling of it in "The Fire Sermon," the formula for the development of such awareness is always triadic and involves therefore the three "moments" or "sides" which human experience of any kind, dialectically understood, always reveals.

The first, so far as *The Waste Land* goes, derives from the implications of what Helen Williams has aptly described as "The Web of Allusion."[1] That web is created for the reader by those "particles" (*SE* 8) of experiential reality, whether they be mythic or modern, literary or otherwise, to which reference or allusion is made by the poet-protagonist of the poem—things seen or heard, remembered or felt, and all suspended within that creative mind whose working he exemplifies. Those particles have already been objectified within the consciousness of the poet-protagonist and exist within the poem therefore as the "objective correlative[s]" (*SE* 124) of his *particular* emotion" or feeling (*SE* 125). Such particles of themselves, however, are only of subordinate interest within a dialectical reading of the poem, as they are also within the dialectical philosophy from which they derive. The second moment involves the dialectical dance of the particles, a dance everywhere generated by the principle of selective and controlled collision—the principle except for which "There would be no dance, and there is only the dance" (*BN* 11). If the particles constitute not experience but only the objective matter of its ceaseless and further becoming, *what* that matter becomes is an ever larger and larger whole—that new and never before existent whole which constitutes the third and final side or moment in the temporal history of developing experience. The "new whole" or "third something" to which we

1. See "The Web of Allusion," chap. 2 of Helen Williams, *T. S. Eliot: The Waste Land* (London: Edward Arnold, 1968), pp. 44-76.

have heard Eisenstein refer earlier (*FS* 9) is the creative issue into which such experience shapes itself but, if we have described the moment of the "third something" as final, that is only a way of saying that what happens thereafter is not something different from what happened before but involves instead merely a ceaseless recurrence of what is ever the same triadic process. The unity of a formal and stabilized experience, in collision with further particles of experience, adjusts itself to them by relaxing its perimeters and by dissolving. It dies unto itself in the sense that its former unity first disintegrates and then is reborn at a higher and "holier" level when, in conjunction with further particles of experience, it shall have been properly integrated once more. Thus the ever-widening gyres of transcendental becoming or of "soul-making" continue as experience broadens and as the spiralling continuities of the dialectical hero whose experienc₃ it is expand from centre to circumference with it. That dialectical hero will shortly be identified with the *significant self-in-becoming* existing at the fulcrum of Eliot's philosophy.

Particles, collision, the "third something" or "new whole"—this is the triadic concept of experiential reality central to the post-Hegelian tradition of process philosophy. To create a literary form which should embody the three-sided and dialectical nature of such developing experience, and in precisely the way in which that nature had been philosophically formulated is, I suggested earlier, something of what I believe Eliot to have been about in *The Waste Land*. In that passage of "The Fire Sermon" which we analysed earlier, we noted Eliot's use and development of a particular literary device which we can now see is exactly correlative to the triadic process outlined above. The technique is simply one of lifting a phrase—a particle of literary experience, together with the meaning which surrounds it in the previous context—and then resetting that phrase in a new and different context which collides with it in an explosively generative way that is creative of enlarged awareness or perception on the one side and, correlatively, of deeper feeling on the other.

It is notable—and we shall make much of it hereafter—that, so far as the poet-protagonist of the poem goes, *Knowledge and Experience,* truth and reality, always develop simultaneously and *pari-passu* with one another for, within Eliot's philosophy, these are the twin correlatives indispensably involved in the process of "soul-making"—a process of becoming (or coming to be) that which one knows. Indeed this is the most remarkable and thoroughly innovative feature of Eliot's presentation of his pilgrim's progress, and it is one which follows precisely upon the account he formulated of such empirical self-development or "unification of sensibility" (*SE* 248) in his doctoral thesis on *Knowledge and Experience in the Philosophy of F. H. Bradley*. To that subject we shall return in our next chapter but, for now, we must turn directly instead to *The Waste Land* itself. As we do so, our first concern must be to reconstruct for ourselves that vision of the whole which originally served the poet-maker in the making of his poem and which, I have suggested, he goes on then to provide immediately and directly for his reader by way of his continuous juxtaposition of mythical titles and modern texts.

Having already dealt in our first chapter with the first and most important of all Eliot's titles—the title, that is, of the poem itself—and with Eliot's reference, by way of it, to that myth of *the waste land* providing him with his primary analogates, we may turn next to a consideration of the poem's epigraph. Eliot has consistently used the device of the epigraph as a tuning fork wherewith to establish the exact pitch of those reverberations his poem will seek to resonate and, as a consequence, his epigraph to *The Waste Land* can provide us with the second of those major indices to the vision of the whole which we are presently concerned to reconstruct.

The Cumaean Sibyl, whose reply to the children dancing about her Eliot quotes in his epigraph to the poem, was the most famous of those prophetic old women of Greek mythology. It was she who guided Aeneas through Hades as Vergil would later guide Dante through the Inferno. In return for her services, Apollo had granted her the boon of as long a life as she had grains of sand in her hand. Having neglected, however, to ask as well for eternal youth, she shrank into a withered old age—not of life but of a death-in-life to which the extinction of total death would have been infinitely preferable. When the children ask of her: "Sibyl, what do you want?", she replies therefore: "I want to die," and thus expresses in the epigraph to the poem the need or desire of virtually every personage within it.

The death-in-life of the Cumaean Sibyl is to life as the imagery of dream is to the reality imaged. It is in *the waste land*—in "death's dream kingdom" (*HM* 11) therefore—that death will rehearse itself in the imagery of death-in-life and in the death desire or "Paralysed force" (*HM* 1) which is its primary insignia. Throughout the poem, however, a second kind of death—the sacrificial death of the Quester Hero through which his transubstantiation is to be effected and culminating, therefore, in what is really life-in-death—is opposed to the death-in-life existence of the various personae dramatized in the poem and whose "voices" we have already isolated within it. What the collision of these two different kinds of death generates is that sense of parody to which I have already referred, and one which encourages us to see that Eliot's "dramatic character[s]" (*OPP* 89)—characters so like those of Pinter and Beckett— together with the lives they lead, constitute but a parody of that self-generative and self-transcendent life "requiring, pointing to the agony / Of death and birth" instead (*EC* 111). It is in the collision of the various titles which Eliot assigns to the various sections of his poem with the texts immediately following upon them that the disparity between these two kinds of death and two kinds of life is further dramatized and enforced.

The relational complex with which we are confronted in the first section of the poem begins its own formulation with the title Eliot derived from the majestic Anglican service for the dead—"The Burial of the Dead." The theme of resurrection, which St. Paul proclaimed in the words "the dead shall be raised incorruptible and we shall be changed," runs everywhere through that service and it is that resurrection motif which Eliot, in the first section of the poem, collides with a series of six tableaux, each of them imaging a kind of death or death-in-life from which only a similarly spurious kind of rebirth can follow. The "third something" resulting from the collision is the suggestion that in the *waste land,* whenever something is reborn, it is not "raised incorruptible" but is degenerated instead so that rebirth in the *waste land* is always an empty simulacrum of the resurrection in just the same way that death-in-life is a caricature of sacrificial death. That is why "April," with its promise of springtime renewal, is seen in the opening lines of the poem as "the cruellest month" and why "Winter" which

> kept us warm, covering
> Earth in forgetful snow, feeding
> A little life with dried tubers
> (5-7)

is preferred to the renewal forced upon "the dead land" by "stirring" its "Dull roots with spring rain." What Eliot does next is suggestively to collide the death-in-life existence of such personages as Marie, who have really died but managed to survive themselves by "going south in the winter" for their revitalization, with the "Dull roots" whose "little life" is similarly fed with similarly "dried tubers." Such rebirth is clearly a parody of that which is promised in "The Burial of the Dead" but what is noteworthy for our purposes is the method by which both the delusive parallel, and an awareness of it, are always and simultaneously created in the mind of poet-protagonist and reader alike—that is, solely by the collision of title and text and in virtue of the internal and constitutive relations by which the two are held together. It is this same dialectical method which Eliot makes such brilliant use of in the remaining four parts of the poem wherein once again the substantive parody is created almost exclusively by means of the collision of titles and text.

What we are given in Part II, for example, is simply two images of married love as it exists within the contemporary *waste land*—one taken from the upper classes and the other from the lower—and these in immediate juxtaposition with the title "A Game of Chess." Marriage, seen as just such a game of strategy and one ending all too often in a very stale mate, is the dialectical substance (or part of it) generated by the memorable dialogues of the neurasthenic wife and her bored and exhausted spouse who, together,

> play a game of chess,
> Pressing lidless eyes and waiting for a knock upon the door . . .
> (137-8)

on the one hand, and of the toothless Lil and her friend on the other. Lil is warned that Albert's "been in the army four years" and "wants a good time,/ And if you don't give it him, there's others will." The strategic failure is one of looking "so antique (And her only thirty-one)" but a new set of teeth should help to "renew" Lil and thereby to revitalize her marriage. So much is given merely by the title itself but the dialectical "meaning" is, of course, underscored for those who know (as does the poet-protagonist) the play to which Eliot's note to line 138 of the poem refers us—that is, Middleton's, *Women Beware Women.* In Act II, scene ii, of that play, Bianca goes with her mother-in-law to visit Livia, a "lady of situations" (line 50), and one who in this instance is in league with the Duke who, in turn, is intent on seducing Bianca. The Duke has arranged that Livia should distract the mother-in-law by means of a Game of Chess which is set on the lower stage but is viewed by the audience simultaneously with the seduction scene set on the upper stage. The scene (à la Flaubert) is, of course, loaded with the double entendres created by the witty juxtaposition of the two scenes—the stages of the seduction everywhere paralleling the analogous stages of the game of chess with both of them ending presumably in a check-mate. One exchange between the ladies on the lower stage is of particular significance to the dialectical meaning of the hyacinth passage in Part 1, and must therefore be quoted here. The mother-in-law says to Livia, "You may see, madam / My eyes begin to fail" and Livia, referring to the final embraces on the upper stage, mut-ters in reply the loud stage whisper, "I'll swear they do, wench."

In Part III, Eliot's title, "The Fire Sermon," refers, as his note to line 308 of the poem tells us, to that particular sermon given by Buddha in which this major "representative of eastern . . . asceti-cism" exhorts his priests to control the fires of passion . . . the fires of hatred . . . [and] the fires of infatuation" by means of that "refining fire" within which Arnaut gladly "hid himself" in the *Purgatorio* of Dante. What Eliot images in the text itself, on the other hand, is that "cauldron of unholy loves" which St. Augustine tells us "sang all about mine ears" when he came to Carthage and to which Eliot's note to line 307 of the poem refers us. It is, once again, in collision with the title that "the cauldron of unholy loves" defines itself as an ironic variant of that "refining fire" both of Buddha and of the Sermon on the Mount to which Eliot's notes also refer us. In another place Eliot has distinguished the two flames from one another as follows:

In purgatory the torment of flame is deliberately and consciously accepted by the penitent. When Dante approaches with Virgil these souls in purga-tory flame, they crowd towards him: . . .

Then certain of them made towards me, so far as they could, but ever watchful not to come so far that they should not be in the fire.

The souls in purgatory suffer because they *wish to suffer,* for purgation. And observe that they suffer more actively and keenly, being souls prepar-ing for blessedness, than Virgil suffers in eternal limbo. In their suffering is hope, in the anaesthesia of Virgil is hopelessness; that is the difference. (*SE* 217)

Similarly, the dialectical meaning" of Part IV of the poem emerges from the simple collision of Death by Water in the baptis-mal sense of its title with the physical sense imaged in its text. The loss of self—or death—required in the first instance is the vehicle through which one is born into a higher life whereas the drowning of Phlebas, if it does entail the fact that he too "rose and fell" while "A current under sea / Picked his bones in whispers," hardly adumbrates in that irregular bobbing the dying and reviving life delineated in the Phoenician fertility cults.

Finally, in Part V, the title, together with Eliot's note to line 402 of the poem, refers us to the Hindu fable of the Thunder which concludes with the following instruction: "This same thing does the divine voice here, thunder, repeat when he says: Da, Da, Da—that is, control yourselves, give, be compassionate. Therefore one should practice these three things: self-control, alms-giving, and compassion." Within the life of the poem's poet-protagonist "these three things" had been parodied in a giving which had consisted in nothing more than "The awful daring of a moment's surrender"; a compassion which had become instead only an act of prideful isolation:

We think of the key, each in his prison
Thinking of the key, each confirms a prison;

and a self-control to which her "heart would have responded / Gaily"—as gaily as did the boat "to the hand expert with sail and oar" if only the "controlling hands" had been there.

It is this spinal nerve of parody which runs through and connects the manifold "particles" of the poem's becoming and substantiates itself as it goes. It is worth noting too, however, that the vision of the whole which the reader can derive very quickly merely by colliding title and text is the same vision which the poem's poet-protagonist progressively generates for himself but only as he moves through the various sections of the poem. Thus two avenues whereby the reader may attain "the substance of the poem" are open to him—the first, by sharing the superior vision of the whole utilized by the poet-maker in his actual making of it and then offered by him to the reader in the manner enjoined by "the mythical method," and the second, by identifying himself experientially with the poet-protagonist of the poem as he retraces those linear and temporal stages leading him progressively to it. What a dialectical methodology of form requires for complete success, however, is the "exact equivalence" (*SE* 125) of those two kinds of vision which are involved and which every maker or artist must have if he is to make anything (even his own soul) successfully—the vision, that is, of the whole and the vision of the stages necessary to its becoming so and which, consequently, can lead him to it. It will perhaps be sufficient for our further purposes now if we return to a somewhat more detailed analysis of the remainder of "The Burial of the Dead" so as to determine whether or not the vision of the whole and the linear and temporal vision leading to it do in fact reveal that "exact equivalence" we have said is necessary to complete artistic success.

The vision of the whole underlying "The Burial of the Dead" derives, we have said, from the collision of those two different kinds of death which the poem as a whole images, as well as from the collision of the two kinds of rebirth consequent upon them. Each of the frames within "The Burial of the Dead", therefore, presents us with an image, not of that sacrificial or redemptive death from which a genuine rebirth may be expected but rather of that death-in-life which leads only to its own final dissolution amidst the wastes of time. Our further analysis may begin with the poem's third frame.

In lines 31-42 of the poem, Eliot is concerned with the death-in-life of romantic love. Once again we shall find that the "meaning" which the passage really has can only be generated by means of the system of relations internal to its "particles" and created therefore by their collisions with one another. The "third something" which results from those collisions in this instance is the sense of that enormous disparity known to the poet-protagonist of the poem between the inflationary expectations of sexual experience in its beginnings and the deflationary failure of the actual "knowledge" so often derived from it at the end. Thus the inflationary beginning and the deflationary end of romantic love are imaged twice over in the passage—first, in the collision with each other of the two operatic particles" from Wagner's *Tristan und Isolde* and then in the collision of both with the contemporary dialogue of the boy and girl in "the hyacinth garden." Both pairs of collision, however, are set against the background of the whole which in this instance is provided by the myth of Hyacinthus.

The life-fulfilling promise of sexual love is announced in the opera by way of a song which a sailor sings as he casts his eyes over the sea "Towards the homeland" where his love is "tarrying." Isolde is on the ship and she listens to this song—so expressive of a lover's eagerness—at a time when she is herself being brought by Tristan to the palace of his uncle, King Mark, whose proposal she has accepted and who awaits her coming with the same eagerness. In the course of her journey, Isolde has alternately felt attracted and repelled by Tristan and she decides finally that he shall die by poison and that she will die with him. She orders her nurse to prepare the drug but, dreading to see the young Princess perish, the nurse prepares an irresistible love-potion instead which Tristan and Isolde both drink. Amazed, they embrace each other in ecstasy just as the ship reaches Cornwall. Later King Mark surprises his bride with her lover in the opera's version of "the hyacinth garden" and when Tristan draws on Melot, the King's courtier, Tristan receives from him a fatal wound. Returned to his castle in Brittany, the wounded Tristan awaits the arrival of Isolde whose healing arts he hopes will restore him to new life. As he waits, and just before he dies, he repeatedly asks of his messengers whether there is any sign of Isolde's ship and repeatedly he receives the reply: *"Waste and empty is the sea."*

Intermediate between these two operatic "particles," juxtaposed in the passage without copula and scoring the beginning and end of that love resulting from an unwilled but irresistible physiological force, Eliot provides a second image of romantic love—one attaining to almost mystic intensity—but ending nonetheless in that state of death-in-life which the young man's side of the dialogue in "the hyacinth garden" reflects with such unmistakable poignancy:

> —Yet when we came back, late, from the Hyacinth garden,
> Your arms full, and your hair wet, I could not
> Speak, and my eyes failed, I was neither
> Living nor dead, and I knew nothing,
> Looking into the heart of light, the silence.
> *Oed' und leer das meer.*

It is only when we recall the orgasmic death referred to in the line "My eyes begin to fail" from the *Game of Chess* and collide that kind of unknowing death (or death-in-life) with the redemptive death (or life-in-death) delineated in the myth of Hyacinthus that we come to see in what sense the former constitutes a parody of the latter. Within that myth,—at least in the pre-Hellenic form relevant to Eliot's poem—Hyacinthus was closely associated with those other dying and reviving gods to whom Eliot refers us in the headnote to his poem. After acknowledging there his general indebtedness to *The Golden Bough*, Eliot adds that he "used especially the two volumes *Adonis, Attis, Osiris."* These volumes, constituting Part IV of the original twelve-volume edition, are grouped together under the title *Dying and Reviving Gods* and also include Frazer's accounts of The Hanged God and of Hyacinthus.

It is said there that it was the god Apollo who, in a game with Hyacinthus, his noblest and dearest companion, accidentally struck the youth the tragic wound that would as with Tristan culminate in his death. In some later accounts of the myth Apollo, kneeling beside Hyacinthus, is said to have wept for the blow, unwillingly struck but fatal no less, and to have cried out: "Oh, if I could but give my life for yours!" With that word, the boy's head fell back as does a flower when its stem is broken but, even as Apollo spoke, the blood-stained grass turned green again and a hyacinthine flower bloomed at the lad's feet.

If the death of Hyacinthus is followed by his rebirth in a new and substantially different form, yet that rebirth or transubstantiation is effected only when the redemptive and Christ-like exchange between god and man, Apollo and Hyacinthus, has occurred first: "Oh, if I could but give my life for yours!" In that chapter of *The Golden Bough* entitled "Oriental Religions in the West" which follows immediately upon Frazer's account of the festival celebrating what in another version of the myth is Hyacinth's resurrection and ascension into heaven, Frazer remarks that: "It appears from the testimony of an anonymous Christian who wrote in the fourth century of our era, that Chriatians and pagans alike were struck by the remarkable coincidences between the death and resurrection of their respective duties."[2] I suggested earlier that it was just such "coincidences" as these which gave to Eliot whatever further warrant he might have required for Christianizing the myth of the *waste land* in the way that he did—that is, by telescoping in his one protagonist the originally disjoined mythical personae of Fisher King and Quester Hero and thus the two aspects of the redemptive process they signalize. In the case of the Hyacinth myth, it is once again and clearly its dying and reviving aspect—its redemptive underpinnings, that is, rather than its romantic associations—which are of primary significance to Eliot, the poet-maker of *The Waste Land*. It is noteworthy, however, that it is only when we set the images of sexual and romantic love developed within the hyacinth passage against the background of the whole provided by the myths both of Hyacinthus and of the Fisher King, and in just the way which is enjoined upon us by Eliot's "mythical method," that we both generate and receive Eliot's dialectical "meaning" at the same time. What we come to see is that the orgasmic death of a sexually

2. Sir James G. Frazer, *The Golden Bough,* one volume abridged edition (New York: Macmillan, 1923), p. 361.

derived love constitutes for Eliot's persona all too often merely a parody of that redemptive love within which each of the partners to it dies unto himself in favor of the whole which together they "unite to form" (*SE* 8). It is only what Eliot elsewhere has called this "higher love" (*SE* 235) which distinguishes "the love of man and woman (or for that matter of man and man)" from that "coupling of animals" (*SE* 234-5) which apes it and ends in "nothing."

If Eliot, the poet-maker, has made his "meaning" in the hyacinth passage clear enough, yet it must be remarked that it is a clarity only progressively attained by the reader and only as he proceeds to follow out in detail the systematic relations within which the "particles" are held and through which they are given the particular thematic substance they achieve. And so it is in the remaining sections of the first part of the poem. These need not, therefore, be elaborated in any great detail but only linked generally to the thematic "substance of the poem" already defined.

In the next frame of the poem, the Tarot cards are "reborn" as "the wicked pack of cards" used by contemporary gypsies to foretell the future of their fashionable clients whereas originally, and within the ancient religious lore of Egypt, they were used according to Weston[3] to foretell the rise and fall of those mysterious waters of the Nile around which the vegetation and fertility myths first formed themselves. The tonalities reflected in the monologue of "Madam Sosostris, famous clairvoyante" who "Had a bad cold" but "nevertheless / is known to be the wisest woman in Europe," are precious with the illusion of hidden meaning but in fact are, like those of Marie, but "Vacant shuttles [that] / Weave the wind" (Ger), for religion never really dies; it is merely "reborn" in the superstitions which constitute a parody of it.

Yet another kind of death-in-life imaged in the contemporary *waste land* is that reflected in the automatism of those mindless mechanisms flowing over "London Bridge" to their work in the "Unreal City" and passing on the way the church of "Saint Mary Woolnoth"—that contemporary version of the Chapel of the Holy Grail—which is set in the heart of London's financial district. By colliding this image of the "crowd" of commuting office workers during morning rush hours with that of an earlier crowd—not passing by the church but making a procession to it—Eliot forces an ironic twist upon the daily march. He compels us to see it as a

3. Jessie Weston, *From Ritual to Romance* (Garden City: Doubleday, 1957), p. 78.

mockery of that earlier Grail procession and one created by people very like those Dante saw on the outer confines of Hell within that circle reserved for those who never were really alive or sufficiently positive to take part either in good or evil. Dante, looking over them, speaks the line which Eliot quotes—the line which links them thereby to the contemporary office workers in that relational system of those neither living nor dead whose structure he has been delineating so carefully.

In the concluding lines of "The Burial of the Dead," we have yet another such ironic reenactment of that sacrificial death from which alone rebirth might genuinely be expected. In this instance, the parody is effected by the collision of the unblooming corpse "planted" by the businessman Stetson (appearing properly enough in this "shot" taken of London's financial district) in the nonvegetating "garden" of economically based wars prepared in just such districts. What distinguishes this passage from the others in the first part of the poem, however, is the appearance in it of what is here an unidentified speaker having, in one sense at least, a "double" consciousness—one above the linearities of time and able therefore to generalize an all-inclusive vision telescoping all wars into one war and, consequently, all times, places, and people as well; and the other within time and yoking the reader along with himself into inclusion in the world of the partly living by way of the line: "You! hypocrite lecteur!—mon semblable,—mon frère!" (76) That speaker we have identified earlier as the poet-protagonist of the poem but his appearance at this particular juncture causes a violent dislocation in formal propriety simply because, as I suggested earlier, it has not in any sense been adequately prepared for.

In conclusion to this dialectical reading of various passages from *The Waste Land,* two points already made or implied should be emphasized. The first is that the use to which Eliot puts his own brand of complex literary allusion emerges from and is a precise literary variant of those aesthetic principles which are central to post-Hegelian process philosophy. The tightly packed wit which is Eliot's most distinctive poetic trademark and which is generated, for example, by his collision of the "typist home at teatime" (222) with the heroine of Goldsmith's *The Vicar of Wakefield,* is a direct result of the concept of dialectical form implicit in such philosophy and summarily outlined in the preceding chapter. It is worthwhile to consider this passage somewhat more carefully for it can serve not only as a final illustration of the way dialectical form works out in practice but also as a way of generalizing now both that simultaneous vision of the whole which was given to Eliot, the poet-maker, and also that linear and progressive vision leading Eliot, the poet-protagonist of his own poem, to it.

It is the line "When lovely woman stoops to folly" (253) that links Eliot's typist to the gentler heroine of Goldsmith's novel but it is the collision of the two images involved which generates as nothing else could a sense of the enormous spiritual distance which divides the joyless and dreary automatism of contemporary sexuality from the life-giving procreative character it once had in an earlier age. The sense of a progressive degradation is both the poetic "idea" and the aesthetic effect generated in the poet-protagonist of the poem as he, and the reader with him, moves dialectically through the various "particles" of any given passage and then, from that passage, into that ever-widening circle of relations created by the various sections of the poem and finally by the poem as a whole. The significant point, as has already been indicated, is that the "idea" and the emotion attendant upon it are not—as in other methodologies of form—merely expounded or reflected upon or given a merely ornamental shading but instead are generated. And, further, they are generated by the reader himself or not at all.

If the reader, in this very important sense, is confronted by Eliot with a "do-it-yourself" poem, it does not follow from this that he can "do it" in any way he likes, for the process is both self-generative and self-corrective as it goes along. What the new methodology emphasizes is that the use of "objective correlative[s]" will provide, as nothing else can, a precisely controlled subjective response and one that is unique in being both subjective and impersonal at the very same time. It is so in the sense that, although it is personally generated and felt, *what* is generated and felt is both guided and restrained by the systematic and therefore impersonal relations whose objective lineaments the reader has retraced. What art begins in, and what it ends in as well, is not "emotion recollected in tranquillity" (*SE* 10) but in "*significant* emotion, emotion which has its life in the poem and not in the history of the poet" (*SE* 11). Thus if, in Eliot's view, "The emotion of art is impersonal" (*SE* 11), that is only because the dialectical dance of the particles is equally so. It is the dancer who must learn the steps and modify himself accordingly.

Eisenstein has also emphasized the import of these suggestions when he says, as regards the nature of the individual "cells" or "frames" that:

These considerations completely exclude a non-dialectic statement of the question concerning the *single-meaningness* of a frame within itself. The film frame can never be an inflexible *letter of the alphabet,* but must always remain a multiple meaning *ideogram.* And it can be read *only in juxtaposition,* just as an ideogram acquires its specific *significance,* meaning, and even pronunciation . . . only when combined with a separately indicated reading or tiny meaning—an indicator for the exact reading— placed alongside the basic hieroglyph. (*FF* 65-6)

What Eisenstein is concerned to stress here is that particular feature of dialectical theory which Pound and Eliot have also stressed—that is, the inherent multiplicity of possible meanings which can arise by altering—not the "particles" or "cells"— but the "relations" in which they stand to one another for it is those "relations" which, being internal to their terms, are in fact constitutive of the substance they create and define at the same time. These "particles" must be seen as Eisenstein and Eliot both indicate, and as Pound has also insisted, far more as vortices of energy—as radiant nodes or clusters capable of entering into a seemingly inexhaustible number of per-mutations and combinations, all of which open up new possibilities of "meaning."[4] When the "relations" are finally fixed, however, so also is the "exact reading" which is internal to it. Thus, to retrace the dialectical or relational dance of the "particles" is as regards the poem not only to retrace the stages of its own becoming but also, and at the same time, to achieve whatever poetic "substance" has in fact come to be.

We have thus far in the present chapter been much concerned to establish that all-pervasive sense of parody which a dialectical reading of the poem creates as the most substantive feature in it, and we have done so as a way of justifying an assertion made much earlier that it is not "[w]hat Tiresias *sees*" but what the poet-protagonist of the poem progressively comes to see that constitutes "the substance of the poem." There is a sense, however, in which

4. See Ezra Pound, "Vorticism," in *Gaudier-Brzeska: A Memoir [1916]* (Hessle: The Marvell Press, 1960), pp. 81-94, and particularly his statement on page 84 that "The imagiste's images have a variable significance, like the signs *a, b,* and *x* in algebra." See further his famous definition of the image on page 92: "The image is not an idea. It is a radiant node or cluster; it is what I can, and must perforce, call a VORTEX, from which, and through which, and into which, ideas are constantly rushing."

the vision attained by the poet-protagonist at the close of the poem may in fact be identified with the extratemporal vision Tiresias had all along. When that sense is properly understood, Eliot's assertion with regard to Tiresias in his endnotes to the poem will then be seen to be at least partially justified. Such an identity of vision, however, will in some sense involve a similar identity of the persona to whom it belongs, and it is that necessity which will introduce us in the chapters which follow immediately to what is perhaps the most central of all those conceptual differences dividing the philosophy of the nineteenth century from that of the twentieth. It is only a clear understanding of that major and indeed seminal difference between the two which will enable us to delineate clearly thereafter the nature of the last of those three underlying and unresolved conflicts which kept *The Waste Land* from realizing its own aims more fully and completely than it did.

5

"soul-making"

In our first chapter we heard Eliot speak of the struggle of the poet "to transmute his personal and private agonies into something rich and strange, something universal and impersonal" (*SE* 117). This concept of creativity as involving a process of transmuting personal experience into new and therefore qualitatively different substance constituted for Eliot, when he expressed it in 1927, merely an expansion of the similar concept he had first introduced in "Tradition and the Individual Talent" in 1919, just three years after completing his Bradley dissertation. In that essay too, Eliot had identified the creative process with a "process of depersonalization" (*SE* 7) but what he had failed to make sufficiently explicit there is that the creation of the new substance is invariably achieved by way of the transubstantiation of the old.

What should have been clear, however, even from Eliot's summary statement of it in that essay, is the importance of the negative link he tried to establish there between this transmutative formula for creation and "the metaphysical theory of the substantial unity of the soul" (*SE* 9) which, if aesthetically applied, would in fact render such a formula logically inoperative. In other words, what Eliot was suggesting in "Tradition and the Individual Talent" was not only that the creative process is to be understood in terms of the process whereby the personal is depersonalized but he was suggesting as well that such a concept of creativity is an expression

90

of, and depends for its operational validity on, a quite different theory of the soul than the one he was "struggling to attack" in that particular essay.

Obversely, the theory of the soul which is necessary to and implied by such an "Impersonal theory of poetry" (SE 7) as Eliot was trying to formulate in "Tradition and the Individual Talent" is an essentially dialectical theory and therefore one that now exists as the common property of the post-Hegelian philosophical tradition. Eliot himself, however, had derived the theory from his study of that New Idealism in which he had immersed himself, first while studying philosophy at Harvard and then again later while writing his doctoral dissertation on Bradley. Within this later phase of the idealistic tradition, the soul is not so much something one has as something one progressively makes and makes, as we suggested earlier, by means of a ceaseless process of transubstantiation. It is to an elaboration of these differing metaphysical theories of the soul that we must now momentarily address ourselves.

Perhaps the most difficult conception of all to grasp within post-Kantian philosophy is not so much that of the Absolute (or Transcendent Self as it is called by such personalistic Absolutists as Josiah Royce, though not by Bradley himself), [1] nor yet that of the empirical self revealed to introspection but, instead, that deeper and essentially paradoxical conception of the *significant self* which is progressively born of their interaction with one another in time and which consequently never really is but is always becoming. To define the true nature of *that* self—"Caught in the form of limitation / Between un-being and being" (EC V)—was the major philosophical task set for the later Idealism by the logical inconsistencies implicit in Kant's metaphysical dualism and in his consequent disjunction of the two selves—phenomenal and noumenal—from one

1. I recognize that there are important differences among the New Idealists concerning the ultimate structure of the Absolute and how it is finally to be read but those differences are not germane to my present endeavour. Because Royce's substitution of the concept of the Absolute or Transcendent Self for Bradley's concept of the Absolute as a superrelational Whole of Experience has more immediate relevance, as we shall see shortly, to the concept of "soul-making," I have adopted it here without reservations of any kind though many are obviously called for. For Royce, the Absolute is not only a self but a self whose nature is such that within it the integrity of finite selfhood is preserved in a manner which to Bradley and Bosanquet would seem wholly untenable. If Eliot's own position in the matter seems to be equivocal (see SE 402), that is due largely to the fact that he never addressed the distinctions involved at a philosophical level. Those distinctions, in short, went beyond the limits of his thesis material.

another. The nerve of Eliot's accepted faith, lived philosophy, and achieved art, on the other hand, rests in the *continuity* of the phenomenal or personal self with the noumenal or impersonal self and in the conviction that the first of these gains actual substance and significance in time only to the extent that it enters into the becoming of the other in time. The dialectic implicit in this continuity, and of expansion through continuity, is what Eliot expresses both in his poetry and in his literary theory as well and I have suggested in my Introduction that this explains why the Quester Hero or *significant self-in-becoming* is the "generic Eliot character," and the process of his formation as such is the generic Eliot theme.

It was that same dialectic of significant self-creation rather than of mere self-expression to which Keats, in a striking anticipation of this aspect of the New Idealism, applied the original and memorable phrase "Soul-making"[2]—a phrase which Bosanquet, if not Bradley himself, took over and used almost a hundred years later as a way of signifying what Keats had called "the use of the world."[3] Thus when Bosanquet at that much later date could say: "The universe is not a place of pleasure, nor even a place compounded of probation and justice; it is from the highest point of view concerned with finite beings, a place of soul-making" (*PIV* 26), his main concern, as was that of the New Idealism generally, was to reformulate in systematic and philosophical terms the primary insight which Keats had so clearly intuited before him, and then used in his own description of the world as a "vale of Soul-making."[4]

What obstructs acceptance of this newer view of the self or soul, however, Bosanquet tells us, is "the superstition" of regarding ourselves "as substances, crystal nuclei, fallen or celestial angels, or both at once" (*PIV* 372). The whole ground of discussion, he tells us, would be changed if we read our phenomenal selves as: "In truth much more to be compared to a rising and falling tide, which is continually covering wider areas as it deepens, and dropping back to narrower and shallower ones as it ebbs, than to the isolated pillars with their fixed circumferences, as which we have been

2. See Hyder E. Rollins, ed., *The Letters of John Keats: 1814-1821* (Cambridge: Harvard University Press, 1958), II, 102, for the first appearance of the phrase "Soul-making."
3. Ibid., p. 102.
4. Ibid., p. 102.

taught to think of ourselves" (*PIV* 372-3). What the new formulations of post-Kantian and specifically Anglo-American philosophy promised then was, in Bosanquet's words, "a liberation from the tyranny of the substantial soul, and a freer construction of the external object" as well,[5] and it was clearly these formulations which constituted the ideological fruit of Eliot's doctoral studies and which lay behind his innovative struggles in "Tradition and the Individual Talent." The "metaphysical theory of the substantial unity of the soul" which Eliot was "struggling to attack" in that essay—the theory, that is, from which the romantic doctrine of "personality" finally derives—is also the theory which the whole of post-Kantian philosophy had already attacked so successfully before him. What Eliot would substitute for that theory is the alternative one of the soul as a temporal vehicle of, or medium for, the essentially creative process of dialectical becoming.

The process of dialectical becoming in post-Hegelian philosophy entails two closely related but distinguishable considerations: one, the dialectical becoming of the Absolute or Transcendent Self and, two, the dialectical becoming within it of the finite or empirical self. Ultimately we shall find that in Bradley's philosophy "these two souls" or selves "are the same" (*KE* 206) and that, consequently, the development of one must even perhaps be seen as continuous with the development of the other. It is this continuity which will make available to the post-Hegelian world a viable methodology of self-transcendence—one which, if obsessively sought by Eliot's romantic predecessors, had nonetheless managed to elude them for reasons which our next chapter will attempt to make clear.

It is *this relation of continuity* between the "two souls" which in reality are one and "the same" that is finally responsible for the paradoxical nature of the transcendental organism Eliot describes in his thesis and attempts, although with only partial success, to delineate in the Quester Hero of *The Waste Land*. Enough has been said to indicate that such an organism is not to be seen as a "substantial unity" (*SE* 9) but as a crucible of intersection wherein two contrary gyres or poles of energy interpenetrate one another and, by their interaction, engender within a phenomenal medium at least the partial becoming or formation of that noumenal or *significant self* which Eliot was seeking to put at the centre of his poem.

5. B. Bosanquet, "Realism and Metaphysic," *Philosophical Review*, XXVI, no. 1 (January 1917), 13.

If it was Tiresias who served Eliot as the symbol for that extratemporal and all-inclusive consciousness which belongs only to the Transcendent or Noumenal Self, it is the poet-protagonist of the poem who represents for him the temporal or empirical self within it. If one proceeds in accordance with these same philosophical postulates, it becomes immediately clear that the vision to which the phenomenal mind (of which the poet-protagonist of the poem is the obvious and adequate symbol) should attain in its linear and temporal fashion is precisely that nonlinear and extratemporal vision of the whole (of which Tiresias is the equally obvious but inadequate symbol) and with whose progressive development his own is continuous. In short, what dialectical philosophy requires is that what the poet-protagonist (and the reader with him) comes to see in the course of his temporal journey through "the arid plain" is identical with "What Tiresias *sees*" and that this identical vision shall then constitute "the substance of the poem." It is essential, however, to that philosophy on which everything else in the poem is predicated that the two visions coalesce harmoniously at the still point "Where past and future are gathered" together (*BN* 11) within the psyche of that transcendental or *significant self-in-becoming* wherein the intersection occurs. The two visions therefore must not be seen as discontinuous with or disjoined from one another but, instead, as always interpenetrating one another and as generating by means of that interpenetration the ever-widening spheres of systematic relation constitutive of it. It is in this sense that the vision of the whole and the vision leading to it can finally be seen as one and the same. And so too are, and must be, the "two souls" (*KE* 206) to whom those visions correspond.

It was when Eliot created two separate and distinct personae as the protagonists of his poem and as symbols for those "two souls," seemingly irreconcilable with one another and yet finally "the same" (*KE* 206), which he had found at the core of Bradley's philosophy, that he diminished the status of his poet-protagonist and obscured both the theme and "the substance of the poem" at the same time. It is the dialectical hero—both man and god, "Torn and most whole" (*AW* 11)—which resides at the heart of Eliot's philosophy and resides as well at the centre of the Fisher King myth. To have introduced the Tiresias figure into *The Waste Land* as a "substantial unity" (*SE* 8) and one therefore distinct from that of his Quester Hero, and then to have assigned to Tiresias the Transcendent, instead of to his Questor Hero the transcendental, the vision constituting "the substance of the poem," was simultaneously to be untrue to his philosophical beginnings and, as a consequence, to wreak havoc with his poetic ends. If Eliot thought to use Tiresias as a shield whereby to distance his reader from the core of his own personal and temporal agony, what he did instead was merely to distance him from his own generic persona and his own generic form and, finally, to create for his reader by means of this subterfuge that sense of inexact focus one feels as one alternates between the two personae, the two plots, and the two visions which divide the poem between them. It is, in short, because the poem is untrue to the philosophy of which it is, in part at least, a literary expression that it also fails to become more fully what it was in fact "aiming to be."

In our concluding chapter, we shall deal with those minimal additional changes which "the better craftsman" ought to have made in this regard when the *ur-Waste Land* was presented to him for correction in order that the poem might become more successful than it actually is but, for now, it might be well to return to our working hypothesis that what Eliot was seeking to create in *The Waste Land* was a neo-epic of the interior life. If it was Eliot's desire, as it had been the desire of the major romantic poets before him, to write the epic poem of his time and one in which the profoundest philosophical thought available to him was given suitable expression, yet clearly the earlier forms of the epic could serve him no longer in creating one mounted upon *le paysage intérieur.* I have said earlier, however, that the landscapes of the mind, together with the inherent drama implicit within them, could attain such epic proportions only if the mind being dramatized was of far greater significance than is that of the merely empirical self or phenomenal ego which is conventionally found at the base of the dramatic monologue—whether in its nineteenth- or in its twentieth-century variants. Thus, various changes in the form of the monologue had to be made first if it were to serve the interests of our time more adequately.

The first step in the transformation of the dramatic monologue came with the development of the direct interior monologue which, in the work of Joyce and Eliot, replaced the earlier form of the monologue completely. For Eliot, the stream of consciousness with its inherent linear thrust was merely part of the material of his art and the direct interior monologue was one of the techniques he developed for handling it. The particular virtue and gain to be derived from the direct interior monologue resides in the degree of internality which it can project. What it does is to introduce the reader directly and without author intervention into the psyche of his persona so that we might better perceive not only the psychic contents or states which may be found there but also the evanescent nature of the life they lead there—that is, the various levels of consciousness to which they attain, the fluidity of the various processes in which they are involved, the associational patterns they develop, the transformations they undergo, the kind of structuring they endure. It is noteworthy too that, within the direct interior monologue, no auditor is assumed and the device makes therefore for levels of depth, candour, and realism which, eventually patterning itself after such personae as Molly Bloom, went on to transform the character and quality of the modern literature in which it appeared. Eliot's concern, however, consonant with his own reticence, was merely to reveal the actual texture of consciousness as that flows fluid and unbound before us, although he had other concerns as well.

If the direct interior monologue may be said to have presented Eliot with the most adequate vehicle possible for delineating "the life of a soul" (*KE* 147), yet that life as Bradley had taught him to read it involves a methodology within which "the epic principle" (the linear, narrative, and historistic) and "the dramatic principle" (the nonlinear, dialectical, and self-generative) come together. The former methodology is that of Kuleshov and Pudovkin and encourages the mere telling or unrolling of theme (so abhorrent to Henry James, that first of the Anglo-American literary moderns); the latter that of Eisenstein requiring an on-the-spot dialectical creation of it. Both methodologies require a persona but the second involves a persona of a uniquely impersonal kind and one who serves as the "living copula" (*PIV* 371) connecting the Transcendent Self beyond time to the empirical self within it. If Eliot was to confer truly epic status on the dramatization of that *significant self-in-becoming* which he attempted to put at the centre of *The Waste Land,* the one essential error to avoid was that error of disjunction as regards the "two souls" which had invariably been made by his romantic predecessors. It was unfortunately that very same error which Eliot did make for one of his most significant failures in *The Waste Land* is that of conceiving the "two souls"—one noumenal and the other phenomenal—as actual but disjoined existents in precisely the way that his romantic predecessors had done before him instead of as terms in a developing "relation" internal to them both and to their actual formation *as existents.*

It is in my view this particular failure with regard to the presentation of "the most important personage in the poem" which, more than any other, is responsible for grounding Eliot's poem at the level of a traditional extended interior monologue with a traditional phenomenal self at its centre. Alternatively what was required, if *The Waste Land* were in fact to become a neo-epic of modernity instead merely of the postromantic long poem of unspecified genre that it did become, was that its poetic centre should not be occupied by such a self at all but by that dynamic and experiential process through which the self—*the significant self*—comes to be and comes to achieve both its heroic proportions and its historic significance as well. It is that process which, in post-Hegelian philosophy, substitutes a growing and dynamic self for what was formerly the static and un-becoming one arrested within a "substantial unity," and likewise substitutes a transcendental and historically developing world for what formerly was a fully existent one of equally static and un-becoming objects. It is, on the other hand, the dialectical interchange between the subjective and objective "sides" of one's own phenomenal experience that progressively expands both and generates, through that expansion, the further reaches of becoming in which both are equally involved. As a consequence, what accompanies such a "development of sensibility" (*SE* 245), and one requiring both "a direct sensuous apprehension of thought" and also "a recreation of thought into feeling" (*SE* 246), is the progressive attainment by the empirical self of what Bradley calls Degrees of Truth and Reality. If, in other words, the empirical self is the temporal vehicle through which more and more of the only reality there is—that is, experiential reality—is progressively generated, what is also and simultaneously generated with it is more and more of the truth about it. As Eliot has shown us in his doctoral dissertation of that title, *Knowledge and Experience in the Philosophy of F. H. Bradley* develop together—and *pari-passu*—or they develop not at all.

To image the innovative dialectical process of empirical self-development or of "soul-making" in his poetry; to reveal that process in the very mode of its operation; to create a poetic technique able to objectify it simply and effectively—these were the exigencies forced upon the poet-philosopher who would give expression to the ideological lineaments of our age as Milton had done so successfully for his. It has been no part of my purpose in the present study to suggest that it was Eliot's conscious intention in composing *The Waste Land* either to rival Milton or even simply to write a modern epic poem. Indeed, such a supposition would be clearly absurd and one quite impossible to defend. It has, on the other hand, been very much a part of my purpose to show that it was precisely the process of "soul-making"—and in precisely the manner Bradley had taught him to read it—that Eliot dramatized so brilliantly and with such complete success in the central section of *The Waste Land*. It is, as a consequence, primarily in "The Fire Sermon" but also within the concluding section of the poem, that the generic Eliot persona, the generic Eliot theme, and the generic Eliot form come together most conclusively. What we are given there is a compelling and thoroughly unified literary presentation of that dialectical process of transcendental becoming which resides at the vivid core of Bradley's philosophy and of which the dialectical hero, the dialectical theme, and the dialectical form of post-Hegelian process philosophy are each of them but variant expressions. It is here, in these two sections of Eliot's poem, that we see most clearly revealed and in a perfectly annealed form the three integrated elements necessary to the successful completion of a new and modern poem having something like the epic stature, proportion, and significance of that earlier genre. It is for these reasons that "The Fire Sermon" in particular may be taken not only as a literary paradigm for the expression of that creative mythology which underlies all process philosophy but also as the best index we have of what *The Waste Land itself* was "aiming to be" and this regardless of what the poet-maker finally left it to become.

It is, of course, regrettable that Eliot for whatever reasons was unable to sustain the achievement of "The Fire Sermon" throughout the poem as a whole and thus to suffuse it more generously with what I believe to be its own informing spirit or entelechy. Perhaps enough is already there, however, to justify a closer look at some of the more important strands within Eliot's "Impersonal theory of poetry" (*SE* 7) which come together within the entelechy concept and which have also provided the point of departure for the present study. I have tried to show in the introductory chapter that my essay departs from a literal acceptance of Eliot's view of the autotelic nature of poetry. I believe with Eliot, that is, that a poem is an independent and viable entity having "its own life" (*TSW* x) and "its own existence, apart from us" (*Use of* 34) and, as with other such objects, having its own intentions therefore as well. Intentions, however, of whatever kind and whether they be those of the poet-maker or of the poem made reveal themselves only tendentially— only, that is, by virtue of what a thing of itself tends toward or aims to be. In the last resort, however, what a poem is "aiming to be" must depend on the nature of those "particles" of lived experience —what we shall shortly hear Eliot describe as "the units of soul life" (*KE* 147)—which went into its making and which, juxtaposed in various dialectical relations to one another, have generated its new and never before existent poetic substance. I have assumed throughout the present essay that many of the "particles" which existed "in suspension in the poet's mind" (*SE* 8) prior to the poem's becoming derive from Eliot's lengthy and profound absorption in the philosophical currents and endeavours of his age and that, along with those various other "particles" which we examined earlier, and to which we are led by way of Eliot's allusions, they entered into and modified the creative process in significant ways. This, however, is hardly matter for assertion or for mere argument. It is instead the very matter to be shown.

Whereas Bradley's philosophy may very readily be seen as providing the metaphysical system from which all of Eliot's major critical concepts derive and by which their specific meanings are consequently everywhere controlled, yet that philosophy enters into his poetry in an altogether more subtle manner and one much more difficult both to apprehend and to assess critically. What one is concerned with now is nothing so simple as the obvious literary variants of philosophical themes, ideas, and doctrines but instead with the applied significance of such doctrines for poetic practice. Bradley's Doctrine of Internal Relations, for example, is nowhere given direct expression in *The Waste Land* but it enters into and affects the making of that poem at a deeper and more important level than do any of those countless other "particles" existing in Eliot's creative pot and serving to shape and modify his mind and art in more obvious ways. This is primarily because such doctrines tend to be directive of the creative process itself rather than merely of its ideal content. Not only, that is, can such doctrines provide the creative impetus and informing vision behind a new work of art and thus determine the selection of some themes and motifs rather than others, but they can also control the development of those innovative literary methods and techniques which are felt to be

99

necessary to the effective presentation of such themes and motifs and thus can function directively too as regards the form, the pattern, and the structure which the poem will eventually reveal.

These, in any event, are the assumptions—perhaps justified, perhaps not—which underlie the account of Bradley's philosophy developed in the following chapter and offered to the reader for critical assessment. It is for these reasons that we shall depart the literary scene entirely in that chapter and attempt instead to provide a gloss on *The Waste Land* by situating the poem within the intellectual and historical context provided for it by the philosophy of its time. As we proceed, we must attempt to determine for ourselves first of all whether there *are* any relational threads connecting Eliot's mind and art to Bradley's philosophy and then, if there are, to determine precisely where they occur and how they serve to affect either or both the poet-maker and the poem made.

Such an approach to the understanding of *The Waste Land* as is here implied cannot, in any sense, be intended to rescue the poem from the irrevocable artistic defects it reveals. *The Waste Land* is, and will always remain in my view, an enormously significant but deeply flawed work of art—indeed, a formal grotesque, if you will. I would suggest further, however, that, if we were to relate Eliot's literary efforts in *The Waste Land* to the various pressures generated both within "the man who suffers and the mind which creates" (*SE* 8) by some of the poem's philosophical antecedents, two worthwhile insights might be achieved. One is that we shall be better able to perceive the new directions which Eliot's early poetry in particular was attempting to announce and this may encourage us to accord to his achievement in "The Fire Sermon," for example, the full measure of awareness and appreciation which that extraordinary—and, indeed, historic—passage deserves. Secondly, we shall perceive as well something of how "intractable" Eliot's philosophical material really is with regard to literary presentation— surely as "intractable" as that which Eliot has told us lay behind *Hamlet* and accounted for Shakespeare's "artistic failure" (*SE* 123) in dramatizing it. If an awareness of that intractability cannot serve to diminish Eliot's artistic problems either, yet it should serve to help us receive and understand them more sympathetically.

We have earlier in the present chapter dealt with the fatal disjunction from one another of the two sides of the *significant self-in-becoming* symbolized in *The Waste Land* by Tiresias on the one hand, and by the poet-protagonist of the poem on the other, and we have indicated there something of the uncertainty which, as a consequence of that disjunction, hovers around the identification in Eliot's poem both of the dialectical hero and of the dialectical theme. By way of conclusion to this transitional chapter, it may be well to return once again, and for the last time, to a consideration of the poem's form and thus to Joseph Frank's helpful account of it. This will serve to clarify one of the further differences dividing my analysis of the artistic problems underlying the genesis of *The Waste Land* from his. We may rely on Frank's suggestive account of Lessing's *Laocoön,* however, as a summary way of stating the problem clearly.[6]

What is of vital importance in the *Laocoön,* Frank tells us, is Lessing's insistence that "symbols indisputably require a suitable relation to the thing symbolized" and his contention therefore that "symbols arranged in juxtaposition can only express subjects of which the wholes or parts exist in juxtaposition; while consecutive symbols can only express subjects of which the wholes or parts are themselves consecutive."[7] Beginning with this formulation, Lessing went on to define what he believed to be the unalterable laws of aesthetic form. The conclusion to which he arrived, summarily stated, was that form in the plastic arts generally and in painting in particular must necessarily be spatial inasmuch as the visible aspects of objects can best be presented in immediate juxtaposition with one another and within an instant of time that is simultaneously held by all of those various aspects. Literature, on the other hand, because it makes use of language and is composed of a succession of words proceeding through time, must be based on some form of linear or narrative sequence. For Lessing, time and space became the two extremes which defined in an unalterable fashion the aesthetic limits of literature and painting.

What Joseph Frank does, on the other hand, in his very important essay is to apply Lessing's dictum to an analysis of some of the major works in the canon of modern literature. As a consequence, he arrives at the conclusion that the most profoundly innovative and distinguishing characteristic of that literature is that it makes the attempt to move away from that linear or sequential form Lessing believed to be necessary to it and instead, "is moving in the direc-

6. It should at least be noted that both Eliot and Joyce have revealed a considerable knowledge of and interest in the *Laocoön.* See Eliot's *Use of,* p. 113, and Joyce's *A Portrait of the Artist As A Young Man* (New York: Viking Press, 1956), p. 211.

7. Quoted by Joseph Frank in "Spatial Form in Modern Literature," *Sewanee Review* 53 (Spring 1945), 223.

tion of spatial form."[8] It is the poetry of Eliot and Pound, and the novels of Proust, Joyce, and Djuna Barnes, from which Frank derives his supporting material.

I indicated earlier the obvious but, in my view, serious inaccuracy involved in applying Eisenstein's term, "spatial form," to a verbal rather than spatial art, and it was a fear of those supple confusions such usage will generate at the level of aesthetic theory which led me to substitute for that term instead the phrase, "dialectical form." I did so only as a way of generalizing the concept sufficiently to include its possible application to all the arts and, at the same time, to affiliate it more closely (as Eisenstein did also) to those major movements both in post-Hegelian philosophy and science of which it is the aesthetic correlative. It would seem wise to establish that affiliation if only because it provides one way, at least, of distinguishing the emergent forms of modern literature from those merely organic and immanental forms deriving from the Kantian and post-Kantian literary theories of the major romantics.

I have now, however, a second reservation to record with regard to Frank's otherwise highly perceptive and, indeed, seminal essay. It has to do with those polarities of time and space which are central to Frank's commentary on modern literature and which he expresses, for example, when he says that "The one difficulty of these poems, which no amount of textual exegesis can wholly overcome, is the internal conflict between the time-logic of language and the space-logic implicit in the modern conception of the nature of poetry.[9] Whereas I would agree with Frank that unresolved formal conflicts do remain in many of these poems, yet with regard to *The Waste Land* at least I would prefer to locate the ground of Eliot's failure in his inability at that time to integrate in a wholly successful way the many aesthetic requirements implicit in the conception of dialectical form and implicit as well in the "programme for the *métier* of poetry" (*SE* 6) he had announced in "Tradition and the Individual Talent."

8. Ibid., p. 225.
9. Ibid., p. 229. If this were a book on Lawrence Durrell's *Alexandria Quartet,* one could indeed use the space/time polarization of Joseph Frank in an ideologically accurate manner and in a way that could illuminate that concept of the Space-Time continuum of Einstein which, Durrell tells us in his prefatory Note to *Balthazar,* the form of his *Quartet* is deliberately intended to recreate in literary terms. One could also make use then of the succinct and memorable expression which Alexander, a contemporary of F. H. Bradley's, gave to that concept when he said that "Time is the mind of Space and Space the body of Time." S. Alexander, *Space Time and Deity* (London: Macmillan, 1920), II, 38.

That "programme," if it does not necessarily involve an irreconcilable conflict between "time-logic" (the linear) and "space-logic" (the nonlinear or dialectical) as Lessing and Frank would suggest—indeed it actually depends on the intersection of the two—yet does involve a paradox that is equally problematic. It is a paradox we have mentioned repeatedly and one which, as we shall see shortly now, lies at the core of Eliot's philosophy and then reappears in his literary criticism under the guise of "the historical sense" (*SE* 4). That sense involves the polarization not so much of space and time as of two discordant and, indeed, seemingly irreconcilable kinds of time—that is, the linear or sequential time of history that underlies the world of succession and of all temporal becoming, and that other kind of "eternally present" time (*BN* 1) intuited by the sensibility whenever that sensibility is at its highest reach and within which there is no "Time before and time after" (*BN* 111) "And all is always now" (*BN* V). I will suggest later that any philosophy (such as Eliot's) which is both historistic and idealistic at the same time must inevitably involve precisely this paradox.

In his early philosophical writings, Eliot confronted the paradox to which I have referred at the level of the "two souls" (*KE* 206) which he tells us underlie the formulation of Bradley's philosophy the transcendent and noumenal on the one side, and the empirical and phenomenal on the other. The "two souls," Eliot says, "are irreconcileable" and yet finally "are the same" (*KE* 206), and so are the two kinds of time proper to each of them. For the former, there are only the "timeless moments" (*LG* V) of the "eternally present" (*BN* I); for the latter, only the world of "Time before and time after" (*BN* III).

The resolution to which Eliot finally arrives in his philosophical writings rests in his conviction that the two orders interpenetrate and are everywhere continuous with one another and that, as a consequence, the "two souls" or selves together with the two time-orders proper to them must do the same. They do not so much conflict, as Lessing and Frank would have it, as intersect at the psychic "still point of the turning world" wherein the logos of the world comes to consciousness of itself within the consciousness of one of its own phenomenal members (*BN* II). It is that intersection alone which can make actual and possible the otherwise "impossible union / Of spheres of existence" (*DS* V) within which "past and future are gathered" (*BN* II). It is within that significant moment that the spheres of being and becoming, noumenon and phenomenon, the timeless and time, vertical and horizontal, intersect and by that intersection generate those further reaches involved in the dynamic process of empirical self-development or of "soul-making." In order that this may be seen clearly and be understood in a conceptual sense as well, we must now address ourselves in detail to Eliot's philosophical beginnings and to the part played in the shaping of his mind and art by his early studies in that New and specifically Anglo-American Idealism which came into being at the turn of the century, and the main line of whose argument received its classic formulation at the hands of F. H. Bradley, Bernard Bosanquet, and Josiah Royce—Eliot's mentor at Harvard. It is that philosophy, Eliot tells us, which performs upon those "who will surrender patient years" to the study of it "that mysterious and complete operation which transmutes not one department of thought only, but the whole intellectual and emotional tone of their being."[10] It was that same philosophy which during those most critical years of his personal life, 1914-16, provided Eliot with that formula for "the process of depersonalization" (SE 7) on which he was to rely ever after for the resolution of his own problems—both personal and artistic.

10. T. S. Eliot, "A Commentary," Criterion III, 9 (October 1924), 2. Signed: Crites. See also Eliot's own brief account of his philosophical history in his Preface to Knowledge and Experience in the Philosophy of F. H. Bradley by T. S. Eliot (London: Faber and Faber, 1964), pp. 9-11.

6

a resume
of bradley's
"great argument"

THE HISTORICAL BACKGROUND TO
BRADLEY'S FORMULATION

In a recent admirable study of F. H. Bradley, its author, Richard Wollheim, says that the main butt of all Bradley's attacks was the native philosophical school of Empiricism—the tradition of thought that flows through Locke, Berkeley, and Hume and which culminates with John Stuart Mill. Thus, it is this "school of Experience," as Bradley mockingly called it, which Wollheim tells us provides "the true background to his metaphysic"[1] and it is this school to which we must return if we would grasp the true import of Bradley's attacks. We must begin with John Locke who with his "new way of ideas" set British philosophy on the course it was to follow for the next two hundred years. Wollheim tells us that "To Locke, as to the majority of philosophers, philosophy was fundamentally the study of human knowledge, its foundations, its scope, its limits."[2] As Locke himself says, he was concerned to determine "what objects our understandings were, or were not, fitted to deal

1. R. Wollheim, *F. H. Bradley* (Harmondsworth: Penguin Books Ltd., 1959), pp. 18-9.
2. Ibid., p. 19.

with"[3] and, clearly, he begins with the assumption that there are such things as objects out there to be understood.

For Locke, our knowledge of things rests in experience but experience, as he conceives it, begins with that matter or material which is provided to the mind through the instrumentality of the senses. Locke assumes that there is an external object which is the source or cause of the experience called "knowledge" and that that object communicates information to something that may be called a "mind." Within his theory, the percept or image or idea "in" the mind is the representative of an external and independent reality "outside" of it. Thus Locke's analysis of the process of knowledge begins from an assumption of dualism—the dualism of the subject-object relation.

Locke knew, however, that when he saw a tree, for example, what really happened was that the light from an external object was reflected through his optic nerve in the form of vibrations and that somehow these vibrations turned into an image in his consciousness. His knowledge or awareness of the tree began in his consciousness of this reflection or representative image.

The important point in a theory of knowledge and its objects is that, for Locke, knowledge or awareness or consciousness is directly of the image or idea and only indirectly of the object which causes the image or idea. The problem of knowledge, however, as the philosopher poses it, concerns this very disjunction between ideas and the objects for which they stand. If ideas are "in" the mind and different from objects, what is it that one finally comes to know—ideas or objects? If it is answered that we know only ideas, then it follows obviously that objects lie beyond the scope of knowledge. If, on the other hand, it is objects that are directly known to us, then ideas would seem to be rather superfluous ornaments. Locke sensed the difficulty here involved in his sundering of ideas and objects but he never faced it squarely. Instead he based his conviction of the "objectivity" of knowledge on a notion of causality which had not yet had to meet the onslaught of Hume's scepticism. Locke believed, that is, that the truth or validity of a man's knowledge was assured by the *correspondence* of the idea with the external object which it represented and against which it could be measured. That external independent object was for Locke, if not for his successors, a thoroughly reliable criterion. Thus

3. J. Locke, *An Essay Concerning Human Understanding,* ed., J. W. Yolton (London: J. M. Dent and Sons Ltd., 1961), 1, xxxii.

the net result of Locke's analysis may be summarized in the words of G. Watts Cunningham as follows: "There is always a mind which knows, an outside and independent object which is known, and an idea 'in' mind through which, as a medium, the knowing of the external object takes place. This is the theory of knowledge which Ferrier later called 'the theory of representative perception'."[4]

The first step, logically as well as historically, in the development of this theory was taken by Bishop Berkeley. He found himself unable to accept the distinction Locke makes between the idea "in" the mind and the object "outside" and independent of the mind. The reasoning which brought Berkeley to the formulation of Subjective Idealism is essentially as follows.

Since by hypothesis ideas alone are present "in" the mind in the act of knowing, it follows that there is no knowable object other than the ideas themselves. All we can mean by an object in so far as the object is known or knowable is merely an idea or a collection of ideas. And if knowledge of the object rests in the correspondence of the inner idea with the outer object, knowledge can never be achieved since it is impossible to compare an idea with something that is not an idea for the purpose of determining whether the two in fact do correspond. It is not possible to compare my idea of a tree with the actual tree it is supposed to represent because there is no way in which I can escape my egocentric predicament and have direct contact with the tree. In other words, it is not possible to perceive any object when it is not being perceived in order to compare the two perceptions with one another. What such a comparison would necessitate—literally—is the act of going out of one's mind in search of a reality that has no life within it. It is the excessive strain implicit in just such saltatory endeavours that the transcendentalism both of romantic thought and of romantic literature equally reflects.

It was at that moment when Bishop Berkeley was driven to enunciate his famous doctrine that "to be is to be perceived" that the earliest form of British Idealism came into being. From it,

4. G. Watts Cunningham, *The Idealistic Argument in Recent British and American Philosophy* (New York: The Century Company, 1933), p. 4. The incidental footnotes which appear hereafter, both to Cunningham's book and also to *Studies in Speculative Philosophy* by James Edwin Creighton, hardly provide an adequate index to the extraordinary indebtedness I feel to both these writers—one of whom (Creighton) taught the other (Cunningham) and both of whom have taught me what little I know about the New Idealism. Without their expert guidance, I should never have penetrated the Bradleian labyrinth nor come to understand the various doctrines which, when properly systematized, constitute his philosophy.

however, no escape from subjectivism was possible for Berkeley's analysis had demonstrated conclusively that to suppose that there are external objects independent of the mind was to make an unwarranted assumption from Locke's premisses. If, when we speak of objects, all we mean or can mean by the term is ideas, then when we speak of the *existence* of objects all we mean or can mean is that they are perceived. The upshot of Berkeley's analysis was to eliminate from the "real" the existence of material objects as distinct from and represented by ideas in the mind. Now all statements concerning the existence of material objects had to be rewritten in terms of the *experience* of objects for by hypothesis Berkeley had shown that objects *per se* are unknown and unknowable. The only "real" existents are "minds" and their "ideas" and experience, as the Empiricist defines it, is the experience hereafter limited to and comprised within that discrete and individual mind.

Hume was to go even further. In Berkeley's hands, "objects" had dissolved into a set of perceptions or ideas. With Hume, a similar fate befalls "minds." Hume held that, if one accepts Locke's view of representative perception as a point of departure, one will inevitably be drawn to Berkeley's conclusion that there is no reason for supposing the existence of an independent object. Hume added, however, that the existence of "mind" is equally, and on essentially similar grounds, open to the same scepticism. As there is no reason for holding that there are objects beyond the ideas which are supposed to image or represent them, so there is equally little logical warrant for holding that there is an independent mind "in" which ideas reside. This was the logic whose inner thrust culminated in the dissolution both of an external "real" world of objects and of an internal "real" world of mind. Materialism and Idealism both floundered and what remained was a collection of images, ideas, and impressions moving about a vacuum. From this desperate situation at the turn of the century, British philosophy in particular and traditional philosophy in general had nowhere to go.

If one would image visually the cognitional impasse to which epistemological theory was inevitably led by the tradition of British Empiricism, one might perhaps do it this way. Let us suppose that the six sides of a room are made up of a hundred panels, each panel being a mirror and distorted as regards its shape in a slightly different way from every other panel. At the centre of the room is a black billiard ball. If we should suppose further that *you* are the ball, what is it that *you* would see? You would see the reality that you are reflected in a hundred different ways and according to a hundred different perspectives or points of view. Each panel would existentially and substantially be identical with, or a unity comprised of, its own point of view and that point of view is all that it could possibly "express" if it had as well the means of expression (Locke). Let us suppose further now that, at the centre of the room, *there is no black ball* (Berkeley). Within such a view, all that remains is a series of distorting mirrors each reflecting the reflectors around it (Hume). Each "point of view" looks out on an infinity of other "points of view" while urging its own.

What these suppositions image visually and are intended to represent is that epistemological theory of the eye (or mind) and of the epistemological self behind it which Bradley confronted when he came upon the philosophical scene and which had been delivered to the Romantic poets and critics by the British Empiricists. It was Yeats—in his own view, one of the "last romantics"[5] and, in ours, assuredly the greatest of them all—who gave sad but consummate poetic expression to this wholly subjectivist theory of the mind's knowledge as little more than a series of "Reflections in a Mirror"[6] when he said:

> Empty eyeballs knew
> That knowledge increases unreality, that
> Mirror on mirror mirrored is all the show.[7]

It is essentially this same epistemological theory which lies behind the contemporary romanticism of those who continue to remain impaled on the metaphysical dualism of Kant or, alternatively, on the tradition of German Rationalism generally.

Professor Muirhead, in his preface to the first volume of *Contemporary British Philosophy,* says that by common consent of the contributors to that volume, it was dedicated to F. H. Bradley as the "foremost figure in British philosophy" and the one who guided that philosophy through its period of recovery from the onslaughts referred to above.[8] It was Bradley, they agreed, "to whom British

5. W. B. Yeats, "Coole Park and Ballylee, 1931," *Collected Poems* (London: Macmillan and Company, 1950), p. 276.
6. *Cf.* Northrop Frye's choice of this Berkeleyan metaphor, "Reflections in a Mirror," as the title of his reply to some of his more negative critics at the English Institute of 1966. See M. Krieger, ed., *Northrop Frye in Modern Criticism* (New York: Columbia University Press, 1966), pp. 133-46.
7. Yeats, "The Statues," *Collected Poems,* p. 376.
8. J. H. Muirhead, ed., *Contemporary British Philosophy* (New York: The Macmillan Company, 1953), p. 11.

philosophy owed the impulse that gave it new life in our time."[9] That "new life" resulted from the formulation by Bradley of what Harald Höffding describes as "the New Idealism,"[10]—an "objective" idealism to be clearly distinguished from the "subjective" idealism of Berkeley and his successors. Bradley's major indebtedness in this formulation is clearly to Hegel for, despite the fact that his borrowings from Hegel are occasional and unsystematic, there can be no doubt that whenever it suited his purposes Bradley did not hesitate in his attacks on the Empiricists to draw heavily, as Wollheim tells us, "on the armoury of German philosophical thought, [and] on the weapons forged by Hegel and his successors."[11]

In the problem we have under review, Hegel served him particularly well. "In England at all events," Bradley wrote, "we have lived too long in the psychological attitude,"[12] and it was the entire theory of the mind and of its knowledge as these had been developed by the British Empiricists which Bradley is here rejecting. Even more emphatically does he reject the very notion of philosophy and logic which underlies it and with which it is indissolubly associated. Bradley's wholesale rejection of subjectivism and of psychologism, however, and Eliot's with him, would perhaps not have been possible save for a suggestion originally offered by Kant as a way out of the difficulty summarily outlined above and later taken up and developed in earnest both by Hegel and Bradley. The suggestion was to the effect that the way out of the Locke-Berkeley-Hume dilemma is through a denial of that separation between mind and objects from which the difficulty arises. It is that suggestion which, when fully developed, goes on to force the great divide between traditional pre-Kantian philosophy on the one hand, and critical post-Kantian philosophy on the other. But if Kant must be credited with having first made the suggestion, he cannot be credited with having systematized his philosophical insights successfully around it and, as everyone knows, he ended by reintroducing into philosophy the very same disjunction between the two worlds of appearance and reality, subject and object, phenomenon and noumenon, which he had set out to breach.

9. Ibid., Dedicatory Page.
10. H. Höffding, *A Brief History of Modern Thought* (New York: The Macmillan Company, 1931), p. 284.
11. Wollheim, *F. H. Bradley*, p. 18.
12. F. H. Bradley, *Principles of Logic*, 2nd ed. (London: Oxford University Press, 1922), p. 2.

Precritical philosophy starts from the unquestioned assumption that mind and the objects reflected in it are existentially distinct entities sharply sundered from one another, and ultimately definable each in its own right without reference to the other. It is on the contrary Bradley's view, and Eliot's with him, that if one begins from the assumption that reality is ultimately dualistic in nature— that is, of two substantially different and mutually exclusive kinds, one real and the other *merely* ideal—then the task of effecting a reconciliation, or even a viable reciprocity, between subject and object in Logic, between self and world in Psychology, and be-tween truth and reality (or between the inner and "mental" world of ideas and the outer and "real" world of things) in Epistemology is a hopeless one, a hopelessness which accounts for the failure of nineteenth-century transcendentalism to sustain the aspirations of Eliot's romantic predecessors. The premiss of disjointedness and mutual exclusiveness between the two realms of being—noumenal and phenomenal, ideal and real—is the corrosive premiss which, on the one side, makes a sound philosophy impossible and, on the other, opens wide the doorway into that romantic agony com-pounded of alienation, scepticism, and melancholy despair which we see reflected everywhere in its literature. The upshot of such metaphysical dualism, however, is not only to debilit the litera-ture mounted upon it; it is also to put philosophy effectively and permanently out of business. Bradley's immediate reaction to this unsettling state of affairs when he came upon the scene was to say with admirable succinctness and clarity that "Where all is rotten it is a man's work to cry stinking fish" (*AR* x). That is not quite all he said about the metaphysical dualism which underlies the odorifer-ous postulates of the British Empiricists and finally underlies the philosophy of Kant as well.

It is the initial disjunction of terms from which pre-Kantian and Kantian idealism begin, together with the subsequent reification of those terms as themselves absolute instead of as mere aspects or "sides" of what is in fact absolute, that not only makes the tran-scendence from one to the other impossible but which obviates the possibility of any genuine reciprocal action between them as well —that kind of "ennobling interchange" between "the discerning intellect of Man" and "the goodly universe" in which Wordsworth had hoped to find the substance of his "high argument" for *The Excursion*. *The Excursion* was to be a genuinely "philosophical poem"—the first in English—and one which was to "chant, in

111

lonely peace, the spousal verse / of this great consummation" between the two discrete realms of "Individual Mind" on the one hand, and "external World" on the other.[13] One must suggest, however, that daily intercourse is hardly feasible between the divorced and that the truth of this unaccommodating fact is everywhere evident, not only in Wordsworth's inability to complete the "philosophical poem" he set out to write but also in the failure of the romantics generally to resolve the relational problem of subject and object, self and world, lying at the heart of their aesthetic aspirations. Rather than the "great consummation" so often promised by romantic literature, we are far more often given instead either a solipsistic withdrawal into the prison of the ego on the one hand, or some Promethean effort at periodic rape on the other. And, given the disjunction from which romantic thought departs, that is all really that the terms will allow. Neither strategy, however, can make for the progressive achievement of a sound philosophy, a viable literary theory, and a mature and stable art—at least not the particular art of equipoise to which Eliot aspired and to which he was led by the triadic rather than the dualistic lineaments of post-Kantian thought.

Thus far I have been concerned merely to recapitulate something of the history of the philosophical problem arising from the relation of subject and object, knowledge and experience, appearance and reality, when that relation is conceived of in dualistic terms and thus to indicate the logical nexus which forced from Bradley the emergence of a new metaphysical premiss within which that relation might be read differently. Inasmuch as it was a metaphysical dualism which first created the problem and then made it impossible to resolve, it was necessary in Bradley's view to attack the problem at the metaphysical level first and to do so by getting behind the omnipresent disjunctions of post-Cartesian philosophy.

It was therefore the view of the Anglo-American idealists that the one thing really needful at the turn of our century was the formulation of a New Idealism, a sane—and paradoxically enough—a realistic idealism which could extricate philosophy from the impasse forced upon it by metaphysical dualisms of whatever stripe, be it those of the Realists and Idealists or those of the Empiricists and Rationalists alike. So desirous was this group of dissociating the new and foundational doctrines of the New Idealism from those upheld

13. See both Wordsworth's Preface to *The Excursion* and also the "Prospectus" which forms the introductory portion of it.

by their philosophical predecessors that Bosanquet finally repudiated the name "Idealism" altogether and suggested that the term "speculative philosophy" be used instead to designate the metaphysical theory to which those doctrines point and which he shared preeminently with Bradley and Royce but with the other New Idealists as well.[14] Bradley himself had said of his philosophy, even before Bosanquet, that "whether it is to be called Realism or Idealism I do not know, and I have not cared to inquire" (AR 485) and Eliot, following suit, concluded his dissertation with the view that: "We may draw, I believe, certain inferences as to the nature of reality which will forbid us to accept either an idealistic or a realistic philosophy at its full value" (KE 153).

It was essential to these writers that the separation between traditional Idealism and this new, post-Hegelian, and specifically *Anglo-American,* Idealism be final and complete, for to sanction any longer or even to allow continued mutual borrowings or accommodations between the two was, in their eyes, to invite that confusion—and one which continues to exist even today—of its new and distinctive doctrines, either with the earlier subjectivist doctrines of Berkeley on the one hand, or with the inadequately grounded transcendentalism of Kant and his German successors on the other. It is that same confusion, further compounded, which encourages so many of our literary critics to associate—indeed, even to identify—Eliot's mind and art with that of his romantic predecessors, and to do so without any precautionary discriminations of any kind.

Alternatively, what Bradley and Eliot insist upon is that we must begin again and begin, as Kant tried but never finally succeeded in doing, by rejecting outright any view which puts the noumenal world of "real reality" (as Bosanquet calls it)[15] on one side, and everything we know of that world through our knowledge or experience of it on the other, and then gives to philosophy the job of

14. See in particular B. Bosanquet, "Realism and Metaphysics," *Philosophical Review* XXVI, 1 (January 1917), 6, where Bosanquet says crisply: " . . . for myself I reject the term idealism," and also his essay, "The Relation of Coherence to Immediacy and Specific Purpose," *Philosophical Review* XXVI, 3 (May 1917), 268 fn. where the same sentiment is virtually repeated. A second and equally fine account of the efforts of the New Idealists to dissociate themselves doctrinally from the old is also given in an essay by James E. Creighton entitled "Two Types of Idealism" in Harold O. Smart, ed., *Studies in Speculative Philosophy by James Edwin Creighton* (New York: The Macmillan Company, 1925), pp. 256-83.

15. B. Bosanquet, *Social and International Ideals* (London: Macmillan and Company, 1917), p. 97.

determining how the two worlds can be meaningfully related (or, in Wordsworth's terms, "exquisitely . . . fitted") to one another at the same time that they are both essentially and existentially disjoined from one another. It is not enough, they tell us, to accept the initial metaphysical premiss of disjunction, as both Berkeley and Kant finally did, and then to inquire as to how that disjunction might be transcended for it has been the negative lesson of philosophical history that this simply cannot be done. Or, as Eliot puts it in his dissertation, "if the existence of subject or object is always relative, then the point to which we elaborate this relativity is a matter of indifference" (*KE* 30), and that is why he is not, he tells us, "satisfied merely that the distinction should be finally transcended, but wish [es] to enquire into its validity as a starting point" (*KE* 34) for philosophy instead. In the view of the New Idealism, philosophy must begin from an entirely different standpoint—'The Standpoint of Experience" itself, as James Creighton will later call it,[16]—but experience, be it noted, not in the way that either an eighteenth-century Empiricism or a nineteenth-century Rationalism defined it but as Bradley and the other New Idealists came finally to understand and to formulate what they believed to be its true nature. Creighton has described that new standpoint as follows:

This historical speculative idealism, as occupying the standpoint of experience, has never separated the mind from the external order of nature. It knows no egocentric predicament, because it recognizes no ego "alone with its states," standing apart from the order of nature and from a society of other minds. It thus dismisses as unmeaning those problems which are sometimes called "epistemological," as to how the mind as such can know reality as such. Without any epistemological grace before meat it falls to work to philosophize, assuming, naively, if you please, that the mind by its very nature is already in touch with reality. Instead, that is, of assuming that there is an entity called the mind, and another entity having no organic relation to mind called nature, it assumes on the basis of experience that these realities are not sundered and opposed, but are in very being and essence related and complementary. The relation or rather system of relations that constitute the bond between what we call mind and that which is termed nature it takes not as external and accidental, as if each of these could be real outside of this system, but rather as internal, essential and constitutive. We can think of a mind apart from an objective order only through an abstraction; to be a mind at all it is necessary to be in active commerce with a world which is more than an order of ideas. If it be said that this is mere assumption, and not proof, I reply that this is the universal

16. James E. Creighton, "The Standpoint of Experience," *Studies in Speculative Philosophy*, pp. 71-92.

114

assumption upon which all experience and all science proceeds. It needs no proof because it is the standpoint of experience itself.[17]

Creighton's statement is an important one not only because of its clarity and succinctness but also because it includes within itself an index of the various doctrines within Bradley's philosophy which we must come to understand if the significance of that philosophy and of the post-Hegelian literature mounted upon it is to be seen and appreciated for what it really is. Rather than turn to a detailed account of those doctrines, however, it will perhaps be more helpful merely to generalize their substance at once and thus gain immediately the point—'the still point" (*BN* 11)—to which both Bradley's philosophy and Eliot's art gather as a whole.

THE PRINCIPLE OF TRICHOTOMY

It was the negative lesson of philosophical history that the ultimate problems of philosophy have resisted solution whenever the philosopher begins his speculations from that dualistic and relational level within which the speculating subject is conceived of as already and existentially disjoined from the object of his speculation. It was this lesson which led Bradley to say repeatedly that "From such premises there is in my opinion no road except to total scepticism" (*ETR* 199). What a new beginning meant for The New Idealism however was first of all the creation of a post-Kantian and triadic logic able to support the metaphysical structure Bradley would later build upon it, and this task Bradley undertook in his famous *Principles of Logic* (1883)—a book which was later significantly refined and corrected by Bosanquet.[18] The most significant implication of Bradley's triadic logic emerges from the new reading of the subject-object relation which it will make both possible and

17. Creighton, "Two Types of Idealism," *Studies in Speculative Philosophy,* p. 266.

18. Bradley never stinted in his praise of Bosanquet's *Logic* as superior to his own. On one occasion, he referred to Bosanquet's *Logic* as "in many points, a great advance on my own work" (*AR* 324 fn.) and, on another, when he had himself misrepresented his own thought rather badly, he insisted that "from the first and throughout, Professor Bosanquet has consistently advocated the true doctrine. The debt which philosophy owes to him here has not been adequately recognized" (*ETR* 29 fn.). Eliot's "correction" of Bradley in Chapter III of his thesis as regards the nature of ideas is in substance a repetition of Bosanquet's earlier refinements but Eliot seems to have arrived at his conclusions quite independently of Bosanquet.

necessary at the same time, and which Bradley and Eliot signalize whenever they substitute the language of correlativity for an earlier language of absolutes. On the epistemological level and on the aesthetic level as well, the concern now must be not with the subject-object relation but with the relation of subjective correlative and "objective correlative" (*SE* 124)[19] within the experiential whole which, in post-Kantian terms, provides its "third side" and the ground of relational adjustment between the related terms. Let us put this even more directly.

The major point of the triadic logic which Bradley and Bosanquet formulated as a base for and in support of the major doctrines of the New Idealism rests in the assertion that wherever you have two terms or termini (let us say, self and world, subjective correlative and objective correlative, knower and known, or perhaps even husband and wife), you have as well as the terms themselves the relation internal to, and therefore constitutive of, them as terms.[20] You cannot, that is, *have* a husband where there is no wife, a knower without something known, a subjective correlative where there is no objective correlative, nor correlatives of any kind apart from a "whole" within which the correlation is in fact operative. Neither "side" of the correlation, that is to say, can be defined out of itself nor can it be rendered intelligible merely in terms of the other. Thus one cannot hope to understand what it is to be a husband merely by probing one's wife. To understand either, both "sides" of the relationship must be referred to and seen within the context of "the whole" which in relation (and only in relation) they can "unite to form" (*SE* 8) and which thus provides the "third side" essential to their intelligibility as terms.

19. To my knowledge, none of the three major Anglo-American Idealists has actually used the phrase "objective correlative" (*SE* 124) though the whole point of the New Idealism may, in one sense at least, be seen as one of distinguishing that "objective correlative" from "the object as it really is" (*TSW* 15). Bosanquet perhaps came closest when he used the phrase "objective correlates" (*PIV* 36). Eliot believed himself to be responsible for coining the phrase when he wrote his essay on "Hamlet and His Problems" and needed a succinct way of expressing this aspect of Bradley's philosophy. He was somewhat chagrined to learn later that Washington Allston (misspelled by Eliot below) had done so before him. See Eliot's "Preface" to his *Essays on Elizabethan Drama* (New York: Harcourt, Brace and Company, 1956), pp. vii-viii, where Eliot says: "The *Hamlet,* of course, had been kept afloat all these years by the success of the phrase 'objective correlative'—a phrase which, I am now told, is not even my own but was first used by Washington Alston."

20. Bradley's doctrine of internal relations is, of course, here implied and underlies everything that follows.

Thus any correlative—simply in virtue of being a correlative—has three sides to it rather than two, as the dualists would have it, and it is that third side which provides the escape hatch from the impasse to which all metaphysical dualisms have led in the past and must inevitably lead in the future. Within the newer view, the underlying premiss is the premiss of the whole whose nature is experiential and within which each "side" of experience (for example, husband and wife, knower and known, subjective and objective) takes of the other and develops its own individual being as a term *pari-passu* with the development of the other. A husband becomes a husband and his wife becomes a wife as both together realize more and more fully the nature and substance not of each other, as within a dualistic framework, but of the "whole" which they can "unite to form" (*SE* 8).

It is this holistic background—one which, "however much transcended," in Bradley's words, "both remains and is active" (*ETR* 161)—which redistributes the focal points of relationship and substitutes a new and triadic economy for the earlier antithetical one of the metaphysical dualists. Within it, one "side" does not inform or suffuse the other with its own life (as with Coleridge), or absorb it (as with Blake), for the nature of the relationship is neither imitative or representative (as in classical theory) nor projective or even strictly reciprocal (as in most romantic theory) but dialectical and therefore of an essentially self-generative and progressive nature. Thesis and antithesis yield to the equipoise of synthesis, and can yield, because the relation of the correlative terms being both internal and constitutive is to be read as a literal vehicle of ascent—the agent of transcendental becoming.

When this holistic context is applied to the traditional problems of philosophy—whether logical, psychological, epistemological, or ontological—those problems will all be seen in an entirely new light. They will no longer be identified, in epistemology for example, with the question: "How is mind *per se* related to the thing *per se*?" as if the difference between "mind" and "thing," or between ideas "in here" and objects "out there," is an absolute difference—absolute enough to guarantee each aspect independence of the other. The true view, Bradley would maintain, is that the difference is only a relative difference within a total experiential situation which alone is "real reality" and which has both an objective and a subjective side to it. The question therefore of how the mind *per se* is related to the thing *per se*, as traditionally posed, was equivalent to asking what was the relation of, or between, one thing. These two "sides"—subjective correlative and objective correlative, mind and thing, ideality and factuality—are not *existentially* two but two aspects of one and the same absolute and experiential whole, and that whole alone is the "real reality" as such. It is that undivided and experiential whole which for Bradley and Eliot constitutes "the given fact" (*ETR* 246) from which a sound philosophy must depart, rather than from those one-sided abstractions from reality which had been reified as absolutes by the Subjective Idealists on the one hand, and by the Objective Idealists on the other.

The effect of Bradley's logic is thus to set a limit to relativity by seeing it as operative within a whole which is absolute, and this is why Bradley can say: "Everywhere on behalf of the real Absolute I have been warning the reader against that false absolutism which in philosophy is to me another name for error" (*ETR* 470). Alternatively, and from the point of view developed here, nothing is more important than Bradley's formulation not, as has often been charged, of one more nineteenth-century theory of relativity, but of a new and twentieth-century theory of correlativity within a Whole which alone is Absolute, and it is precisely because the "relativism" of Bradley and Eliot is everywhere shored against this Absolute that their philosophy is free of that corrosive scepticism which so frequently enervated the aspirations of their earlier nineteenth-century predecessors.

It was the initially Kantian insight that subject and object are in some sense reciprocal which led Bradley to begin his philosophizing by reopening the question as to "what is given at the start" (*ETR* 199). Unlike Kant, however, he answered it by setting that reciprocity against the background of the whole which introduces a new and vertical perspective, as it were, into the discussion of the relational problem of subject and object, appearance and reality, self and world. That perspective enables us now to read the problem of transcendence in a very different way than it was both by romantic philosophers and by the poets and critics who were their literary counterparts. What the new way makes possible is not that linear or horizontal leap of transcendence from one term or side of a disjunction to the other—a transcendence, that is, from left to right or obversely from right to left—but rather the interaction with one another of reciprocal terms which, set against the vertical background of the whole, effects that *intersection* of horizontal and vertical planes which in turn generates upwards the self-transcendence of each side *pari-passu* with the self-transcendence of the other.

It is that intersection which, to put the matter visually, will divide Bradley's circle of the Absolute or Whole of Experience into the four quadrants of the mandala Eliot will use later as the structural model for his *Four Quartets*. In order to see how this comes about and to trace the curve of Bradley's "great argument" a few steps further, we must define now some of the implications which a triadic logic has for that process of "soul-making" which is our special concern here and this, in its turn, must involve first an account of that concrete universal which is seminal to an understanding of all post-Hegelian thought.[21]

21. Before departing from the subject of Bradley's triadic logic, mention should be made of Coleridge's valiant efforts to formulate such a logic for himself and for his time. In his sound and penetrating study entitled *Coleridge as Philosopher,* Muirhead has had this to say concerning Coleridge's dissatisfaction with the earlier logic of Kant:

Kant, Coleridge held, had introduced new matter into the old logic. He had enlarged its scope, but he had thereby only in the end brought into clearer evidence the limitations imposed upon it by the dualistic assumption of the independence of thought and reality, without himself being able to get beyond them. In effect his work had resulted only in riveting the chains more securely to this dualism. Yet he had indicated a way of deliverance in the hint of a new triadic logic, and Coleridge's own metaphysics may best be considered as an attempt to carry the dialectic of Kant's thought a step farther and turn criticism against the Critic. "Kant", he had said, "had begun again and completed the work of Hume." He himself aimed, if not at beginning Kant's work again, at any rate at beginning where Kant had ended and completing what he had begun. (p. 89)

What Muirhead is speaking of here, however, has to do more with Coleridge's aspirations than with what he actually managed to accomplish. Even Muirhead gives witness to this when, albeit most reluctantly, he indicates in another place that it was left to the professional philosophers of the seventies, eighties, and nineties, whom Coleridge had so clearly anticipated, "to complete the work which Coleridge had planned, but had let drop from his hands" (J. H. Muirhead, ed., *Contemporary British Philosophy,* p. 311). One can only be grateful to Muirhead as well for acknowledging that the task of removing those radical inadequacies within Kant's *Logic* which Coleridge was perhaps one of the first to see and to see clearly was a task which it remained for F. H. Bradley and the others of his school to accomplish. Muirhead says:

What seemed to be chiefly required henceforth was to carry this central principle [the principle of trichotomy, that is] into all departments of philosophy and use it as a key to a detailed reconstruction of them. How brilliantly this work was begun in Ethics and Politics by Green and Bradley, in Logic and Metaphysics by Bradley and Bosanquet is now an old story. The more we realize what these writers accomplished the less one wonders that their work seemed to us in the 'eighties and 'nineties to be a fresh and convincing verification of the truth of the idealistic hypothesis on which it was founded. (Ibid., p. 315)

119

It was the achievement of Kant's successors to create out of his earlier Transcendentalism a new and radically different metaphysics than his and one that was both idealistic and historistic at the same time. It was so in the sense that it involves a metaphysic of Spirit or Mind conceived of as incarnating itself through the temporal linearities of that world history or evolution whose becoming it inspires and whose ideal substance is only progressively concretized by means of that history on the paradigmatic model provided by the concrete universal.

The New Idealists have all of them made it abundantly clear that it is the concept of the concrete universal which underlies and which alone can sustain the most central of all their major conceptions—the conception, that is, of the Transcendent Self or Absolute-in-Becoming—and it is to that concept therefore that we must now turn our attention directly. The first and essential point to understand concerning the nature of the concrete universal is the way in which it differs from the nature of a nominal or abstract universal and this must include an understanding of how each is arrived at.

The abstract universal is the end result of that sort of generalization which seeks identity apart from differences and its operative method is one of omission. Such a universal, Bosanquet tells us, is "framed by attending to the common qualities of a number of individuals, and [by] disregarding their differences" (*PIV* 35). Ultimately therefore it turns out to be a bare generality which, at best, is of indefinite "meaning," and if such a process of generalization is carried to its logical goal as regards any noun or individual whole, whether it be singular or collective in nature—man, poem, poetry, house, let us say—the resulting universal tends increasingly to vanish into complete emptiness. The universal man, for example, cannot as actually existent in one's conception of him be either tall or short, white or black, fat or thin. The universal man is in fact no man at all but merely an empty and "meaningless" generality.

The Idealists on the other hand—really from Plato on down—prefer to use "concrete universals," by which they mean universals which accommodate all the differences within them, as the paradigm of a true and genuine (rather than merely abstract) universality and the one which must therefore guide all logical inference during the progressive course of knowledge. If we began our intellectual life, let us say, in a society where all the men were white and tall, our idea of man would include whiteness and tallness; if we later met men who were short and black and yellow and a number of other things, we should have to adjust our definition to include these differences. These new facts must be included in the concept and thus the "meaning" of the word "man"—the meaning, that is, intended by the Word itself as distinct from what *you* may or may not mean by it—progressively expands by taking account of the differences which are internal to, and constitutive of, the reality being defined and progressively being concretized in time.

The complete conception of man must follow upon this progressive concretization and upon a real experience of it and this, of course, is why only *degrees* of truth are available to the empirical self and only as its experience follows upon the development of reality itself. Even partial truths, however, include an awareness both of that universal by which all men are recognized as men and all the differences by which one particular man is distinguished from another as well. In short, a truly concrete universal is that total and systematic whole or "ideal order" (*SE* 5) which is *intended* by every noun—man, gladness, house, poetry. Bosanquet has described it as: "a system of members, such that every member, being *ex hypothesi* distinct, nevertheless contributes to the unity of the whole in virtue of the peculiarities which constitute its distinction" (*PIV* 37). Thus the concrete universal—even as already partially existent in time—is in its nature, and will always remain, an identity-in-difference or a many-in-one and that, in what is surely the most succinct expression possible, is precisely how Bradley and Bosanquet delineate the structure of the Absolute.

When the concept of the concrete universal is applied to the conception of the individual self or soul, as it was by Royce and other personalistic Absolutists, one comes necessarily to view those selves not as having each of them what Eliot calls a "substantial unity" (*SE* 8) and Bosanquet "a fixed essence" (*PIV* 289) but instead as constituting *together* the expression of that actually and concretely real selfhood to the formation of which "the individual Talent" or self contributes, rather than is. Within this context, the Absolute (or Transcendent Self) is a universal community of selves —a unity of selfhood which includes within itself the particular and individual selves of the many. As Bosanquet says, it is because "our type of individuality has been from the first what we described as the concrete universal" that its form will be that of an "identity-in-difference" (*PIV* 319) or of a oneness that progressively makes itself out of the fusion of the multiple and diverse.

To speak of the Absolute or Transcendent Self, as I have already done, however, in terms of a universal community of selves or as a unity of selfhood is really to delineate what we may call a merely structural concept. Let us say now that the "matter" or "filling" of that Absolute or Transcendent Selfhood is experiential in nature rather than material or spiritual as in earlier, and specifically dualistic, metaphysical systems. It follows that there will be only one real experience—the developing Experience of the Whole—and that all particular experience must be viewed as a constitutive element within that Whole of Experience which is had (if we may put it so) not by you or by me but by the Transcendent Self of which you and I are, on the one hand, the genuine but limited temporal vehicles and, on the other, the agents of its progressive becoming.

One of the major implications of a monistic system such as Bradley's, however, is that it requires some significant redefinitions of traditional terms so as to make them more or less compatible with that developing logic of the concrete universal which underlies the system as a whole. Such earlier concepts as self and world, subject and object, subjectivity and objectivity, must now all be given new meanings. What in fact happens as a result of the redefinitions involved is that they lose their independent status as substantives and become adjectival instead—the adjectives, that is, of a developing or transcendental Subject and Object and, thus, what was formerly viewed as a subject is now seen instead as a subjective correlative, and what formerly was thought of as an object now becomes an "objective correlative." One might say that these concepts have all in a sense been depersonalized or desubstantiated as the correlative sides now of the one and only "real reality" or substance there is—the experiential substance, that is, of the concrete universal, or of the Absolute-in-Becoming. One of the least regrettable effects of the redefinitions involved is the loss of the logical base for the romantic concept of "personality" and its subsequent disappearance into that limbo created for, and composed of, discarded philosophical rejects. One of the thorniest and multi-faceted problems inhering in such a philosophy, however, is that of defining with exactitude the nature of the "relation" existing between the extratemporal whole or Absolute and those Bosanquet describes as the "pilgrims of the Absolute" (*PIV* 7) or, more precisely, between the Transcendent Self and the empirical self. Given the form of the concrete universal as the paradigm for the structure of the transcendent and whole, it should be clear even from the cursory account of it which has been given here that such a relation is, to say the least, paradoxical. It is so simply in virtue of the fact that neither of the parties to it really *is* but, instead, is involved in the ceaseless process of its own becoming, and yet it is this continuing relation between what we may call temporal is-nots which itself generates the continued becoming of what *really* is—that is, *the significant self-in-becoming.*

We can perhaps clarify this aspect of Bradley's problem by providing an analogy and by suggesting that neither a whole orange, for example, nor a whole anything—either before or after it has been segmented into quarters—can really be said to be capable of "relation" with any one of those quarters. Before segmentation, the parts which would make such a relation possible do not yet exist and, after segmentation, the whole which is equally necessary to such a relation does not exist. A relation between a whole and any of the parts *constitutive* of that wholeness, as is required by the logic of the concrete universal, can therefore only be of an "ideal order" (*SE* 5) for the only thing that can be said to exist *temporally* is not the relation of the whole orange to one of its own parts but the relation of one part of the orange to another, with all the parts together sharing in, at the same time that they serve to create, the "real" substance of that "ideal order" (*SE* 5) of the orange to which they belong.

Returning now from this inexact analogy to the problem at hand, it should be clear that to speak of a relation between the subject of individual or personal experience and the subject of universal experience; between what Eliot elsewhere calls "the limited *ich*" and *"the ueberindividuelles ich"* (*KE* 72); or, finally, between the empirical self and the Transcendent Self is, for the reasons given above, not strictly possible and it is this problem which Eliot has in mind when he speaks of "the impossible union / Of spheres of existence" (*DS V*) in the *Four Quartets.* It is nonetheless, and paradoxically enough, precisely what we may call this vertical relation of real and ideal, temporal and eternal, personal and impersonal, which must be posited—a relation more properly understood as a bond or connection rather than as a relation— together with the impulse of the former to enter into the more abundant life of the latter by following out the *nisus* to wholeness

123

implicit in all phenomenal experience. Within this view, to endure personally and within time the expansion of developing experience is progressively to move in the direction of the whole and thus, in the most literal sense of that word, to become "holier" and therefore more and more absolute.

To speak of "the impossible union / Of spheres of existence" may be poetically viable and indeed suggestive, yet it is philosophically unsound.[22] If, on the other hand, we were to ask directly and in philosophical terms just how we are to conceive of this impossible relation between the "two souls" or selves—one whole and beyond time, the other a fragment and within it—the answer for the New Idealists is not far to seek. Basing themselves always on the logic of the concrete universal, they reply that the subject of universal experience (that is, the Transcendent Self) is not *numerically* distinct from the subject of individual experience (as it finally is with Kant) but is instead continuous with it and its development. *It is this same subject at a later stage of itself and of its own becoming* whereas the *significant self,* on the other hand, is the temporal instrument of that extratemporal spirit which, from below time, cooperates to drive that developmental becoming. It can do so because it shares in and is led by that spirit—what Bosanquet describes as "the spirit of the whole" (*PIV* 267)—which is also its own spirit and which underlies and informs alike all the processes of temporal becoming. Thus the Transcendent Self is simply the empirical self not, as with romanticism, a qualitatively unique and already existent substance or "personality" whose quiddity is first self-consciously experienced and then externalized but a being ever involved in the process of expansion, and of transubstantiation through expansion.

It has been our major point thus far in the present section that the Transcendent Self and the empirical self are not, within post-Hegelian Absolute Idealism, numerically distinct from one another. In order to avoid the plague of disjunction and of discontinuity inherited from Kant, it had become necessary to conceive of the "relation" between the two selves in particular, and between the two realms of being—noumenal and phenomenal—in general, as consisting in a self-generative process of continuity from one to the

---

22. Bradley himself expressed this same view when he said that "We cannot speak of a relation, between immediate experience and that which transcends it, except by a licence. It is a mode of expression found convenient in our reflective thinking, but it is in the end not defensible" (*ETR* 176).

other instead of as involving first a disjunction, and then a leap of transcendence from one to the other. It had been the negative lesson of our philosophical history that such a leap could not logically be sustained within a metaphysical dualism of any kind—neither that of Kant nor of anyone else—and it was the bankruptcy of dualism at the turn of the century which had provided the logical nexus for the emergence of Bradley's new premiss and for his substitution of a monistic metaphysical system for the earlier dualistic systems he challenged so effectively.

Bradley's philosophy, and Eliot's with him, begins with the assertion as Bradley himself would say that "neither the [empirical] world nor the [empirical] self is an ultimately given fact. On the contrary each alike is a construction and a more or less one-sided abstraction" (*ETR* 247). Each is, in short an artefact—a made thing and one only progressively made (and never fully made) at that. It is this view which is finally responsible for the new, and much more fluid and dynamic, conceptions of the self and its world that we have heard Bosanquet and Eliot describe earlier and which have become current in post-Hegelian thought—conceptions which, by intention therefore, lack the hard edge of the earlier ones and return us now to that triadic process of empirical self-development which constitutes the second major consideration of the present section.

It was when Royce and the other personalistic absolutists applied the more rigorously conceived Bradleian doctrine of experience to the concept of the Transcendental Self or soul that the particles of experience which constitute the matter or filling of that self or soul became for Eliot what he describes in his thesis as "the units of soul life" (*KE* 147)—units existing, as it were, "in suspension" (*SE* 8) within "the mind which creates" (*SE* 8) and involved therefore in its dynamic and developing life. That mind, however, is not the poet's own—nor is it personal to him. It is, within dialectical philosophy, a mind which is of an essentially creative and incarnational nature and one which serves therefore to inspire and inform the becoming of all that will in fact come to be. It is also a mind in which the empirical self, below time, can share and does share whenever it acts to unify and make whole that which formerly was partial (or particled) and disparate within it, for in Eliot's view, as in Bradley's before him, "it is not the 'greatness,' the intensity, of . . . the components, but the intensity of the artistic process, the pressure, so to speak, under which the fusion takes place, that counts" (*SE* 8). It is here, of course, that the principle of collision

125

becomes operative and effects, through the bombardment by one another of the various particles of phenomenal experience, that disintegration of the old substance which makes way for the continuing dialectical creation of the new.

What the empirical self becomes by way of this process is a self-generative and ever self-transcendent maker or poet, and what he progressively makes is the poem which is himself. As always within Bradley's triadic economy, the two "sides" of the process develop correlatively to one another and here we may recall with profit that particular analogy which, in our introductory chapter, we saw Eliot use to clarify his dynamic concept of "soul-making." Eliot told us there that "Soul is to body as cutting is to axe: realizing itself in its actions, and not completely real when abstracted from what it does" (*KE* 195). And so it is, we may say, with the phenomenal poet or maker. He becomes a poet only in proportion as he makes his poem: realizing himself (or making himself real as a poet) only as he acts creatively to unify his experience and to make it a new and substantive whole. Thus the only thing that a creative poet (*qua* poet or maker) can *express*—being what he is—is the creative act, and he is significant only to the extent that he does so. It is not what "the man who suffers" *is* that the poet expresses but instead what "the mind which creates" *does* (*SE* 8), and what it does is to unify and to make whole. Thus what the creative poet of the twentieth century must inevitably express if he is to be true to the aesthetics of his own age is the creative process itself—and that, at the very moment of its happening, and in the very mode of its working. It is that process of becoming whole that both the poet and his poem will equally express and which, as a consequence, it will become the generic theme of dialectical poetry to express. It is for these reasons that Eliot cannot think of the poet as having merely a " 'personality' to express" (*SE* 9) instead of the process whereby he in fact becomes one. On the merely phenomenal level, what the poet is instead, is "a particular medium, which is only a medium and not a personality, in which impressions and experiences combine in peculiar and unexpected ways" (*SE* 9). He is "in fact a receptacle for seizing and storing up numberless feelings, phrases, images, which remain there until all the particles which can unite to form a new compound are present together" (*SE* 8).

If it would seem that, up to this point, the empirical self or phenomenal poet is to be defined more nearly as a vehicle within which a process occurs rather than as a personality having something to express, he becomes a self—a creative and therefore *significant self*—only as he acts to unify his experience and thus to endow it with whatever integrity or wholeness it is capable of realizing. It is this process—what Eliot in his thesis characterizes as "the painful task" of unification (*KE* 147)—with which he also identifies what he calls there "the life of a soul" (*KE* 147), and it is obviously that same process to which Eliot is referring in his theory of unified sensibility (*SE* 247-48).

We have seen earlier that "the mind which creates" is the mind which informs and vitalizes the development of the whole and, to that extent at least, it may be said to exist before, and above, the linearities of time, history, and process. And so too in a sense does the phenomenal mind of its temporal agent—the *significant self-in-becoming* or poet-maker—inasmuch as, within this philosophy, one is continuous with the development of the other. To whatever extent the poet-maker shares in that creative mind of which he is himself, to use another phrase of Keats, "a Member,"[23] to that extent his own will be a mind permeated by its characteristic spirit —the "spirit of the whole" (*PIV* 267). That "spirit" is given to the poet-maker along with the living (and therefore inspirited) particles of experience accumulating in his pot, as it were. It is in those moments when he is led by the "spirit of the whole" and is following out the *nisus* to wholeness inherent in the particles, that the poet as pot or receptacle yields to and becomes the poet as maker and thus, patient becomes agent, the static becomes dynamic, and the partial and fragmented becomes whole. What happens as a result of that agency—the agency leading to the fusion of the particles in "a new [and never before existent] compound" (*SE* 8)—is that "the spirit of the whole" is fulfilled by being substantiated. It is, in short, given body (or embodied) and made incarnate in time.

23. How well Keats's genius had enabled him to understand some aspects of dialectical philosophy even before that philosophy had been fully formulated may be seen in the whole of that important letter from which I have abstracted the phrase used above. Keats speaks suggestively there of those two differing theories of the soul, with which we also have been much concerned, as follows:

As to the poetical Character itself, (I mean that sort of which, if I am anything, I am a Member; that sort distinguished from the wordsworthian or egotistical sublime; which is a thing *per se* and stands alone) it is not itself—it has no self—it is everything and nothing—it has no character . . . it is a wretched thing to confess; but is a very fact that not one word I ever utter can be taken for granted as an opinion growing out of my identical nature—how can it, when I have no nature?

Hyder E. Rollins, ed., *The Letters of John Keats: 1814-1821*, (Cambridge: Harvard University Press, 1958), I, 386-87. Coleridge's adumbration of the concept of "soul-making" in his poem "Self-Knowledge" (1832) should also be noted.

Within such a theory as Bradley's, there can clearly be no warrant for viewing experience—even from below time—as a "private" or "personal" affair or as something that either separates the experiencing self from the reality experienced or isolates one experiencing self from another.[24] Experience is something available and common to us all and the exclusive property of none. We all of us share in its substance as the orange shares in the being of orangeness, the poem in the reality of poetry, and the dog in quintessential dogginess. It is precisely in virtue of that sharing *and by means of it* that the orange defines itself as an orange (rather than as a lemon) and that the poem defines itself as a poem "and not another thing" (*TSW* viii). So then must it be with the experiential self which defines itself as a self—that is, the *significant self* it progressively becomes rather than is—as it more and more partakes of and acquires the essential character of experience, which character is that of greater and greater wholeness or integrity, a character involving both the *expansion* of its limited material and its increasing *unification* at a higher level as well. It is the dialectical method, exactly as Bradley formulated it, that provides the formulae both for that creative expansion of material which constitutes one side of the process of empirical self-development, and for that "unification of sensibility" (*SE* 248) which constitutes the other. Implicit within the process as a whole is the never-ending necessity to depersonalize oneself by dying to the more limited perimeters of one's subjective experience so as to be remade or reborn at a higher (because wider and more generous) level thereafter as one absorbs the constitutive and ever-widening relational lineaments implicit in one's own objective experience instead.

It is because this dialectical process of expansion is central to Eliot's conception of the *significant self* that he refuses outright to accept as valid the earlier view of the self or soul as "static"—that is, "as *merely* a substance with states" (*KE* 206). Similarly, Bosanquet always describes the *significant self* in some such terms as the following: "What we call 'the individual' then is not a fixed essence, but a living world of content, representing a certain range of externality, which in it strives after unity and true individuality or completeness because it has in it the active spirit of non-contradiction, the form of the whole" (*PIV* 289). It is this dialectical conception of the *significant self-in-becoming* that Eliot opposes to the earlier

24. It is for this reason that Bradley never wearies of saying again and again that "nothing in the end . . . is simply private," or merely subjective (*ETR* 248).

conception of the self as a hard and unyielding nucleus of psychic experience "closed on the outside."[25] The opposition of the two makes its way into his poetry as a polarization between the dynamic and therefore growing and developing Quester Hero we meet in *The Waste Land,* and the static or arrested and therefore literally un-becoming Anti-Hero to whom we are introduced in those personae who (like Prufrock, for example) act as its foil. It is also this same *significant self-in-becoming* which, throughout the whole of his literary career, Eliot went on to oppose both suggestively and systematically to the phenomenal "personality" he found at the base of romantic literary theory and practice.

But how, we may well ask, in actual fact, does the *significant self* acquire that integrity or experiential wholeness to which we have referred and thus distinguish himself from his static and merely role-playing counterpart? What process must he endure? In brief, the answer to these questions lies in viewing experience itself as a developing affair (and one which develops according to the model provided by the dialectical logic of the concrete universal) rather than as something which simply is or as a lump which one passively endures, and of seeing the *significant self* as that which develops with it, thus making of the universe a "vale of Soul-making" indeed. It is, however, to a further and deeper understanding of this vital process that the next section of the present chapter must address itself.

THE PROCESS OF EMPIRICAL SELF-DEVELOPMENT OR OF SOUL-MAKING

If the process of "soul-making" may be viewed as the keystone in the arch of Bradley's philosophy, yet it is one which is formed out of and expresses the interrelationship of various other Bradleian doctrines which, when viewed systematically, lead us inevitably to it as to a crowning glory. Two such doctrines are those of Immediate Experience at the beginning of time and Absolute Experience at its end—the ideological perimeters within which Bradley's philosophy defines and completes itself. Both Bradley and Eliot use the term "Immediate Experience" to represent that positive, nondistin-

25. See Eliot's note to line 411 of *The Waste Land,* and also my footnote on this subject, p. 36, n. 9.

guished, nonrelational Whole of Experience from which all distinction, including the distinction of subject and object, later breaks out. The "Absolute," on the other hand, represents the whole or unity in which all distinction is later transcended and made good. The first has to do with the kind of wholeness which exists *before* the emergence of relational or phenomenal consciousness, whereas the second has to do with the very different kind of wholeness or unity which comes into being *after* the diremption of Immediate Experience has first occurred and then progressively been made up. What exists between the two extratemporal worlds of Immediate Experience *before* time and Absolute Experience *after* time is the temporal world of the "meantime" within which the two intersect, thus creating that "still point of the turning world" (*BN* 11) which, in its turn, initiates the dialectical journey of transcendental becoming or of "soul-making." What it is that is in fact coming to be is the Absolute or "ideal order" itself—the Absolute, however, understood now as a concrete and therefore temporally incarnated universal Whole of Experience and of the Transcendent Self whose experience it is. Any account of the dialectical journey, however, must begin with an account of that particular kind of experience in which it begins and thus with a resume of Bradley's Doctrine of Immediate Experience.

The Doctrine of Immediate Experience. In an essay entitled "On our Knowledge of Immediate Experience" (*ETR* 159-91), Bradley described the nature of such experience as follows:

We in short have experience in which there is no distinction between my awareness and that of which it is aware. There is an immediate feeling, a knowing and being in one, with which knowledge begins; and though this in a manner is transcended, it nevertheless remains throughout as the present foundation of my known world. And if you remove this direct sense of my momentary contents and being, you bring down the whole of consciousness in one common wreck. For it is in the end ruin [as the history of philosophy has demonstrated] to divide experience into something on one side experienced as an object and on the other side something not experienced at all. (*ETR* 159-60)

In another place, Bradley has described Immediate Experience even more clearly. He says there that

It means for me, first, the general condition before distinctions and relations have been developed, and where as yet neither any subject nor object exists. And it means, in the second place, anything which is present at any

130

stage of mental life [after subject-object relations have developed] in so far as that is only present and simply *is*. In the latter sense we may say that everything actual, no matter what, must be felt. (*AR* 406-7).

This nonrelational felt unity of many in one "of which I am immediately aware" is what Bradley means by Immediate Experience, and this is his understanding of the "given" from which speculation, art, and criticism must all begin. Not only do they begin there; they also rest there. It is against Immediate Experience as the "given" that they are themselves defined and judged, for Bradley insists

that immediate experience, however much transcended, both remains and is active. It is not a stage which shows itself at the beginning and then disappears, but it remains at the bottom throughout as fundamental. And, further, remaining, it contains in itself every development which in a sense transcends it. Nor does it merely contain all developments, but in its own way it acts to some extent as their judge . . . . (*ETR* 161)

or as their *criterion*. [26]

It should be clear from what has been said that Immediate Experience is not to be confused with personal experience, and yet it is precisely that confusion which continues to support the now systematized misunderstandings of well over a hundred years. Instead, such experience must be viewed as occurring within what Bradley designates as a "finite centre" (*AR* 460) and Bosanquet describes as "a living world of content" (*PIV* 289). From such temporal and finite centres of experience, particular souls or selves will eventually arise and *become* selves, but only as they act to unify and make whole the experiential matter and substance of such selfhood. For now, however, we must accept Bradley's unequivocal and repeated assertions, first, that "A centre of experience, first, is not the same thing as either a soul or, again, a self" (*AR* 468) and, second, that at the level of Immediate Experience such substantial unities do not as yet exist.

That Bradley's doctrine of Immediate Experience is subtle, I would not care to deny, but it is not esoteric. Once one has lived with the notion and conquered the almost unconquerable identification of Immediate Experience with "my" experience, a certain profound simplicity in the notion comes to the fore. In order to make this clear, I shall introduce a personal example. The other evening I heard for the first time a particularly impressive recording of Synge's *Riders to the Sea* and the experience, in its totality and immediacy, was very nearly one of transport. Within that experi-

26. See my footnote regarding Bradley's "doctrine of the Criterion" on p. 67.

ence, I was not I; I was not consciously present as a subject, nor was the play there before me distinct as an object. The actual fact of the matter is that there was just what Bradley says there is—a manifold simply felt and felt as one whole, a blur with differences that are felt but not discriminated. This simply felt whole or unity, this kind of deep-lying felt totality, is Immediate Experience and is nonrelational in the sense that the "I", as Eliot has indicated in his dissertation, "is no more consciously present than is the intercellular action" (*KE* 154). Nor is the play as "my" object—that is, as the object of "my" consciousness or attention—any more present. In this moment of bare immediacy, subject and object *as* subject and object, self and world, feeling and felt, are not yet discriminated and, when later they are so, they are discriminated as derivative aspects of the nondifferentiated and nonrelational unity from which they have broken out.

This is the kind of experience which for Bradley constitutes the "given" and which, from an initial limbo of dimness, works itself out into the reciprocally correlative directions of subject and object —something deeply and consciously felt now on one side, and something dim and unknown but correlative to the feeling, on the other. Even after the level of relational consciousness has been established, and subject and object, feeling and felt, I and *Riders to the Sea,* may be thought of as at least distinguishable from one another, it is possible for that derivative and only progressively emergent empirical self to push back to that "felt whole of which I am immediately aware" and within which—as such—it did not even exist.

Clearly, what must be avoided at all costs is the identification of Immediate Experience with "my" experience and yet that identification was urged upon Bradley time and time again and he would reply time and time again with the same quiet restraint: "This is the ground, inherited of course from others, on which I may say that I have based myself always. If you take experience as above, then all the main conclusions which I advocate are assuredly wrecked. And nothing, I presume, is gained by simply urging against myself and others a result on which we ourselves have consistently stood" (*ETR* 199). In short, if and whenever Immediate Experience is confused with "my" experience, all is lost for we have unwittingly returned to the relational level from which all prior philosophy had begun and which ended by leaving "reality. . . outside uncomprehended" (AR 29). Immediate Experience must be understood in exactly the way defined above. It is not so much a form of experience as the form of all experience: it is not personal to anyone and yet is available to everyone; it is not within time nor yet out of it; it is almost inconceivable but, were we to make the attempt, we might best conceive of it as a point—perhaps as "the still point of the turning world" (BN II)—or as a moment—perhaps "the unattended/Moment, the moment in and out of time" (DS V).

More precisely, we have seen Bradley refer to Immediate Experience as a moment of "immediate feeling, a knowing and being in one," a moment "in which there is no distinction between my awareness [as subject] and that of which it is aware [as object]." Bradley's metaphysical speculation, like Eliot's art and criticism, begins in an experience that is—both at its beginning and at its end —already metaphysical and impersonal. If it were not so in the beginning, and if it did not remain so throughout, that transcendent and impersonal nature could never be achieved at the end.

Accordingly, the first step required in solving the hitherto insuperable problem of knowledge is to accept Immediate Experience, at least hypothetically for the moment, in exactly the way in which Bradley has defined it. The second major step in the formulation of the process of "soul-making" emerges from that diremption of Immediate Experience which initiates the development of the phenomenal realm of subject-object correlation—that realm of the "meantime" within which the process of empirical self-development occurs and which exists between Immediate Experience at the beginning of the temporal order, and Absolute Experience at its end. However, Eliot's particular concern in the Bradley thesis is not, he tells us, with either "the beginning or end of our journey" (both of which he, like Bradley, views as "hypothetical limits") but with "some of the intermediate steps" (KE 31) involved after Immediate Experience has first canalized its energies into the downward gyre culminating in the phenomenal realm of subject-object correlation, and then reversed its movement to initiate the upward and ever-widening gyre leading it to the Absolute. It is, as we shall eventually see, the markedly different reading which Bradley and Eliot give to these "intermediate steps" of the dialectical process which will dissociate Bradley's particular brand of Absolute Idealism irrevocably from Hegel's and, as a consequence, Eliot's mind and art from that of his romantic predecessors.

The Phenomenal Realm of Subject-Object Correlation. Enough, I think, has been said already about the nature of Immediate Experience itself. Our concern now is to give an account, as Eliot has also done, of the temporal "development of subject and object out of immediate experience" (*KE* 15), and then to go on from that to view the dialectical opposition created by the diremption of such experience as itself the generative vehicle for the achievement of self-creation or of "soul-making." Our account of this later phase in the process of empirical self-development may begin with Eliot's stunningly brief explication of it in his Bradley thesis. In Immediate Experience, Eliot tells us, "the subject and object are one. The object becomes an object by its felt continuity with other feelings which fall outside of the finite centre or subject, and the subject becomes a subject by its felt continuity with a core of feeling which is not related to the object" (*KE* 21). As Immediate Experience moves or breaks out from itself, WHAT was felt that is, the "real reality" of experience) is loosened and dissociated from the THAT (the finite centre of sensibility) which feels, and it is in this temporal "dissociation of sensibility" (*SE* 247) from the experiential substance of sensibility that relational consciousness is born. Perhaps it will be helpful at this point to return to the example used earlier of the experiential "event" in which I and *Riders to the Sea* were both comprised so as to make the basic distinctions involved in the present discussion somewhat clearer.

With regard to that event, I have asserted with Bradley that it is possible to distinguish an order of impersonal or Immediate Experience prior to and yet continuous with the development of my own later personal and subjective experience. I can, that is, distinguish two moments in the total experience which later diremped itself as *my* experience of *Riders to the Sea:* an earlier moment when I, as such, was not even there, and a later moment when the original experience broke up and I and the play seemed to take up separate existence from one another. The first phase of the argument with which Bradley and Eliot are concerned rests in the empirically verifiable assertion that "We in short have experience in which there is no distinction between my awareness and that of which it is aware." Putting this kind of experience entirely to the side now, we are given next Bradley's conception of that form of *relational* experience into which Immediate Experience somehow passes and within which I and the play—a phenomenal subject having before itself a phenomenal object of consciousness—make their initial, but as yet *insubstantial,* appearance in time.

It is part of Bradley's general premiss that Immediate Experience does not last as such because it is not its nature to do so. Something happens to it; it breaks up from within and develops in various directions. In short, there is no Immediate Experience in which we can remain standing. It is not correct to say that Immediate Experience dissolves or crumbles away; it just moves into another way of being, or on to another plane—the relational plane now of subject-hood (feeling) on the one side and object-hood (felt) on the other. If I were to relate this second moment to the example I introduced earlier for purposes of clarification, I would say that the locus of the discussion which follows may be found in that moment when I raised my head from the pillow and became conscious or aware on *my* side of an object called *Riders to the Sea* on the other. We might say that the dawn of personal consciousness was to be found when I asked the question: "WHAT was THAT?" The question (with which we may identify the entire problem of knowledge) could never even be formulated as a question except from a ground in which the answer is already implicit. Unless, that is, the "real reality" or WHATNESS of the play has first and in some sense been "given at the start," we would not later be able to say of the play we attend to in judgment that it is this or that or the other thing. This kind of affirmation is knowledge in the only true sense of the word—knowledge as recognition (re-cognition or the knowing again) by the phenomenal or conscious mind, as mind, of an identity *felt* in one sense and therefore known already but never before explicated by the mind. Knowledge, judgment, criticism, are all alike impossible if there is not first "an immediate feeling, a knowing and being in one, with which knowledge begins" and in which both its truth and its coherence is grounded.

It is noteworthy that what this second moment seeks is not reality, but light—the truth about reality. In a sense we may say that reality, in all its transcendent impersonality, has already, as Bradley says, been "given at the start" (*ETR* 199) although it has not yet been taken and made "my" own in knowledge. Experience as immediate—that is, experience as "really real"—simply *is,* and this alone is the real *as such.* But on this level there is not a word to be said about it. Knowledge of experience, and of the reality with which it is identical in substance, constitutes a later stage and involves its death as real at the moment of its birth as truth, except that Immediate Experience does not die for "it is foundational throughout." In other words, WHAT the THAT is can only be known in time and through the dialectical agency of phenomenal selves in active commerce with their phenomenal objects for in Immediate Experience as such "knowing and being are one." The important point here is that even in this world of dirempted experience where "knowing and being are [not] one," and where knowledge of WHAT we experience is temporarily dissociated from the fact of its having been experienced, it is nonetheless the reality of Immediate Experience which, lying behind the "dissociation of sensibility" (SE 247) from its own experiential content, can provide the holistic background within which the "unification of sensibility" (SE 248) can be made up.

I have suggested that phenomenal consciousness comes alive to itself simultaneously with the awareness of something felt now as external and in opposition to it—something to be known. The phenomenal "I"—albeit in a merely potential form—falls out of the primary experience and will go on then to become an actual (if only temporal and therefore temporary) self or knower as it progressively incorporates into its self-hood the substance of the reality to be known. What serves to make such experiential reality develop, however, instead of remaining merely static, is the creative commerce with one another of its now dirempted "sides"—the subjective or personal side held within feeling, and the objective or impersonal side held within the reality felt. Perhaps a few examples can serve to make the actual nature of that commerce clearer than a further elaboration of the doctrines themselves would do. What we shall find is that the transcendental or *significant self-in-becoming* existing "above" its own sides grows or develops proportionately with the growth implicit in the developing (because relational) life of its objects. The *significant self,* that is, is the self which comes into fuller and fuller being as it leaves the restricted confines of mere *feeling*—that with which the subjective side of its experience may now be identified—and allows itself instead to be led outward from such feeling into the relational and therefore expanding life of the whole to which the "objective correlative" of such feeling is indissolubly connected. Before turning to those examples directly, however, we may consider a trenchant footnote of Bradley's wherein he has given as succinct expression as is possible to this seminally important aspect of his philosophy. He says there:

We never in one sense do, or can, go beyond immediate experience. Apart from the immediacy of 'this' and 'now' we never have, or can have, reality. The real, to be real, must be felt. This is one side of the matter. But on the other side the felt content takes on a form which more and more goes beyond the essential character of feeling, i.e. direct and nonrelational qualification. Distinction and separation into substantives and adjectives, terms and relations, alienate the content of immediate experience from the form of immediacy which still on its side persists. In other words the ideality, present from the first, is developed, and to follow this ideality is our way to the true Reality which is there in feeling. (*ETR* 190 fn.)

On another occasion, and even more simply, Bradley has put what is essentially the same matter this way: "What is fundamental is . . . the presence in everything finite of that which takes it beyond itself" (*ETR* 272).

For Bradley, then, it is the way of relations alone which can lead that which is finite and personal "beyond itself"—a way identical with what Eliot in his literary criticism first designated as a "process of depersonalization" (*SE* 7), and then put at the centre of his poetic theory. The following statement by Eliot on feeling which is merely externalized or objectified is an important one because it implies, first of all, that it is only through relations that anything expands "beyond itself" and also because it clarifies some of the subtler implications of the "process of depersonalization" better than Eliot has managed to do in his literary criticism. Eliot says: "The feeling which is an object is feeling shrunk and impoverished, though in a sense expanded and developed as well: shrunk because it is now the object of consciousness, narrower instead of wider than consciousness; expanded because in becoming an object it has developed relations which lead it beyond itself" (*KE* 22-3). It is noteworthy here that the same relations which enable an object to expand and thus "lead it beyond itself" can also lead the subject whose object it is "beyond itself" when it likewise follows them. What is perhaps even more important is Eliot's polarization here of the divergent concepts separating the strategies of self-creation from those merely of self-consciousness. If we would understand the importance of those differences, we have only to contrast the dyadic relations underlying the earlier romantic disposition of "immediate experience" or feeling with the triadic relations underlying Bradley's later treatment of it.

It should be clear from what has been said already that, in the first instance, there is virtually nothing one can do with "feeling" other than to "express" it and thus, in a sense, to externalize or objectify it. This, Bradley tells us, may be said to give us "one side of the matter" (*ETR* 190 fn.)—the side embraced in self-consciousness. To make the inner outer, however, or to give an objective *form* to what is essentially of a subjective *nature* (as is the case with phenomenal self-consciousness), can never lead one to the transcendence of one's subjectivity and thus to the attainment either of the real or of the truth about it. Nor can such effusion lead to that process of self-creation or of "soul-making" which is central to the post-Hegelian tradition. For this, what Bradley describes as "the other side" (*ETR* 190 fn.) of the matter referred to above is also, and equally, required—the side, that is, which effects the expansion or development of one's object world. It is to an elaboration of these two sides of the process of transcendental becoming and of the two variant conceptions of objectivity underlying them that we must next turn our attention and this will return us to a further, and final, implication of Bradley's triadic logic.

I have indicated earlier, and repeatedly, that within a triadic logic, to speak of the subjective and objective "sides" of experience is not yet to speak of the self, for to identify the self—that is, the empirical or phenomenal self—with the subjective "side" of experience (as both romantic philosophy and literature had finally done) is, Bradley tells us, "a mistake at once fundamental and disastrous" (*ETR* 189).[27] Instead, the *significant self* exists above its own "sides" and is that which evolves, or which is progressively generated, through the interactive (but subsequently resolved) tension between them, and thus between the subjective and objective aspects of its own experience. Thus the vital point in Bradley's philosophy and what distinguishes that philosophy from others is that, within the triadic economy he formulated, "knowing and being," feeling and felt, subjective and objective, develop, and can only develop, *pari-passu* inasmuch as they constitute two sides of

27. Alternatively, see J. Hillis Miller, *Poets of Reality,* (Cambridge: Harvard University Press, 1966) pp. 159-60, where Miller has made some grossly misleading statements such as the following: "Everything is already subjective for Eliot, and the mind can never bump into anything other than itself, anything stubbornly recalcitrant to its devouring power to assimilate everything." Compare with this statement of Miller's the one from which I have taken the excerpt used above: "This my world, of feeling and felt in one, is not to be called 'subjective', nor is it to be identified with my self. That would be a mistake at once fundamental and disastrous" (*ETR* 189). This, it seems to me, is precisely the mistake Miller makes and it vitiates not only his understanding of Bradley's philosophy but his reading of Eliot's mind and art as well. See further Appendix II.

one and the same developing experience and of the developing self whose experience it is.

In his essay on "Lancelot Andrewes," Eliot has provided what for him is a remarkably clear example of that proportional ascent whereby the self or soul involved in it progressively develops as it moves from that realm of mere sense or feeling constituting the subjective side of its experience through the relational realm of the reality felt and held within its objective side. What Eliot is depicting here is what Wallace Stevens has called "the act of the mind"[28] —an act involving the movement of the mind through the real nature of the reality felt and whose structure is determined by the relational system within which it exists. To travel the way of relations, therefore, is to perceive the nature of that reality at its joints as it were—the joints both of its being and of its further becoming —and to travel that way is the quintessential "act of the mind." In the passage which follows, what is important is not only Eliot's display of the "act of the mind" at work, but also the contrast between Andrewes and Donne through which he takes note of the "exact equivalence" (*SE* 125) of feeling and felt, subjective and objective, towards which the classical, as opposed to the romantic, tradition attempts to bring that "act." Eliot says:

When Andrewes begins his sermon, from beginning to end you are sure that he is wholly in his subject, unaware of anything else, that his emotion grows as he penetrates more deeply into his subject, that he is finally "alone with the Alone," with the mystery which he is seeking to grasp more and more firmly . . . . Andrewes' emotion is purely contemplative; it is not personal, it is wholly evoked by the object of contemplation, to which it is adequate; his emotions wholly contained in and explained by its object. But with Donne there is always the something else. . . . Donne is a "personality" in a sense in which Andrewes is not: his sermons, one feels, are a "means of self-expression." He is constantly finding an object which shall be adequate to his feelings; Andrewes is wholly absorbed in the object and therefore responds with the adequate emotion. (*SE* 308-9)

If the key distinction here is undoubtedly the distinction between personal emotion on the one hand and *"significant* emotion" (*SE* 11) on the other, yet what is more important is Eliot's identification of "significant emotion" with emotion that is, in Bradley's sense of that word, "purely contemplative"—that is, wholly "evoked by the object of contemplation" and determined, therefore, both as to

28. W. Stevens, "Of Modern Poetry," *Collected Poems* (New York: Alfred A. Knopf, 1969), p. 239.

nature and degree, by that object. The contrast of Bishop An-drewes' emotion with that of Donne is, of course, particularly instructive as regards the romantic tendancy to create in imagina-tion the object to which one responds in reality. In Bradley's philosophy, on the other hand, it is always the object itself—the reality felt—which controls and which everywhere acts as the *crit-erion* through which such feeling is itself continuously modified and rendered proportional. Within the New Idealism, thought (or imagination) does not create its object; it finds it, and then goes on to penetrate its real nature by retracing the relations actually con-stitutive of its unique and particular being.

But, we may well ask, if to follow the pathways of ideality is assuredly to attain to degrees of truth, yet in what sense can the attainment of degrees of truth become the attainment of degrees of reality as well? It is this question which returns us once again to that principle of trichotomy with which we were concerned earlier and which alone makes an answer possible for, as was shown in our account of that principle, it is the relation itself between any two terms which actually constitutes the being, and also controls the becoming, of the terms related. The terms or parties to a relation, that is, expand precisely by virtue of the relation itself which the terms equally embrace and within which they are equally bound, and they do so whether the relation be one of likeness or difference. To see anything "in relation," therefore, is not only to see it more clearly, but also to see "more" of it—the "more" released by the relation itself. When, for example, the poet-protagonist of *The Waste Land* sees the typist "in relation" to Goldsmith's earlier heroine, he not only sees her in a different light; he sees her as well in a light which illuminates what she *really* is more clearly. As a consequence, his actual experience of her is both widened and deepened at the same time, and so too is his experience of Gold-smith's heroine. Likewise, if one wants, let us say, to experience profoundly the poetic reality of Dylan Thomas' "Fern Hill," one can do so best by reading it in conjunction with other poems of its own kind within the already "existing monuments" of the "ideal order" (*SE* 5) such as Emily Dickinson's "I taste a liquor never brewed." What the "identity-in-difference" implicit in the conjunc-tion will release is the rich particularity—indeed, the unique reality —of either and thus make it available to an apprehension which is both sensuous (real) and thoughtful (ideal) at the same time. This, of course, is why Eliot constantly urges that "Comparison and analysis . . . are the chief tools of the critic" (SE 21), for it is the forced collision—the telescoping—of the terms of a relation which in fact, and simultaneously, generates both something more to be known (the "third something") and an experiential knowledge of it.

This correlativity theory which Eliot developed in his thesis on *Knowledge and Experience in the Philosophy of F. H. Bradley* merely represents his reexpression of Bradley's doctrine of Degrees of Truth and Reality and also of the major point which Bosanquet had made with regard to Bradley's theory of judgment. In his book, *Implication and Linear Inference,* Bosanquet stated the substance of that doctrine summarily when he said that truth is merely the form which reality assumes when expressed through ideas in particular minds and that, "If you suppose a course of ideas inexpressive of reality, or a reality which has no expression in ideal form, you have destroyed the essence of truth."[29] The whole point of Bradley's theory of judgment would seem to be that, within judgment and the progressive attainment of truth, ideality and reality, knowledge and experience, thought and sense, are never even for a moment disjoined from one another as they are, for example, in Kant. To follow out the relational pathways of ideality, therefore, is to attain not only degrees of truth but degrees of reality as well. What knowledge in fact *is* is the unceasing conversion of that reality which constitutes one side of experience into that truth which constitutes the other—a conversion effected through the instrumentality or mediumship of mind. To live the life of the mind is progressively to enter into the very substance of reality itself and to attain thereby the very truth about it. And if the "course" of reality is itself the temporal and dialectical course of its own becoming on the model provided by the concrete universal, then to experience that course sensuously and concretely by retracing its relational lineaments is progressively to embody in truth a concrete and experiential realization of the whole. It is, in short, because knowing, in the philosophy of Bradley and Eliot, is a way which being has that it can also be a way of becoming (or coming to be) that which one knows.

What we have encountered already in the preceding discussion is Bradley's Doctrine of Degrees of Truth and Reality—one of the two doctrines which alone, Eliot tells us, he would accept "Out of Absolute Idealism" unequivocally and without reservations of any

29. B. Bosanquet, *Implication and Linear Inference* (London: Macmillan and Company Ltd., 1920), p. 148.

kind, the other being Bradley's Doctrine of the "Internality of Relations" (*KE* 153). What these doctrines in fact do is to confer ontological status not on the life of the mind abstracted from the life of
sense but on that three-sided life of developing experience as Bradley defined it in his philosophy and Eliot embodied it, in particular,
in "The Fire Sermon" of *The Waste Land* as well. We must turn
finally now to a brief consideration of these remaining Bradleian
doctrines inasmuch as they provide, when systematically conceived, a new and distinctively different reading of the nature of
developing experience than was possible before.

"Degrees of Truth and Reality and the Internality of Relations"
(KE 153). The gap which separates the moderns generally from the
romantics is nowhere more pronounced than in their divergent
views of the life of the mind and of the nature of ideality. It is
Bradley's special theory of the nature of judgment which, in particular, restores to the realms of mind and thought and ideality the
classic valuations which a romantic generation of writers, both
everyday and philosophical, had so seriously obscured. The mas-
sive and insidious antiintellectualism of our own time is perhaps the
most obvious, as it is assuredly the most regrettable, result of that
obscuration. Bradley's reinstatement of the life of the mind as at the
core of man's essential dignity, however, brings with it the necessity
of demonstrating both how that life is properly to be lived and the
goal it is intended to reach. The two together are what Bosanquet
defines as "The Pilgrim's Progress of Philosophy" (*PIV* 7). In short,
the life of the mind must have a method to it—a working principle
—and it is that principle which the New Idealists first observe in the
progressive and dialectical "working" of the concrete universal
towards its own temporal and systematic completion and then use
equally as the paradigm for acquiring the truth about it. To retrace
below time, and in truth, the progressively expanding lineaments of
any systematic and relational whole or "ideal order" beyond it is
progressively to embody in truth an experiential realization of the
whole and, thus, progressively "to see the object as it really is"
(*TSW* 15).

The vital point in Bradley's philosophy and what distinguishes
that philosophy from others is, as I have tried to show, that within
the triadic economy he formulated, knower and known, self and
world, develop *pari-passu* and correlatively with one another inasmuch as they constitute two sides of one and the same process of

142

developing experience. The knower becomes a knower in proportion, and only, as he comes to know, and to become what he knows, and if the *matter* of "real reality" is experience itself—felt on one side, and known on the other—then to go back and forth from one "side" of real experience (sense) to the other (thought) is to effect what Eliot has called "a degree of development of sensibility" (*SE* 245) inasmuch as it involves what he further describes as a "sensuous apprehension of thought or a recreation of thought into feeling" (*SE* 246). Thus, to follow out the pathways of ideality—pathways whose structure is provided by the inherently developing logic of the concrete universal or "ideal order" (*SE* 5) —is to attain, not only degrees of truth but degrees of reality as well, but only, Bradley would insist against Hegel, when knowledge and experience, thought and sense, ideality and reality, everywhere "move in measure, like a dancer" (*LG* 11). What the adjectival or empirical self accomplishes by this movement is the progressive creation of itself. It becomes substantial and, therefore, *significant* —a unity progressively made, and then unmade, only to be made again as it journeys along the pathways of dialectical becoming, pathways which involve that unceasing transubstantiation through which the empirical self is led from centre to circumference within the circle of the Absolute-in-Becoming.

If we were now to schematize the import of those various doctrines which we have attempted to generalize here, and all of which are implicatively involved with one another within Bradley's philosophy, the resultant diagram might look something like the one on the following page.

If our diagram is strongly reminiscent of the interpenetrating cones of Yeats's gyres, that only serves to show that Yeats's "authors," if not Yeats himself, had taken the odd course or two in the post-Hegelian "singing school" of dialectical philosophy and that they had gained their certification as specialists, not from Madame Blavatsky really, but in that school of the "higher mysticism" (*PIV* 251), as Bosanquet has called it, to which the central insights of post-Hegelian Absolute Idealism must inevitably lead.[30]

30. Yeats's statement regarding his wife's reading should be recalled here inasmuch as it was she who served as the medium for the system he then went on to construct in *A Vision:*

Then I took down from my wife a list of what she had read, two or three volumes of Wundt, part of Hegel's *Logic,* all Thomas Taylor's *Plotinus,* a Latin work of Pico della Mirandola, and a great deal of medieval mysticism. . . . I did not expect to find

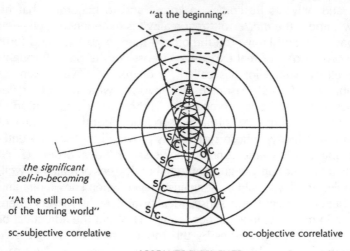

IMMEDIATE EXPERIENCE

"at the beginning"

the significant
self-in-becoming

"At the still point
of the turning world"

sc-subjective correlative   oc-objective correlative

ABSOLUTE EXPERIENCE
of the
TRANSCENDENT SELF

"at the end"

Within that philosophy whose totality can best be visually ac-
commodated by the inclusion of Yeats's gyres within the Great
Wheel of Eliot's mandala, "the way up is the way down, the way
forward is the way back" (*DS* 111). Eliot's concern, however, as
it was Bradley's before him, was to give particular salience to the
spiral of dialectical ascent within the circle of the Absolute. If we
would perceive that salience clearly, we must perceive as well that
the spiral is only made possible by the dying and reviving god who
is to be found at its centre and who, by dying to himself, turns the
wheel of transcendental becoming. It remains finally to distinguish
that dialectical hero from his earlier romantic counterpart and thus
to take an initial step in distinguishing from one another as well the
variant literary traditions which have developed around them. It is

---

that the communicators echoed what she had read, for I had proof they were not
dependent on her memory or mine, but did expect to find somewhere something
from which their symbolic geometry had been elaborated, something used as they
had used *Per Amica Silentia Lunae*. . . . Although the more I read the better did I
understand what I had been taught, I found neither the geometrical symbolism nor
anything that could have inspired it except the vortex of Empedocles. *A Vision* (New
York: Macmillan, 1961), pp. 19-20.

Had Yeats read Hegel's *Logic*, he might perhaps have found the particular source
he was seeking for his wife's inspiration.

to this task that the next and last section of the present chapter must now turn.

THE DIALECTICAL VS THE BYRONIC HERO, OR BRADLEY VS HEGEL

If one were, as I am, fortunate in not having in philosophy a reputation to lose and if, enjoying such freedom, one were to attempt in the most flagrant of summary terms to differentiate the dialectical philosophy of Hegel from that of Kant, one could more or less safely lay the entire burden of that differentiation on the one cardinal point I have tried to elaborate in the present chapter—the continuity of the "two souls" or selves, noumenal and phenomenal, together with the self-generation from one to the other, within the Hegelian tradition, as opposed to their disjunction from one another within the earlier Kantian tradition. If one dared to proceed further and wanted to distinguish turn-of-the-century Anglo-American Absolute Idealism from its German counterparts, and to do so in equally summary fashion, one could proceed only by understanding the markedly different reading given by Bradley to that process of dialectical becoming delineated before him by Hegel. If thirdly, and finally, the import of these two seminal distinctions were then to be applied to a reading of our literary history, an initial step might be taken towards a distinctive characterization of *The Modern Tradition,*[31] and one which would view its literature not merely as an extension of romanticism from the nineteenth into the twentieth century but sometimes, at least, as representative of a fully conscious and deliberate reaction against it.

Northrop Frye has told us that "Anti-Romanticism . . . had no resources for becoming anything more than a post-Romantic movement" and, in doing so, he has echoed what is at present the prevailing critical view of our modern literary tradition.[32] Alternatively, I would suggest that the resources are certainly there but that

31. *Cf.* R. Ellmann and C. Feidelson, Jr., eds., *The Modern Tradition* (New York: Oxford University Press, 1965), particularly the Preface, pp. v-ix.
32. N. Frye, "The Drunken Boat," *Romanticism Reconsidered* (New York: Columbia University Press, 1963), p. 24. This view has also been variously expressed and supported by such otherwise widely diversified critics as Langbaum, Kermode, Krieger, Foster, Winters, Vivas, and even by M.H. Abrams in *The Mirror and The Lamp.* In his more recent study, entitled *Natural Supernaturalism: Tradition and Revolution in Romantic Literature* (New York: W.W. Norton and Company, 1971), however, Abrams has modified his earlier view significantly as may be seen in the following statement:

145

they are available only within the discipline provided by the history of ideas and that if we were to relate our modern English literature to the lineaments of post-Kantian English and American Absolute Idealism, rather than exclusively to Kantian and post-Kantian German Absolute Idealism, we would be enabled to find them within the implications of that process to which Keats applied the phrase "Soul-making" and then enjoined upon those who, like himself, would aspire to transcend the limits of what we have already heard him call "the wordsworthian or egotistical sublime." Perhaps enough has been said already to substantiate the first of those three points summarily stated above. The second and third, however, require further elaboration.

I have noted (p. 59, n. 6) Bradley's reservations concerning the use to which Hegel put the dialectical method. In various passages in his *Principles of Logic* and in other writings, Bradley has made abundantly clear the particular reasons which led him to those reservations and to his consequent inability to "accept what is often understood as the process of Hegel's dialectic" (*ETR* 278). In brief, his reasoning was this. The point which Kant had made in his *Critique of Pure Reason* was that experience must conform to the structure of thought in order to be knowable. To Hegel, it seemed necessary to conclude from this that the order of thought and the order of reality are one and the same. As a consequence, the unfolding of reason is identical with the course of the real and, thus, within Hegelian Absolute Idealism, logic and ontology become identified as one and the same, thereby giving rise to that panlogism with which Hegel's philosophy has frequently been associated.

It was precisely this Hegelian brand of ontological rationalism which, in Bradley's view, represents one of the twin aberrations of nineteenth-century thought, the other having been provided by the tradition of the Empiricists. One rests in the disjunction of thought from sense, and the other in the disjunction of sense from thought.

In this, as in earlier chapters, I have stressed analogues in post-Romantic literature to the ideas and forms that were developed during that period of astonishing creativity, the several decades after the French Revolution. Such an emphasis may appear to align my point of view with the recent tendency to break down the traditional opposition between what is Romantic and what seems to us distinctively "modern" in literature. . . . The fact is, however, that many of the chief figures in the modernist movement—including in England and America, Hulme, Pound, and Eliot—identified themselves as, explicitly, counter-Romantic; and from any comprehensive view of their basic premises and literary practice, it seems to me that in this judgment they were manifestly right. (p. 427)

It was the Hegelian aberration Bradley had in mind when, in a celebrated passage which Eliot has quoted before me, Bradley spoke as follows of it:

It may come from a failure in my metaphysics, or from a weakness of the flesh which continues to blind me, but the notion that existence could be the same as understanding strikes as cold and ghost-like as the dreariest materialism. That the glory of this world in the end is appearance leaves the world more glorious, if we feel it is a show of some fuller splendour; but the sensuous curtain is a deception and a cheat, if it hides some colourless movement of atoms, some spectral woof of impalpable abstractions, or unearthly ballet of bloodless categories. Though dragged to such conclusions, we cannot embrace them. Our principles may be true, but they are not reality. They no more *make* that Whole which commands our devotion than some shredded dissection of human tatters *is* that warm and breathing beauty of flesh which our hearts found delightful.[33]

Alternatively, it was Bradley's view that "the union in all perception of thought with sense, the co-presence everywhere in all appearances of fact with ideality—this is the one foundation of truth" (*AR* 335). It is on this alternative foundation that Bradley's philosophy rests, as does also Eliot's theory of unified sensibility—that literary variant of it whose exposition in his essay on "The Metaphysical Poets" Eliot could tell us somewhat disingenuously is "too brief, perhaps, to carry conviction" (*SE* 248).

Thus the vital point in Bradley's philosophy, and what distinguishes that philosophy most significantly from Hegel's when it is applied to the process of empirical self-development or of "soul-making," concerns his insistence that subject and object, self and world, knower and known develop, and can only develop, *paripassu* and correlatively to one another. It is this insistence of Bradley's, as we have already seen, which gives "exact equivalence" (*SE* 125) to the life of sense and the life of thought and, in addition, a complete mobility and freedom of exchange between the sensuous real and the equally sensuous ideal. It is also this insistence which will lead Eliot to seek out as his models poets like Chapman and Donne, as well as Marlowe, Webster, Tourneur, and Shakespeare—poets in whom "there is a direct sensuous apprehension of thought, or a recreation of thought into feeling" (*SE* 246). Poets like them, Eliot tells us, "feel their thought as immediately as the odour of a rose" (*SE* 247) and have that "same essential quality" he so admires "of transmuting ideas into sensations, of transforming an observation into a state of mind" (*SE* 249). On an earlier occasion,

33. Bradley, *Principles of Logic,* pp. 590-91.

Eliot had described that same quality as one of "sensuous thought, or of the senses thinking, of which the exact formula remains to be defined" (*TSW* 23).

With Hegel, however, a variety of readings is of course possible. Those who, for example, take their primary insights from the later works beginning with the *Logic* (1812-16)—and Bradley would seem to have been one of these—are inclined to emphasize Hegel's application of the dialectical method to objects of thought and to read it, therefore, primarily as a conceptual dialectic leading to the panlogism Bradley found so distasteful. More recently, however, there are those who argue that Hegel's earlier and much neglected *Phenomenology of Mind* (1807) reveals his true vision much more felicitously than does the *Logic* and that the dialectical method there is applied not, as Bradley would have it, to some "unearthly ballet of bloodless categories" but to certain preeminent and very concrete types of human experience. If Bradley would probably accept this later corrective to his view, yet there is an even more important reservation that I think he would bring to bear on the *Phenomenology*, and one which would lead him to reassert his earlier objections even more vigorously than before, if perhaps in a somewhat different way.

It should be clear from what was said earlier that there are basically only two things that can happen to the reality given in "immediate feeling " or in "immediate experience." It can remain static—that is, at the level of those *states* of consciousness which are subsequently externalized in self-consciousness—or it can develop. Simply put, the strategy involved in the former is that of jumping out of one's skin, as it were, and then of taking as the object of one's consciousness those shrivelling and dissociated fragments of the self one has left behind and which, underlying the fractured ironies of the Byronic hero, generate that romantic self-mockery and sometimes even that romantic self-contempt to which its literature gives such ample expression. It is in such irony that Schlegel found the ideological essence of romanticism that he elaborated as its cardinal principle. My concern here, however, is with the particular use to which Hegel put the dialectical method in his *Phenomenology* and, in this matter, J. Loewenberg can be of special assistance to us inasmuch as he has clarified that use effectively as follows:

The dialectical method, as exhibited in the *Phenomenology*, means two things: it means a subjective pose and it means an objective situation. The attitude demanded for the application of the dialectical method is a certain kind of impersonation. The only way to understand a point of view is by intellectual sympathy to impersonate it. For no point of view, so Hegel teaches, can be grasped from without. To appreciate it truly one must insert oneself inside it and reproduce by an act of sympathetic imagination its intrinsic nature. The dialectical critic's art is like that of the dramatist or of the actor: he must identify himself with the character he is portraying. To be sure, only a great artist—a Shakespeare—can with skill hide his own true face behind an alien mask. Dramatic or histrionic sincerity is not ordinary sincerity: the artist must always pretend to be what he himself is not. He must play a part. On its subjective side, then, the dialectical method is simply a method of portrayal, requiring an initial distinction, so Hegel tells us in his characteristic language, between what a thing is *für uns* and what it is *für sich.* [34]

Loewenberg goes on then to show that if the histrionic art made use of by Hegel in his application of the dialectical method represents only one side of that method—that is, the subjective side externalized in self-consciousness—yet the kind of Idealism to which such a one-sided and histrionic use is conducive is not unlike the Idealism suggested by that cardinal principle of romanticism referred to earlier. Loewenberg goes on then to say that "The comparison will shock those who regard Hegel as the apostle of 'panlogism' of which romanticists are indeed the passionate adversaries. None the less, the dialectical logic as a method of Impersonation may be seen to lie cheek by jowl with the spirit of romanticism." [35] Loewenberg's conclusion is equally apposite to my own, and follows upon his description of the nature of irony as

the power to impersonate in rapid succession heterogeneous moods, passions, and attitudes, with apparent seriousness and sincerity, in order to show through subsequent parody and ridicule the artist's complete mastery over them. Romantic irony is an art essentially histrionic. It is the actor's art of concealing himself behind a character not his own, and then, the play being over, appearing without his mask to receive the plaudits for his masterly simulation, thus destroying the illusion of identity between himself and his role. Admiration for his creative art is enhanced by the recognition of disparity between his true and his assumed character. [36]

There is in the histrionic strategy—implicit particularly in Hegel's kind of Idealism but implicit as well as in German Absolute Idealism generally—that recessive strain of subjectivism in which the romantic literary tradition finds not only its cardinal ideological principle,

34. J. Loewenberg, ed., *Hegel Selections* (New York: Charles Scribner's Sons, 1929), xix-xx.
35. Ibid., xxviii.
36. Ibid., xxix.

but also the peculiar environment productive of its role-playing heroes and central themes as well. It is a strain which can only look backwards to Berkeley and Kant rather than onwards to *The Modern Tradition*. Bradley, on the other hand, gives salience as I have tried to show earlier to a dialectical ascent mounted upon the "exact equivalence" (*SE* 125) of the subjective and objective sides of developing experience and this, it seems to me, represents the distinguishing mark of his philosophy as well as the distinguishing characteristic of Eliot's best poetry. The difference between the two variant applications of the dialectical method which are here involved may perhaps be summarized as the difference between an interior life mounted upon feeling externalized or acted out in the various roles one enjoys playing ("I have seen my head [grown slightly bald] brought in upon a platter"), and an interior life progressively enriched by the creation of a self in which the roles are actualized and made real rather than merely acted out or impersonated. Inwardness as feeling expressed, or inwardness as outwardness absorbed—these seem to be the major ideological polarities dividing the post-Kantian German Absolute Idealism of Schlegel and Hegel from the post-Kantian English and American Absolute Idealism of Bradley and Bosanquet and, as a consequence, the romantic literary tradition from the modern.

It would not, I think, be inaccurate to say that the dialectical conception of "soul-making"—the conception, that is, of the *significant self-in-becoming* with which Eliot identifies his Quester Hero in *The Waste Land*—is the most seminal of all his critical concepts and provides the hidden root from which everything else proliferates. At whatever point one engages Eliot's life, his mind, or his art, it is that concept which one finds lying in the midst of all —so much so that it can provide to the student of Eliot's work a convenient thread with which to weave his elaborate embroideries on the doctrine into one luminous and significant tapestry. Whether the concept of "soul-making" came first, was accepted on its own merits as philosophically viable, and then its fruits applied to the "personal and private agonies" (*SE* 117) of "the man who suffers" (*SE* 8), or whether it was in fact the relevance of the theory to his own situation that led Eliot to accept the doctrine of creative transubstantiation provided for him by the New Idealism is not for us to say. Suffice it to recall here that the critical years, both in his personal life and in the formulation of his philosophy were the same, for it was during the first two years of his marriage (1915-

1916) that Eliot wrote the major portion of his Bradley dissertation.

What, on the other hand, is so remarkable about *The Waste Land* is the way in which Eliot's life, his poetic theory, and his philosophy converge there to provide the poem with the dialectical hero, the dialectical theme, and the dialectical form necessary to the successful emergence of a truly modern neo-epic of the interior life. It is just such an epic which, in my view, *The Waste Land* was "aiming to be," for it is just such an epic which the "particles" belonging to "the man who suffers" had it in them to become. It is not such generalized "particles" as those Eliot has himself referred us to in the phrase, "numberless feelings, phrases, images" (*SE* 8), that have been of particular interest to us in the present study but rather the "particles" specific to the phenomenal Eliot himself, and to which the elaborate web of his allusions has led us: the "rude unknown *psychic material*" bequeathed to him by his first marriage, the particles of philosophy he derived mainly from his study of the New Idealism, *le paysage intérieur* he absorbed from Baudelaire, the Christianized doctrine of the purgatorial ascent which came to him from Dante and from an earlier mythology, and so much more. If Eliot in 1921 was unable successfully to participate in that "mind which creates"—the mind, that is, through which those particles of his own experience might have been fused into "a new whole" the reason, I have suggested, lies in those three major unresolved conflicts which *The Waste Land* reveals, and which I have attempted to detail in the present study—the conflicts, that is, between the underlying postulates of public and private, scenic and psychic, and romantic and modern. It is because of those conflicts that Eliot's presentation of the dialectical hero and of the dialectical theme is sometimes obscured, and that his usage of dialectical form is sporadic and uncertain. In our concluding chapter, it will become one of our special concerns to suggest those minimal changes in the poem's presentation which could have led to the resolution at least of the last of those three conflicts.

7

the
wafte land
refurbifhed

In the course of this study, it will have become progressively clear that if the process of "soul-making" is as central to the mind and art of T.S. Eliot as it is to the philosophy of F.H. Bradley, it is a process which in the various forms of itself in which it appears in the work of both men yet obeys a single logic—that triadic and stepladder logic of the concrete universal which the later idealism opposed to the dualistic logic of Kant. If the development of that logic was preeminently the achievement of Hegel in German philosophy and of Bradley and Bosanquet in English philosophy, yet it was Eliot who attempted to internalize for the first time in our literary history, and both in his literary theory and in his poetry, the radical alterations in vehicle, perspective, theme, and structure which are made necessary by it.

It is, I think, no exaggeration to say that, from the time of Kant to the present, the New Idealism has primarily been concerned not only to formulate a philosophically exact conception of that Transcendent Self which sustains, at the same time that it impels, "the Pilgrims . . . of the Absolute" (*PIV* 9) in the course of their never-ending quest but also to help us perceive and understand the nature of that "relation" between pilgrim and Absolute which is internal to the definition of either and through which both are, in time, qualified and given substance. We have spoken earlier, and in considerable detail, of the paradox which underlies that relation and now we must consider a final implication flowing from it with regard to the presentation of the Tiresias figure in *The Waste Land*.

It is because of the impossibility of this metaphysical relation— what we have already heard Eliot describe as "the impossible union / Of spheres of existence" (*DS* V)—that *awareness* of the Absolute or Transcendent Self from below time always enters the world of Eliot's poetry in much the same way that it enters Bradley's philosophy—that is, by way of an intuitive immediacy and ultimately, therefore, as a matter for faith. As Eliot has said of Immediate Experience in his thesis, it is logically speaking "a timeless unity which is not as such present either any*where* or to any*one*" (*KE* 31).[1] In Eliot's early poetry, therefore, the Absolute always appears tentatively and suggestively rather than in an explicit manner. It comes as a voice heard or as a presence felt and, in Bradley's words, "merely felt within me" (*ETR* 179), whereas later, as in the *Four Quartets,* it is presented to us in the form of a conceptual paradox to be thematically explored. In "The Love Song," the Absolute invades Prufrock's consciousness in the form of

> Streets that follow like a tedious argument
> Of insidious intent
> To lead you to an overwhelming question . . .

and also as the "human voices" which "wake" him in the end to a realization of his final dissolution amidst the wastes of time. In *The Waste Land,* the entry of the Absolute into the poem is announced by way of what I have designated earlier as "the voice of the prophet," and also by way of the "aethereal rumours" which "Revive for a moment a broken Coriolanus" (414-16) and, through him, revive as well the flagging efforts of the Quester Hero or *significant self* to "set my lands in order" (425). In *Ash Wednesday,*

1. We may recall here with profit Bradley's statement that "Philosophy demands, and in the end it rests on, what may fairly be termed faith. It has, we may say, in a sense to presuppose its conclusion in order to prove it. It tacitly assumes something in general to be true in order to carry this general truth out in detail" (*ETR* 15).

Eliot repeats what is essentially the same sentiment when he says: "A philosophy can and must be worked out with the greatest rigour and discipline in the details, but can ultimately be founded on nothing but faith: and this is the reason, I suspect, why the novelties in philosophy are only in elaboration, and never in fundamentals" (*KE* 163). Thirty-six years later, in his "Introduction" to J. Pieper's *Leisure the Basis of Culture* (New York: Pantheon Books, 1952), p. 15, Eliot will refer once again to "the necessary relation between philosophy and theology, and the implication in philosophy of some religious faith."

the Absolute appears in the Christian variant of it which Bradley himself eschewed but which Josiah Royce and other personalistic Absolutists approved—that is as

> the Word unheard,
> The Word without a word, the Word within
> The world and for the world . . .

against whose "centre" "the unstilled world still whirled" (*A W* V).[2] In the *Four Quartets,* finally, the Absolute appears variously —sometimes, as earlier, in a suggestive way as, for example, in the reference to that which is "heard, half-heard, in the stillness / Between two waves of the sea" (*LG* V) but more often, and more significantly now, the Absolute appears in the paradoxical form required both by Bradley's own formulation of its nature and by the Christian doctrine of Incarnation as well. It appears as "The point of intersection of the timeless / With time" (*DS* V) and its existence therefore is metaphorically defined both as a "moment in and out of time" (*DS* V) and as "the still point of the turning world" (*BN* II) except for which "There would be no dance, and there is only the dance" (*BN* II).

To those who have never heard those "Whispers of Immortality" which are engendered within us by the presence there of the Absolute, nor raised them if heard to the level of consciousness, Eliot must always remain a poet with little or nothing to say, but Eliot's personae are not of these. They *have* heard them and that is precisely their problem for to have heard them is ever after to be possessed by the requirement internal to the experience of the

2. Bradley's position in this matter is clear, crisp, and consistent with his philosophy as a whole. He says: "I have not, I know, to repeat to those who are acquainted with my book that for me the Absolute is not God" (*ETR* 248). Contrast with this view, shared in by both Bradley and Bosanquet, the alternative views of such other Absolute Idealists as Josiah Royce, Thomas Hill Green, Andrew Seth Pringle-Pattison, and A. E. Taylor, some of whose work Eliot refers to approvingly in a footnote (*Use of* 135) and who says, for example: "I have never disguised it from myself that when I speak of the 'absolute' I mean by the word precisely that simple, absolutely transcendent, source of all things which the great Christian scholastics call God. I would add that when, following the tradition of my own teachers, I speak of the 'creatures' as 'appearances' of the Absolute, I mean by this precisely what St. Thomas, for example, meant by the doctrine that they have being by 'participation'." A. E. Taylor, *Elements of Metaphysics,* 7th ed. (London: Methuen and Company, 1924), p. xiii. This substitution of the "absolutely transcendent" in the scholastic sense for the "transcendental" in the dialectical sense represents what is clearly a metaphysical no-no for Bradley. I cannot think that very much of his philosophy, and certainly nothing of primary significance, would be left standing if that substitution were to be rigorously applied.

Absolute—the need, that is, to endure that "process of depersonalization" (*SE* 7) which its becoming makes necessary for them. That process—a process of transmutation in service of the whole and one "Costing not less than everything" (*LG* V)—is the process through which *the significant self,* "Timeless, and undesiring" (*BN* V), itself finally comes to be.

Thus, at one end of Bradley's philosophy and of Eliot's poetry as well is the Transcendent Self and, at the other, the empirical self. The Quester Hero or *significant self-in-becoming,* on the other hand, is not identical in *substance* with either but is instead that paradoxical organism which exists at "the still point" (*BN* II) of Eliot's polarities and serves to resolve his antinomies as they did those of Bradley before him. It is this transcendental and self-generating organism, partially in time but finally not of it, which is to be found at the centre of Eliot's mind and art and to which his poetry introduces us. It is also this same *significant self-in-becoming* which, throughout the whole of his literary career, Eliot went on everywhere to oppose, both suggestively and systematically, to the phenomenal "personality" he found at the base of romantic literary theory and practice.

In the task of formulating a philosophically exact conception of the Transcendent Self and also of its first cousin that "living copula" (*PIV* 371) or *significant self* by which its becoming is temporalized—unqualified success was hardly to be looked for. What was more often given to us by the philosophers instead was each time only "a different kind of failure" (*EC* V). It was nonetheless to that same task that Eliot devoted much of his poetic art for, being both philosopher and poet, it was inevitable that the task of giving luminous and concrete expression to these subtle and difficult philosophical conceptions should devolve preeminently upon him. In *The Waste Land,* however, he failed as so many of the philosophers had done before him and returned us once again to the discontinuities of Kant. What Eliot has presented us with in *The Waste Land* are two protagonists—the Quester Hero or poet-protagonist of the poem on the one hand, and Tiresias whom he has described as "the most important personage in the poem" on the other. In my first chapter, I have suggested some of the possible reasons for his having done so. The present chapter, on the other hand, has begun with an account of some of the ways in which the Absolute or Transcendent Self (of which Tiresias and the other prophet figures in the poem are the obvious symbols) *normally*

155

enter the world of Eliot's poetry—ways all of them consonant with the philosophical doctrines of which they are a literary expression. Those examples can serve to show us how minimal indeed were the changes Eliot needed to make in *The Waste Land* with regard to the presentation of the Tiresias figure in order to bring that figure into harmony with his own philosophical postulates and into conformity with the requirements of that neo-epic of modernity which his poem, in my view, was "aiming to be."

It is in the typist scene that the Tiresias figure makes its only appearance and if we examine this scene exactly as we see it on the page, we will find that what I regard as shifts in the tonality of "one voice," the voice of the poet-protagonist of the poem, others regard as actual shifts in personae and, consequently, in point of view, with lines 207-14, for example, assigned to one voice, and lines 215-56 to another. The first voice has never, to my knowledge, been identified, and the second is assumed to be that of Tiresias. What "relation" the two have to one another has apparently not seemed worth questioning. The fact that these two "voices" are tonally and temporally the same, and decidedly different from the gentle lyric melancholy of Tiresias' voice as it was heard and recorded many generations ago "by Thebes below the wall" (245) should have alerted the sensitive reader to the fact that what is involved here is not an actual shift from the persona of the poet-protagonist to that of Tiresias but a momentary fusion of their similar "observations" and "states" within that mind in which they both share.

The same reader would have been disturbed by two other problems which appear in this scene: one, the breakdown of Eliot's syntax in lines 218-23 and two, his inconsistent, and therefore unintelligible, use of parentheses in this passage (and, we may add, elsewhere in the poem as well). Technically in this instance, all that was required of "the better craftsman" when the *ur-Waste Land* was presented to him was the substitution of a period for the comma which follows the word "sea" in line 221, and the enclosure of all three of the Tiresias bits in parentheses, instead only of one. This would have rendered Eliot's punctuation in this passage consistent with itself and with the dialectical form we have seen Eliot give to the technique of the interior monologue which he was using and which we have analysed earlier in "The Fire Sermon." It would be clear then that what we are hearing in the typist scene is a continuation of that voice of the protagonist as observer or as cinematic narrator which we identified earlier, and which Eliot utilizes to unroll the whole dreary business before our eyes and before those of the Quester Hero with whom our angle of vision is identified. The momentary intrusion of the Tiresias bits would not disturb that angle of vision nor the psychological continuity which encloses it but would function instead as one more literary memory from a historical past that, in collision with "observations" from a contemporary present, universalizes the situation and effects, in protagonist and reader alike, the lyric melancholy arrested for us in the plaintive rhythm of the lines. That the fusion between the protagonist and Tiresias is at this juncture in the poem very nearly complete does not, in short, justify the shift in point of view which even so perceptive a reader of Eliot's poetry as Kenner postulates.[3]

The voice of Tiresias is one of those five portentously solemn voices in the poem which are so reminiscent of the gods and of their prophets and which I referred to earlier as "the voice of the prophet." That voice is heard first in the sinister lines addressed to the Son of Man (20-30); next, perhaps, in the pubkeeper's "HURRY UP PLEASE ITS TIME" in Part II; then in the typist scene presently under review; again, in the Augustinian lines climaxing Part III; and finally in the brief words attributed to the Thunder and his auditors near the close of the poem (400-91, 410-11, 417-18). What really distinguishes these "dramatic voices" (dramatic in the sense defined earlier of being voices "heard" by the protagonist and internalized by him but readily distinguishable from his own) from the others in *The Waste Land* is the superior angle of vision they share. These prophetic figures do not themselves reside permanently in the *waste land* as the protagonist does, nor are they really of time—historical time, that is. Hence the gloss of extratemporal inclusiveness which they provide and the sense which they create of an immemorial and transcendent racial wisdom—an unwobbly pivot, as it were—against which the temporal pilgrim in time can stabilize himself or even, perhaps, shore his ruins. To confuse any one of these voices, however, with that of the poet-protagonist of the poem is to destroy irrevocably any possibility of perceiving the only unity to which this poem can aspire, and the fact that Eliot himself has led us to this disastrous confusion does not, in my view, give to his critics a warrant for compounding that confusion indefinitely.

3. H. Kenner, *The Invisible Poet: T. S. Eliot* (London: Methuen, 1965), p. 143.

Within the stepladder logic of the New Idealism, as we have seen earlier, "the way up is the way down, the way forward is the way back" (*DS* III). Given this context, "the voice of the prophet"— whenever it appears in Eliot's poetry—may always be taken as symbolizing "the way down" or as representing the downward spiral of the Absolute in its invasion of the temporal order and of the patient "finite centre" of experience Bradley describes as residing there (*ETR* 414). Accordingly, *awareness* of the Absolute from below time and within such a "finite centre" must then be viewed as representing the moment wherein the two contrary gyres or movements of the timeless and time intersect "At the still point of the turning world" (*BN* II)—the moment wherein the mind of the universe comes to consciousness of itself within the phenomenal minds of its dialectical heroes: "To be conscious is not to be in time" (*BN* II). It is that visionary moment of intersection between awareness and awared, truth and reality, which then initiates a new and further stage in the process of transcendental becoming through the now self-conscious and purposeful creativity of its temporal vehicles—the process indicated in the movement of that upward spiral to the Absolute shown in our diagram.

In this commentary on the diagram of Bradley's philosophy provided earlier, I have been attempting to suggest something of the way in which the dialectical hero, his theme, and the form proper to its expression, all come together both in Eliot's philosophy and in his poetry as well. To demonstrate that Eliot, in his *Four Quartests,* managed finally to create in our time "the new (the really new) work of art" (*SE* 5) which is so precisely to the extent that its persona, theme, and form, constitute a precise literary correlative of what the deepest insights of twentieth-century philosophy and science have cooperated to make possible may well be the generative impulse to another book. What can be done here instead, and by way of conclusion to this study of *The Waste Land,* is to demonstrate that it is the ideological links provided by Bradley's philosophy that can alone serve to reveal the full integrity which Eliot's poetry does indeed have and thus to endow it with the further dignity of an *oeuvre.*

The significance of a turning point in literary history such as that delineated in the poetry of T. S. Eliot is that one can descry in the distance the end to which the new road leads and on which the first step has now already been taken. That end for Eliot was, to a great extent, predetermined by his early and profound absorption in the

New Idealism of F. H. Bradley and it has been at least part of my concern in the present study to detail the relevance of Eliot's philosophical beginnings to his poetic ends. That relevance is not all of a piece nor, in each new poetic venture, is it of equal importance but in one way or another the influence of Bradley's thought runs everywhere through Eliot's mind and art and creates there a shadowed underpattern which is worthy of some relief and which it may be worthwhile to resume here.

Those of Eliot's readers who have managed, one way or another, to get through his early philosophical writings, and through the latter half of the present study as well, will have been apprised of the fact that, in probing the relation between *Experience and the Objects of Knowledge in the Philosophy of F. H. Bradley*,[4] what Eliot was attempting to do was to formulate for himself a viable theory of the mind which, if already closeted together with its objects, would make possible nonetheless the transcendence of the egocentric predicament of nineteenth-century psychology, epistemology, and art, and thus make possible as well the attainment of limited but genuine Degrees of Truth and Reality. That theory—ultimately neither realistic nor idealistic in kind and departing from Bradley's own formulation in some peripheral and other not so peripheral ways—is nonetheless, Eliot has assured us, "in substantial agreement with *Appearance and Reality*" (*KE* 153). Each of his four major poems—"The Love Song of J. Afred Prufrock," *The Waste Land, Ash Wednesday* and *Four Quartets*—reveals some aspect or other of that theory and of "the general doctrine to which . . . [it] points" (*KE* 154), and the four together may be said to constitute as complete a poetic equivalent of its philosophical substance as we are ever likely to achieve.

It is in the *Four Quartets* that Eliot finally attained the unique stature of a philosophical poet, thereby at a stroke rivalling Milton and approximating the grandeur of Dante, for it is in the *Four Quartets* that he gave consummate poetic expression to the significant historical lineaments of post-Hegelian English and American philosophical thought and thus achieved in fact the composition of that philosophical poem to which the romantic poets before him could only aspire.

It is in the mandala whose structure underlies that of the *Quartets* that those lineaments can be most quickly and most clearly discerned for, if the four quadrants of the mandala are created by the

4. This was the original title of Eliot's dissertation. See *KE* 11.

intersection of its horizontal diameter by a vertical one within a closed circle, that structure merely images in a concrete visible form each of the pivotal doctrines within post-Hegelian Absolute Idealism on which the wheel of that philosophy finally turns. Within the circle of the Absolute, it is "The dove descending" (*LG* IV) which, by its vertical descent into and intersection with, the linear order of time establishes the cross as at the centre of all absoluteness. Thus the Way of the Cross will become the one and only way for the self stretched upon its intersecting beams to enter, by degrees and "With the drawing of this Love and the voice of this Calling" (*LG* V), into the life of the Absolute and the wheel of its Becoming. It is a life and a way within which the self, "In response to / The unheard music in the shrubbery" (*BN* I) and to "The dove descending," is progressively unhinged, as it were, from the merely linear world of "Time before and time after" (*BN* III) and urged into a spiral of ascent—an unsymmetrical movement which, being spiral, is therefore no longer either totally linear or totally vertical in nature but one whose ever-widening coil is created by the interactive tension of the opposing forces involved.

If Eliot, in the *Four Quartets,* has not so much embodied Bradley's philosophy as replaced it with "its complete equivalent in vision" (*TSW* 161), he has in the three major poems which preceded the *Four Quartets* given expression to the impact made upon him by one or other of the various doctrines within that philosophy which, at the particular time involved, was uppermost in his mind. Anyone attempting, therefore, to define the relation of Eliot's other major poems—"The Love Song of J. Alfred Prufrock," *The Waste Land,* and *Ash Wednesday*—to the *Four Quartets* cannot but be reminded of Wordsworth's Preface to his own projected but never completed philosophical poem, *The Recluse,* a poem which he described in terms of "a gothic church." "(H)is minor Pieces," Wordsworth added, "when they shall be properly arranged, will be found by the attentive Reader to have such connection with the main Work as may give them claim to be likened to the little cells, oratories, and sepulchral recesses, ordinarily included in those edifices." And so it is, we may say, with Eliot's poetry as well for, if Eliot would not likely have compared the *Four Quartets* to a gothic cathedral, yet he would certainly have approved the conception of a significant poet's work as comprising an "*oeuvre*" (*SE* 171) which, in the unity it effects, expresses his total poetic vision. In Eliot's case, the curve of that vision follows precisely that of the history of the *significant self-in-becoming* which had been progressively delineated by Bradley, and by others as well, in the various doctrines of late nineteenth- and early twentieth-century philosophical thought, and to which the Keatsian phrase, "Soul-making," was then applied.

When, in turn, we apply to Eliot's poetic world the historical and philosophical perspectives implicit in the consideration of it as "a vale of Soul-making," what we find is that if, on the one hand, the poetry offers what is perhaps one of the easier, and assuredly the comeliest, of all possible vehicles for understanding at least something of the philosophy of Bradley and Eliot, an understanding of their philosophy on the other hand provides one of the more effective entrées into the layered depths of Eliot's poetry and into a clearer perception of just what is there to be perceived.

In "The Love Song of J. Alfred Prufrock," what is there to be perceived is the peculiarly Bradleian ambience created in Prufrock's person by the *continuity* of the two selves within it and by the spiral of ascent to which its dialectic urges him. The imperatives of Prufrock, however, being pre-Kantian and romantic in nature, are uncategorical ("No! I am not Prince Hamlet, nor was meant to be") and, as a consequence of the early nineteenth-century theory of the nuclear self and of its mind which underlies his Byronic postures, Prufrock forms within himself not the character of the Quester Hero to which Eliot will eventually lead us but the character instead of the Anti-Hero in which he finds its precise literary foil. Thus, what Eliot gives us in "The Love Song" is a minor masterpiece of negation—a satiric commentary on an earlier and debased theory of the self-enclosed mind and its debilitating effects on the man arrested within it and unable therefore "to force the moment to its crisis."

It is in *The Waste Land* that Eliot sought for the first time, but with only partial success, to delineate the character of the Quester Hero and to reveal that character to us in the process of its actual formation as such. *The Waste Land,* however, is Eliot's *Hamlet*—his most notable "artistic failure" (*SE* 123)—and one in which the two selves —that of the poet-protagonist or Quester Hero and that of Tiresias —are seen as external to, or disjoined from, one another instead of as continuous with and integral to the formation of one another. The premises are once again dualistic and what Eliot gives us in *The Waste Land* is accordingly "two souls" (*KE* 206) or selves (empirical and Transcendent), not as operative within one Whole of Experience which mediates the expansion of one through the progressive working of the other (and also unifies the poem in the process) but as two distinct protagonists whose points of view serve instead to split the poem apart.

This technical defect is made up in *Ash Wednesday* and what we see delineated as a consequence is the second of the two major forms under which the process of empirical self-development or "soul-making" takes place. Bradley has indicated what those two forms are in the following statement: "Under what main aspects then, let us ask, is experience found? We may say, speaking broadly, that there are two great modes, perception and thought on the one side, and will and desire on the other side" (*AR* 405). Eliot's immediate concern in *The Waste Land* was clearly with the former of these two aspects and therefore with the attainment of a substantive truth whereas, in *Ash Wednesday,* he was just as clearly concerned to dramatize the depersonalization of personal will and of personal desire inasmuch as "soul-making" must involve *all* the faculties of the soul. What we are allowed to see in *Ash Wednesday* is the struggle of the personal will as it transcends itself in a coiling spiral of ascent which, in this poem, is also and primarily a spiral of assent as well to the working of what Bradley calls the "indwelling will" of the divine within us (*ETR* 435).

Thus what one finds in the poetry of T. S. Eliot is not so much the philosophy of F. H. Bradley as a precise literary variant of it and of its central motifs. Literal identity between the two is not to be looked for, for that is neither possible nor desirable even if it were. What a historical perspective allows instead to those who would apply it to the illumination of poetry is evidence of those mutative effects which result when the material of philosophy is transformed by its relocation in a different context and charged thereby with the new and visionary *telos* of poetry. At an interesting juncture in his *Speculations* T. E. Hulme introduces the following suggestive image: "The fountain turned on. It has a definite geometrical shape, but the shape did not exist before it was turned on . . . . But the little pipes are there before, which give it the shape as soon as the water is turned on."[5] Taken as a metaphor, the view implied is that if the proliferous flesh of Eliot's mind and art is to be seen as composing one *oeuvre* or body, that body must be seen as gathered around the spinal cord of Bradley's philosophy. In short, "the

5. T. E. Hulme, *Speculations,* ed. Herbert Read, 2nd ed. (New York: Harcourt, Brace and Company, 1924), p. 240.

little pipes . . . which give it the shape" and the order it has are his, and if we were, therefore, to place ourselves at the centre of Eliot's philosophic vision, not only would we understand the many different things it has made him say throughout his life, but we would see as well how undeviatingly true he has been to his philosophical beginnings. It is from this perspective that Eliot's four major poems may be seen as four quadrants in search of a circle—the circle of Bradley's Absolute—and it is also but only from this perspective that *The Waste Land* can be judged a failure. It is, in short, a failure only in Bradley's sense of that word—relative, that is, to the attainment of the Absolute. Of such failures, it can only be said that we could certainly use more of them.

appendix I

TOWARDS AN UNDERSTANDING OF ELIOT'S LIFE

"People change, and smile; but the agony abides." (*DS* II)

Because of continuing copyright restrictions, the biographical material relevant to an understanding of those "personal and private agonies" (*SE* 117) which provided Eliot with the "creative germ" (*OPP* 97) of *The Waste Land* must be pieced together by the diligent reader for himself from three fairly recent and notable publications: Mrs. Eliot's editorial introduction to *The Waste Land: A Facsimile and Transcript of the Original Drafts Including the Annotations of Ezra Pound* (London: Faber and Faber, 1971), ix - xxix; the three volumes of *The Autobiography of Bertrand Russell* (London: George Allen and Unwin Ltd., 1967, 1968, and 1970 respectively); and, finally, Donald Adamson, ed., *T. S. Eliot: A Memoir by Robert Sencourt* (New York: Dodd, Mead & Company, 1971).

In her editorial introduction to the Facsimile Edition of *The Waste Land,* Mrs. Eliot has directed her primary efforts towards a recreation of the enormous financial stress under which Eliot laboured between the years 1915 and 1924. A most sympathetic portrait of the struggling and finally exhausted poet emerges, and does so largely because Mrs. Eliot has allowed her husband to speak to us directly and for himself through his own letters. Mrs. Eliot has refrained from any extended commentary on the correspondence she quotes, and thus interposes nothing of an interpretative or critical nature between the reader and the letters themselves. Many of the letters make reference to Eliot's own ill-health as well as that of his first wife and, as the final breakdown late in 1921 draws near, Eliot—writing from The Albemarle Hotel at Margate—gives us his own diagnosis of the malaise by which his lands have been laid waste: "I am satisfied, since being here, that my 'nerves' are a very mild affair, due not to overwork but to an aboulie and emotional derangement which has been a lifelong affliction. Nothing wrong with my mind—"(xxii). Having written those lines to Richard Aldington, Eliot might well have written the following lines immediately thereafter:

"On Margate Sands.
I can connect
Nothing with nothing.
The broken fingernails of dirty hands."
(*TWL* 300-6)

What *The Autobiography of Bertrand Russell* adds to our understanding of these critical years in Eliot's life derives from the insights it provides into what can only be described as the almost bizarre union of T. S. Eliot and Vivienne Haigh-Wood in 1915, for it would be difficult indeed to find two less likely candidates for a successful marriage than were these. Eliot married Vivienne Haigh-Wood on June 26 of that year. Just a few days after the wedding, the Eliots dined with Russell and, in one paragraph of a letter he wrote to Lady Ottoline Morrell, his mistress at that time, Russell described their evening together as follows:

Friday evg. I dined with my Harvard pupil, (T. S.) Eliot, and his bride. I expected her to be terrible, from his mysteriousness; but she was not so bad. She is light, a little vulgar, adventurous, full of life—an artist I think he said, but I should have thought her an actress. He is exquisite and listless; she says she married him to stimulate him, but finds she can't do it. Obviously he married in order to be stimulated. I think she will soon be tired of him. She refuses to go to America to see his people, for fear of submarines. He is ashamed of his marriage, and very grateful if one is kind to her. (II, 54)

This letter, perhaps more than any other, suggests the nature of that "rude unknown *psychic material*" which, my argument proposes, led Eliot to tell "that particular story" (*OPP* 110) which he did—the "story" of *The Waste Land* and its impotent Fisher King.

The further story of the relationship which soon developed between Russell and Eliot's first wife, together with the progressive breakdown of the marriage thereafter, is pieced together—somewhat uncertainly and with a good deal of irrelevant emotion—by Robert Sencourt in his *T. S. Eliot: A Memoir*. However this may be, the marriage ended finally in 1932. In the fall of that year, when Eliot made his triumphal return to America and to Harvard to deliver the Charles Eliot Norton lectures there, he returned alone and, in February of 1933, while he was still occupied with the fifth of those lectures, Eliot instructed his solicitor to prepare a deed of separation from his wife and to deliver personally with it the letter he wrote breaking the news to her. When Vivienne's brother, Maurice, asked Eliot if he could not find some other, less cruel, way of telling her than by writing to her through his solicitor, Eliot replied despairingly: "What other way *can* I find?" (p. 197).

The lurid light cast upon Eliot's "La Figlia Che Piange"—a poem written four years before he had even met Vivienne Haigh-Wood and twenty-two years before he had separated from her—is too remarkable to let pass unnoticed. In that poem, we see Eliot's persona acting out a future yet unborn:

So I would have had him leave,
So I would have had her stand and grieve,
So he would have left
As the soul leaves the body torn and bruised,
As the mind deserts the body it has used.
I should find
Some way incomparably light and deft,
Some way we both should understand,
Simple and faithless as a smile and shake of the hand.

In the concluding lines of the poem, Eliot's persona is bereft finally both of his cruelty and of the "gesture and . . . [the] pose" he used to dramatize it. When twenty-two years later, Eliot himself needed "Some way incomparably light and deft" whereby to mediate both for his wife and for himself the rending pain of final separation, he too was bereft of any effective resources with which to do so. He could only gather into his own "heart of darkness" that "horror" of which a prevision seems to have been given him in 1911.

In my introduction, I have indicated Eliot's general aversion to biographical criticism, together with his stated reasons for it. It was the rooting instinct, when it was applied by such critics as F. W. Bateson to the digging up of "the real secret" (*OPP* 122) behind a man's work, that particularly invited Eliot's censure in his essay on "The Frontiers of Criticism." The state of literary criticism has unfortunately not changed very much since Eliot wrote that essay, and neither has Mr. Bateson. When Eliot's own correspondence, together with that of Bertrand Russell, begins to be amplified by the psychology of rumour and is then sliced with a liberal degree of innuendo as well, we may be certain that the emergence of "the real secret" behind Eliot's poetry and criticism will henceforward and relentlessly be urged upon us. The first salvos in that ungallant war have already been fired in Sencourt's *Memoir* and, even before that, in John Peter's "A New Interpretation of *The Waste Land,*" (*Essays in Criticism,* XIX, 2 (April 1969), 140-64). It is noteworthy, I suppose, that John Peter's publisher was the same Mr. F. W. Bateson referred to above. It would seem that old grudges never die; nor do they even fade away. They just reappear in libel suits instead. The only safeguard available to Eliot's life, his mind, and his art against "such information or conjecture as that of . . . Mr. Bateson" on Wordsworth's love for his sister (*OPP* 112), or that of Mr. Peter on Eliot's romantic attachments, must be in the publication of his letters in full—a release Eliot has himself authorized and one which we can only hope will occur soon.

appendix II

". . . to be restored, our sickness must grow worse." (EC IV)

The convictions underlying the perennial methods of historical scholarship have been so seriously eroded in recent years that some readers will perhaps regard the philosophical material included in the present study as a somewhat unsightly wart disfiguring an otherwise not unamiable face. As a consequence, a word of explanation may be in order regarding both the genesis and the development of the Bradleian vein in Eliot studies generally. What follows therefore is a chronological (and I believe exhaustive) bibliography isolating that vein and, in the first instance, annotating its primary material. Entries involving secondary material are briefly annotated as well in the commentary which follows.

THE BRADLEIAN VEIN IN ELIOT STUDIES: A CHRONOLOGICAL AND ANNOTATED BIBLIOGRAPHY

1. 1916   ELIOT, T. S. "Leibniz' Monads & Bradley's Finite Centres." *Monist* XXVI, 4 (October 1916), [566]-576. (Gallup A75b, c; C35)

This essay, if it constitutes Eliot's first published commentary on the philosophy of F. H. Bradley, yet was written concurrently with (or just after the completion of) his doctoral dissertation on Bradley entitled *Experience & the Objects of Knowledge in the Philosophy of F. H. Bradley*. (See entries 17 and 18, and Eliot's Preface to *Knowledge and Experience*, p. 11). When, in conjunction with Mr. Eliot, I was editing the Bradley thesis for publication, I had occasion to write to him concerning this essay as follows:

I am in disagreement with your view . . . that it is at most a page that is missing from the concluding chapter of the thesis. If I may hazard a guess, I would say that it is some seven or eight pages that are missing, and that they very probably are missing because they were removed (and never restored) during the preparation of your article on "Leibniz's Monads and Bradley's Finite Centers." In any event, that article, in my view, constitutes the completion of the argument which is left in mid-air at the end of the thesis. The closeness of the relationship existing between the two is what leads me to suggest the advisability of including the two *Monist* articles as appendices to the Bradley essay itself instead of allowing me to reprint them as appendices to my study—something which you yourself suggested at our meeting in November. (10 February 1963)

2. 1922   Eliot's first published literary reference to Bradley by way of his note to line 412 of *The Waste Land.*

3. 1924   ELIOT, T. S. "A Prediction in Regard to Three English Authors: [F. H. Bradley, J. G. Frazer, and H. James]." *Vanity Fair* XXI (6 February 1924), 29, 98. (Gallup CI53)
The source of Eliot's memorable but problematic statement that:

Bradley is wholly and solely a philosopher. . . . Philosophy may be futile or profitable, he seems to say, but if you are to pursue it at all, you must work with such and such data —which are neither literature nor science. All we can do is to accept these data, and follow our argument to the end. If it ends, as it may well end, in zero, well, we have at least the satisfaction of having pursued something to the end, and of having ascertained that certain questions which occur to men to ask, are unanswerable or are meaningless. Once you accept his theory of the nature of judgment, and it is as plausible a theory as any, you are led by his arid and highly sensitive eloquence (no English philosopher has ever written finer English) to something which, according to your temperament, will be resignation or despair—the bewildered despair of wondering why you ever wanted anything, and what it was that you wanted, since this philosophy seems to give you everything that you ask, and yet to render it not worth wanting. (pp. 29, 98)

4. 1924 ——————. "A Commentary." *Criterion* III, 9 (October 1924), 1-2. (Gallup C157)

Eliot's obituary notice on Bradley in the *Criterion,* and source for the following statement made use of in the present study:

Few will ever take the pains to study the consummate art of Bradley's style, the finest philosophic style in our language, in which acute intellect and passionate feeling preserve a classic balance: only those who will surrender patient years to the understanding of his meaning. But upon these few, both living and unborn, his writings perform that mysterious and complete operation which transmutes not one department of thought only, but the whole intellectual and emotional tone of their being. To them, in the living generation, the news of his death has brought an intimate, and private grief.

F. 1927 . "Bradley's Ethical Studies." *Times Literary Supplement* 1352 (29 December 1927), [981]-982. Unsigned. Later reprinted as "Francis Herbert Bradley" in T. S. Eliot, *Selected Essays* (London: Faber and Faber, 1932), pp. 394-404. (Gallup C239 and A12, 21, and 31)

Eliot's fullest literary treatment of Bradley's historic significance. Notable too for the following statement on the continuity of the "two souls" (or selves) germane to the present study: "The distinction is not between a 'private self' and a 'public self' or a 'higher self', it is between the individual as himself, and no more, a mere numbered atom, and the individual in communion with God" (p. 402).

6. 1938 CHURCH, R. W. "Eliot on Bradley's Metaphysics." *Harvard Advocate* CXXV 3 (December 1938), 24-26. (Gallup C440)

7. 1949 SMIDT, Kristian. *Poetry and Belief in the Work of T. S. Eliot.* Oslo: I Kommisjon Hos Jacob Dybwad, 1949.

8.   1952   ELIOT, T. S. "Introduction" in Josef Pieper, *Leisure the Basis of Culture* (London: Faber and Faber, 1952), pp. 11-17. (Gallup B65)
Contains yet another of Eliot's problematical—indeed almost perverse—statements on the philosophy of Bradley and on the source of its particular persuasiveness: "I would mention also the work of such a writer as F. H. Bradley, which owes its persuasiveness to a masterly prose style. The charm of the author's personality stimulates an agreeable state of feeling: and such books will continue to be read as literature, for the enlargement of our experience through a contact with powerful and individual minds" (p. 17).

     1954   Transfer of Eliot's Bradley thesis from the archives of the Department of Philosophy in Eliot House to the Houghton Library of Harvard University.

9.   1956   SMITH, Grover. *T. S. Eliot's Poetry and Plays: A Study in Sources and Meaning.* Chicago: University of Chicago Press, 1956.

10.   1958   MATTHIESSEN, F. O. *The Achievement of T. S. Eliot (1935).* 3rd ed., revised and enlarged. New York: Oxford University Press, 1958.
The third edition of Matthiessen's book was the first to include the Biographical Note (xiv-xxiii)—added I believe by C. L. Barber—in which some mention is made of Eliot's philosophical background and training, though still not of his Bradley thesis.

11.   1960   BOLGAN, Anne C. "Mr. Eliot's Philosophical Writings, or What the Thunder Said." Unpublished doctoral dissertation. University of Toronto, 1960.

12.   1960   KENNER, Hugh. *The Invisible Poet: T. S. Eliot.* London: W. H. Allen, 1960.

13.   1961   ELIOT, T. S. "To Criticize the Critic." The sixth Convocation Lecture delivered at the University of Leeds in July 1961. Later reprinted in T. S. Eliot, *To Criticize The Critic* (London: Faber and Faber, 1965), pp. 11-26.
Contains another Eliot statement concerning the nature and extent of Bradley's influence upon him as well as the following somewhat misleading statement

concerning the length of his own philosophical studies:

> But I am certain of one thing: that I have written best about writers who have influenced my own poetry. And I say 'writers' and not only 'poets', because I include F. H. Bradley, whose works—I might say whose personality as manifested in his works—affected me profoundly. . . . I include, in fact, any writers whether of verse or prose, whose style has strongly affected my own. . . . I spent three years, when young, in the study of philosophy. What remains to me of these studies? The style of three philosophers: Bradley's English, Spinoza's Latin, and Plato's Greek. (pp. 20-21)

14. 1962   BOLLIER, E. P. "T. S. Eliot and F. H. Bradley: A Question of Influence." *Tulane Studies in English* XII (1962), 87-111.

15. 1962   FREED, Lewis. *T. S. Eliot: Aesthetics and History.* La Salle, Illinois: Open Court Publishing Company, 1962.

16. 1963   THOMPSON, Eric. *T. S. Eliot: The Metaphysical Perspective.* Carbondale: Southern Illinois University Press, 1963.

17. 1963   MOE, Charles. "T. S. Eliot and F. H. Bradley." *Delta* (Summer 1963), 40-42.

A review of Mr. Eliot's own earlier and aborted edition of *Knowledge and Experience in the Philosophy of F. H. Bradley.* That edition is described by Gallup (Item A75a) as follows:

> Not published. 4961 sets of sheets were printed and 2961 were bound and delivered to the warehouse of the publishers in May 1963; the remaining 2000 sets of sheets were pulped by the binders. All save "a very few" of the bound copies were destroyed by the publishers. This abortive edition (of which an advance bound copy was inscribed by the author to his wife on 12 February 1963) was eventually replaced by the published (corrected and expanded) edition described below. (45 proof copies, so marked, bound in printed paper wrappers, were circulated and one review actually appeared—in the issue of *Delta,* Cambridge, for Summer 1963—but most of these copies were recalled by the publishers and also destroyed.) *On verso of title-leaf: First published in mcmlxiii.*

It was the large number of serious textual errors that this earlier edition of *Knowledge and Experience* revealed which, in November 1962, led me first to advise its total abandonment and then, at Mr. Eliot's invitation, to undertake the preparation of the edition which finally appeared in February 1964. I still retain one of those "very few" remaining copies of the unpublished edition and it has become now something of a bibliophile's rarity.

18. 1964 ELIOT, T. S. *Knowledge and Experience in the Philosophy of F. H. Bradley.* London: Faber and Faber, 1964. Entered by Gallup as item A75b, and described as follows:

A dissertation completed and submitted in 1916 in partial fulfilment of the requirement for the degree of Doctor of Philosophy at Harvard. The original title of the dissertation was "Experience and the Objects of Knowledge in the Philosophy of F. H. Bradley." Printed as appendices are "The Development of Leibniz' Monadism" and "Leibniz' Monads and Bradley's Finite Centres," both reprinted from the *Monist,* Chicago, Ill (October 1916)—C34 & C35—with translations of passages quoted added for this edition.

In the Preface to *Knowledge and Experience* which Gallup quotes, Eliot has alluded as follows to some of the changes made in the published version. "[Professor Anne Bolgan] has . . . . made important corrections and suggestions; she has most painstakingly edited the text. . . . She has also checked my references . . . . and has prepared a select bibliography, the index, and valuable notes." *Preface,* p. 10.

19. 1964 WOLLHEIM, Richard. "Eliot, Bradley and Immediate Experience." *New Statesman* LXVII (13 March 1964), 401-2.

20. 1964 SINGH, D. P. "The influence of F. H. Bradley on T. S. Eliot." Unpublished doctoral dissertation. University of Patna, 1964.

21. 1964 HOWARTH, Herbert. *Notes on Some Figures Behind T. S. Eliot.* Boston: Houghton Mifflin Company, 1964.

22. 1966 LU, Fei-Pai. *T. S. Eliot: The Dialectical Structure of His Theory of Poetry.* Chicago: University of Chicago Press, 1966.

23. 1966 MILLER, J. Hillis. *Poets of Reality.* Cambridge: Harvard University Press, 1966.

24. 1968   WHITESIDE, George. "T. S. Eliot's Dissertation." *Journal of English Literary History* XXXIV (September 1967), 400-24.
25. 1968   SOLDO, John J. "Knowledge and Experience in the Criticism of T. S. Eliot." *Journal of English Literary History* XXXV (June 1968), 284-308.
26. 1969   GALLUP, Donald. *T. S. Eliot: A Bibliography* (1952). 2nd ed. London: Faber and Faber, 1969.
27. 1970   WOLLHEIM, Richard. "Eliot and F. H. Bradley: an account", in Graham Martin ed., *Eliot in Perspective: A Symposium*. London: Macmillan; 1970, pp. 169-93.
28. 1971   BOLGAN, Anne C. "The Philosophy of F. H. Bradley and The Mind and Art of T. S. Eliot: An Introduction", in S. P. Rosenbaum ed., *English Literature and British Philosophy*. Chicago: University of Chicago Press, 1971, pp. 251-77.
29. 1971   AUSTIN, Allen. *T. S. Eliot: The Literary and Social Criticism*. Bloomington: Indiana University Press, 1971.

It may be helpful now to generalize the categories into which the various entries listed above may be seen to sort themselves, and then to comment briefly on some of the critical problems common to the Bradley/Eliot vein of studies generally. That vein may be conveniently subdivided into the following seven distinguishable categories, and includes:

a) the primary material which derives, of course, from Eliot himself and which may be further subdivided into those literary remarks he has made concerning Bradley or Bradley's influence upon him on the one hand, and into his own contributions to philosophical literature on the other (entries 2, 3, 4, 5, 8, and 13 comprise the former material, and entries 1 and 18, the latter);

b) those entries involving merely a reference to Eliot's philosophical writing but providing no analysis of, or extended commentary on, it—that is, entries 9 (Smith), 10 (Matthiessen), 21 (Howarth), 22 (Lu), 26 (Gallup), and 29 (Austin);

c) one or two-page reviews of *Knowledge and Experience*—that is, entries 17 (Page) and 19 (Wollheim);

d) summaries or paraphrases of *Knowledge and Experience,* together with the assertion of relevance to Eliot's thought, but with virtually no analysis or demonstration of that relevance—that is, entries 6 (Church) and 24 (Whiteside);

e) full-length studies (books or theses) concerned exclusively with the relevance of Bradley's philosophy to Eliot's literary criticism or aesthetic theory—that is, entries II (Bolgan), 15 (Freed), 16 (Thompson), and 20 (Singh);

f) journal articles, essays, and chapters of a book devoted to illuminating some specific aspect or other of Bradley's influence on Eliot's literary criticism or aesthetic theory—that is, entries 7 (Smidt: "Poetry and Belief"), 12 (Kenner: primarily a tonal and stylistic influence), 14 (Bollier: the kind of scepticism common to Bradley and Eliot), 23 (Miller: *Poets of Reality*, hence of "immediate experience"), 25 (Soldo: the source of Eliot's "objective correlative" and unified sensibility concepts), 27 (Wollheim: three "elements in Eliot's thinking that have a distinctly Bradleian character"—the "impersonal theory of the poet," the "connection between emotions and their objects," and the "dissociation of sensibility" theory), 28 (Bolgan: Eliot's concept of the "process of depersonalization" and of *the significant-self-in-becoming);*

g) books, articles, or chapters of a book concerned with the relevance of Bradley's philosophy to Eliot's poetry—that is, entries 16 (Thompson: *The Waste Land, Burnt Norton*), 23 (Miller: virtually all of Eliot's poems are referred to), 28 (Bolgan: "The Love Song of J. Alfred Prufrock," *The Waste Land, Ash Wednesday, Four Quartets).*

What is so remarkable about the publication of Eliot's philosophical writings is that here, with an amplitude and in a manner that is unique in our literary history, we have given to us by a poet, critic, and philosopher that specific metaphysical framework of ideas in relation to which his literary principles emerged and his poetic practice was formed. The particular emphasis which Eliot has himself given to the matter of Bradley's influence upon him, however, has centred around Bradley's prose style, and around the comparison which he has seen fit to invite between it and his own. In his Preface to *Knowledge and Experience,* for example, he has put the matter this way: "I can present this book only as a curiosity of biographical interest, which shows, as my wife observed at once, how closely my own prose style was formed on that of Bradley, and how little it has changed in all these years" (*KE* 10-11). That the comparison is dubious—indeed in the main quite preposterous—

has already been remarked by Richard Wollheim whose significant and thoroughly critical study of Bradley's philosophy qualifies him to speak with authority on the subject of Bradley's thought and on Bradley's method and stylistic manner of expressing it as well. Apart, however, from Wollheim's simple and direct statement that "It is possible—in fact, not hard—to disagree with Eliot's comparison of his style to Bradley's. . ." (entry 26, p. 169), the various problems inhering in Eliot's comparison have generally evaded scrutiny. Had they not done so, one of the things which would have become apparent very quickly, I should think, is that although Eliot has written often and successfully of Bradley's style, he has only rarely been able to imitate it with equal success. If Eliot's prose, that is, does indeed sometimes reveal Bradley's economy, yet it lacks the faultless clarity and precision that accompanies that economy in Bradley's case and serves to fortify the trenchant and acerbic wit which made Bradley, in Eliot's phrase, so "triumphant in polemic" (*SE* 401).

It is for these reasons, perhaps, that no one of us presently involved in the Bradley/Eliot vein (with the exception of Kenner, as will appear shortly) can quite take Eliot seriously as regards the wishful identification of his prose style with that of Bradley. Nor can we, by way of the exaggerated emphasis given to the stylistic influence, enter into the diminution of the conceptual influence which that emphasis sometimes serves to invite. Kenner (entry 12) provides an instructive example of the way in which the process of diminution begins with the influence of Bradley on Eliot, and then goes on to disparage the conceptual content of Bradley's philosophy as well. Kenner's view of the Bradleian influence, together with the general tone of his work, can perhaps most quickly and most accurately be suggested by way of direct quotation. He says:

. . . it is precisely as a stain, imparting colour to all else that passes through, that Bradley is most discernible in Eliot's poetic sensibility.

He was uniquely equipped to exert that sort of tonal influence on a disciple . . . [for it] is as a colouring, not as a body of doctrine, that he stays in the mind. (p. 39)

Naturally, a few odds and ends of what the plain reader of Bradley [are there any "plain" readers of Bradley?] would call Bradleian "doctrines" do turn up in Eliot's writings. (p. 41)

Bradley has an attractive mind, though he has perhaps nothing to tell us. He is an experience, like the taste of nectarines or the style of Henry James. (p. 54)

It is just such desultory comments as these that Kenner gives us in the one brief chapter of his book (pp. 35-59) which he devotes to a consideration of Bradley's influence on Eliot. The chapter provides no direct treatment of the Bradley thesis nor any evidence that Kenner has in fact read it, and it may be for these reasons that the conceptual influence of Bradley on Eliot seems to him to be of such negligible importance. If, on the contrary, there is any one view that is held in common by all the other writers listed above as regards the relative importance of the conceptual over the stylistic influence, that view might well be suggested by saying that wherever one scratches Eliot's thought, it is in fact Bradley's mind which bleeds.

To those who know the work of both these men, it is already abundantly clear that it is in Bradley's philosophy that we shall find the source not only for every major critical concept appearing in Eliot's literary criticism but also for that informing ideology which gives rise to the controlling images and symbols of his poetry. R. S. Crane has perhaps taken more careful notice than has anyone else of the way in which literary concepts are frequently related to and often derived from those hidden but nonetheless controlling philosophical postulates that as a consequence determine in large part their actual meaning.[1] Thus, in Eliot's case, if we would enter more profoundly into an understanding of those seminal ideas which have served to make his literary criticism so incisive and his poetry so beguiling, it would seem clear that we must examine them, not as so many of our contemporary commentators have done, in ignorance of the philosophical antecedents by which they are everywhere controlled but, rather, within the context provided for them by that particular philosophy in which they find ther genesis and within which alone their actual meaning can therefore be determined. To say this much, however, is hardly to have introduced us into Eliot's rose-garden where "all shall be well" (*LG* V) but, instead, merely to concentrate in a few lines some of the many hazards central to the critical enterprise at hand, for to suggest that the only way really to understand Eliot's poetry and criticism is by way of Bradley's even more dazzling conceptual intricacies is not unlike saying that "to be restored, our sickness must grow worse" (*EC* IV).

1. See Ronald S. Crane, ed., "Introduction," *Critics and Criticism, Ancient and Modern* (Chicago: University of Chicago Press, 1952), pp. 1-24.

It is at this juncture that the writers listed above have tended to fall somewhere between the two stools Northrop Frye once suggested to me when he said that what one finally writes in studies such as these must be too elementary for philosophers on the one hand and too peripheral for literary critics on the other. By way of reply, I could only suggest that if it is reasonable to assume that literary and philosophical achievements do interact with one another in any given age, then it must also be reasonable to assume that a method can be found for demonstrating such interaction effectively. Instead of accepting Frye's disjunction as final, that is, what one can try to do is to throw some bridges between the various disciplines involved and thus encourage in philosophers and literary critics alike the occasional stroll into one another's territorial specialties. It is to that procedure—despite the notorious difficulties involved—that all of the writers listed above have, each in his own way, devoted their various energies.

The critical task implicit in the Bradley/Eliot vein of studies is not merely one of asserting that Bradley influenced Eliot but one of determining just how and to what extent he did so. It is also important to recognize that there are times when he did *not* do so for, as Church has rightly emphasized, Eliot is not to be thought of as "merely a zealous student of Bradley, without range among the works of his author's opponents and critics" (entry 6, p. 26). When Eliot diverges from Bradley, therefore, it is with reason, and the divergencies are as significant as are the agreements. Finally, however, the most important thing of all is to determine accurately just how that influence is in fact to be read when it is obviously there, and obviously affecting the ideological content either of Eliot's poetry or of his literary theory and criticism. An example here may serve to illustrate the point better than any further discussion would do, and what better example can be found than that provided by Eliot's first literary reference to Bradley's *Appearance and Reality* in his Notes to *The Waste Land.*

In the first instance, that note refers the reader to that line of Dante's *Inferno* which translates: ". . . and below, I heard the door of the horrible tower being nailed up." This line is part of that passage in which Ugolino tells Dante how he and his sons were immured in a tower to starve. When the actual historical Ugolino was imprisoned, the keys of the tower were even thrown into the Arno. Eliot then quotes the following brief passage from *Appearance and Reality:* "My external sensations are no less private to

179

myself than are my thoughts or my feelings. In either case my experience falls within my own circle, a circle closed on the outside; and, with all its elements alike, every sphere is opaque to the others which surround it. . . . In brief, regarded as an existence which appears in a soul, the whole world for each is peculiar and private to that soul" (*AR* 306). What Eliot has done in quoting this abbreviated passage from *Appearance and Reality* is to transpose the theme of enclosure, equally expressed within the Dantean passage, to that epistemological realm within which it reappears as the prison of solipsism, the circle of experience "closed on the outside." The immediate assumption of Eliot's commentators has been that both he and Bradley therefore approve, or concur in the validity of, such a solipsistic view. It is something less than inspiring to find that in almost fifty years of commentary on *The Waste Land* no one seems to have looked up the original for, to date, the work of Eliot's critics on the implications of this note represents little more than a finely chiselled monument to this wholly unexamined assumption.

What Eliot is quoting here is a reply that Bradley made to those critics who, like the romantic epistemologists before him, would try to escape from what J. Hillis Miller, commenting on these lines, describes as "the inescapable privacy of each ego" (entry 22, p. 172), but who would do so by resting on the illusory superiority of what Bradley calls "the outer world of experience" over "our inner worlds." It is a personal variant of that solipsistic but mistaken epistemological view from which the persona of Eliot's poem suffers, and Eliot's reference to *Appearance and Reality* merely provides the reader with a convenient index both to the nature of the malady and to the direction of its cure.

Bradley's own final view of the epistemological theme of enclosure may perhaps be more accurately suggested by such statements as the following: "How I am to transcend my finite centre and to climb the walls of my pit, is, . . . [my critics] urge, inconceivable. But that they themselves argue here from premises which I reject they seem not to realize" (*ETR* 413). And again: "In short I cannot suppose that those critics who charge me with Solipsism can have much of an idea as to the position in which I stand" (*ETR* 420). Eliot's similar view of Solipsism is developed most fully in the sixth chapter of the Bradley thesis where he begins by telling us that "Solipsism has been one of the dramatic properties of most philosophical entertainers" in the past (*KE* 141), and then goes on to dispel those confusions from which he believes "the stuffed solipsism of the philosophers" (*KE* 142) to have arisen. If, on the other hand, one would see various examples of the "premisses" which both Bradley and Eliot "reject," one has only to read the commentaries, for example, of those who identify Eliot's philosophy with that of his romantic predecessors and do so without reservations of any kind.

What the example selected has been intended to show is the particular degree of truth implicit in Frye's polarization of "elementary" and "peripheral." When various accounts of the Bradley/Eliot relation have been developed in a philosophically reliable manner, as is the case with Church (entry 6), Freed (entry 15), and Wollheim (entry 27), they have tended—and almost in proportion to their skill and exactitude—to be virtually unintelligible to the general reader and peripheral, therefore, to the more nearly practical concerns of the literary critic. When, on the other hand, the accounts have been written by those whose orientation is primarily literary, as is the case with Smidt (entry 7), Kenner (entry 12), and Miller (entry 23), the results are sometimes not only elementary but inaccurate and misleading as well.

In conclusion a personal word regarding the genesis of the Bradley/Eliot vein of studies and of those events which led finally to the publication of Eliot's philosophical writings in 1964 may be allowed. It was eighteen years ago, in 1954, that quite literally I fell upon Eliot's Bradley thesis for the first time. That summer I was reading in the Houghton Library of Harvard University in preparation for the writing of my own doctoral dissertation and, having completed a perusal of all the catalogued Eliot items, I was preparing to leave Cambridge when I was invited to visit the library's private stacks. Having managed somehow to trip on the bottom two steps leading to them, I landed with an arm and hand firmly placed upon—if not quite driven into—a largish academic-looking volume which later turned out to be the Bradley thesis and which was lying on the small table which had broken my fall at the foot of the stairs. The volume to which I was thus pointedly (and somewhat rudely) directed had, that very day, arrived at the Houghton Library from the archives of the Department of Philosophy where it had lain undisturbed and virtually unknown for almost forty years. If my fortuitous "discovery" of the Bradley thesis came to me at that moment with all the stunning force usually reserved to apocalyptic visions, it was due entirely to the kindly beneficence of my own ignorance, for although Eliot in his many references to Bradley had himself never made mention either of his thesis or of his extensive philosophical background and training, others had. I soon learned, and somewhat to my chagrin, that there had already been two published references to the Bradley thesis, both of which had escaped me—one by Kristian Smidt (entry 7) who knew of its existence but had never read it, and the other by the philosopher R.W. Church (entry 6) who had not only read it but had also provided a two-page outline of it for the *Harvard Advocate* as early as 1938.

I had so long thought of Eliot as a poet and critic—indeed as the literary dictator of the twentieth century—that it was almost impossible for me on that particular day in 1954 to accept very readily the evidence that he had been a philosopher first. My resistance was quickly dissolved, however, when I flipped open the cover of the thesis and found there the letter in which the opinion of Josiah Royce that the thesis represents "the work of an expert" (*KE* 10) was quoted for Eliot by Professor J.H. Woods. I was hardly back up the stairs before my first letter to Mr. Eliot, requesting permission to read his doctoral thesis and to use it as the basis of my own, had already drafted itself in my mind. The requested permissions were immediately forthcoming and, some six years later, my doctoral thesis on Eliot and Bradley was finally completed.

When I met Mr. Eliot for the first time during the summer of 1961 and had tea with him in the offices of Faber and Faber, I buttressed my own convictions concerning the seminal importance of the Bradley thesis by referring to those implicit in Royce's remarks. I found then that the letter Professor Woods had written to Mr. Eliot in which Royce's phrase is quoted had apparently never reached him so that, when I told him of Royce's accolade, his eyes widened in delight and then, with a kind of boyish wonder and pride in his voice, he went on to ask somewhat sceptically, "Did he really like it?" I can still recall my astonishment, as I sat in the presence of my master, at seeing Eliot's eyes glisten as he was told of the praise of his own. I could not help but recall as well Yeats's lovely description of the sages in "Lapis Lazuli":

Their eyes mid many wrinkles, their eyes,
Their ancient, glittering eyes, are gay.

And so I left him, inwardly convinced that, with Royce's help, I had urged the case for the publication of his early philosophical writings somewhat more successfully than I had been able to do before. Soon after, however, I learned that Eliot had reverted to his earlier reluctance to publish his early philosophical writings at all.

I decided then to continue independently with my own examination of the Bradleian influence on Eliot, and this despite the unavailability of the primary documents which could alone sustain the endeavour in anything like an adequate manner. I informed Mr. Eliot of my decision and returned to London once again during the fall of 1962 to begin further work. No sooner had I arrived than Mr. Eliot rang up to say that, at his wife's prodding, he had decided to release the Bradley thesis after all, and that he had already begun to prepare it for publication. Scarcely two months later, in early November, I received the page proofs of the edition Mr. Eliot had prepared. That edition is the one described in entry 17 and which unfortunately had later to be abandoned.

Much that is negative is presently being written both about Eliot's work and about his character as a man. I want here only to record my own rather different impressions. The radiance of his being at this time of his life, his great simplicity, his innocent and delighted joy in his second marriage—something he never failed to mention despite its total irrelevance to the subject of our meetings—all of these things I remember. I also remember—indeed I shall never be able to forget—that his kindliness and generosity went so far beyond the conventional limits that he not only read various early drafts of the present study in manuscript, making corrections and suggestions in the margin as he read, but also went to extraordinary lengths to help me through a period of penury all too familiar to him from his own past by writing an embarrassing number of letters in support of the various applications for funds which I had made. In one such letter of reference, dated 21 November 1962, which he wrote both to the American Association of University Women and to the American Council of Learned Societies, Eliot indicated that my exploration of Bradley's influence on his literary criticism seemed to him "to break new ground." In the decade that has passed since that letter was written, however, the "new ground" has become old—and so have we. If the enthusiasm of those presently cultivating it has sometimes been diminished by finding that Eliot's thesis in particular is, in Wollheim's words, "a painfully obscure work" (entry 27, p. 170), yet the recognition of the historic significance of Eliot's early philosophical writings has invariably served to rekindle it. It is almost inevitable now that those writings will go on to develop as long and complicated a literary history as Coleridge's have already done, and this despite the fact that their continued exploration involves a task which is not likely to gratify the usual academic vanities. Neither the genesis of the Bradleian vein of Eliot studies, however, nor its further exploration has, for myself at least, ever really been a matter of choice. The event bears witness to the truth of a remark made, I believe, by Arthur Miller that it is not in what one accidentally comes upon that the lineaments of one's own fate may be discovered but, rather, in that from which one simply cannot walk away.